MY LIFE IN FOOTBALL

Kevin Keegan's glittering career includes domestic and European glory with Liverpool and Hamburg and leaves him as the only English footballer in history to win the Ballon d'Or twice.

As a player, Keegan's six years at Liverpool included three league championships, the European Cup, two UEFA Cups and the FA Cup before leaving Anfield in 1977 to cement his superstar status with Hamburg, leading them to a Bundesliga title and a European Cup final.

Keegan captained the England national team and won the Golden Boot at Southampton before finishing his playing career in dramatic style at Newcastle United, the club he later transformed in his now-legendary spell as manager.

Famously, Keegan guided Newcastle from near-extinction to the brink of a Premier League title, playing a style of football that earned them the nickname of The Entertainers and featuring the never-forgotten 1995–6 championship chase with Manchester United. He went on to manage England, in between spells at Fulham and Manchester City, and later returned to Newcastle, desperately hoping he could bring success to the city that knew him as the Messiah.

Daniel Taylor is the chief football writer for the *Guardian* and the *Observer*. He has been named Football Journalist of the Year three times by the Sports Journalists' Association, as well as winning numerous other awards. He started working at the *Guardian* in 2000 and has covered five World Cups for the newspaper. This is his fifth book.

KEVIN KEEGAN

WITH DANIEL TAYLOR

MY LIFE IN FOOTBALL

THE AUTOBIOGRAPHY

MACMILLAN

First published 2018 by Macmillan
an imprint of Pan Macmillan
20 New Wharf Road, London N1 9RR
Associated companies throughout the world
www.panmacmillan.com

ISBN 978-1-5098-7721-8

3 5 7 9 8 6 4 2

A CIP catalogue record for this book is available from the British Library.

Typeset by Palimpsest Book Production Ltd, Falkirk, Stirlingshire
Printed and bound by CPI Group (UK) Ltd, Croydon, CR0 4YY

For Jean

and dedicated in the memory of Bill Shankly.

Two people who have given me so much.

I want people to dream about their football club.
We should all be dreamers at heart. Some people are
the opposite and say, 'We can't do that,' but when
you ask them why, they can't give a reason.
Well, I say, 'Why not?'

CONTENTS

1

GOING BACK

Nobody has ever officially told me I am banned from St James' Park. Sometimes, though, you know when you are not welcome, and it is almost a decade now since it became apparent that, as far as the people at the top of Newcastle United are concerned, I will always be persona non grata as long as the Mike Ashley regime remains in place.

The saddest thing is that I would not want to go back anyway after everything that happened in my second spell as Newcastle manager and, though my feelings for the club won't fade, that policy is set in stone until Ashley has gone, and more than a hundred years of proud football history is removed from his business portfolio.

The only time I have made an exception came after an invitation to a private function at St James' Park one night when there was no football on. It was a leaving do for a lifelong Newcastle fan. My first response was to send my apologies and explain it would be impossible for me to attend. Then I started feeling bad because the guy was leaving for a new life in America and I knew everyone wanted me to be there for his send-off. I didn't want to let him down. And, besides, I have always loved a challenge.

I improvised. I put on a pair of glasses, I found a flat cap and I turned up the collar on my overcoat to complete the disguise. I found a quiet place to park my car, a safe distance from the ground, and then I walked in the back way, sticking to the shadows and avoiding eye contact with passers-by. It was dark and nobody had recognised me until I made it to the stadium entrance. Then one of the staff came over straight away. 'Hello, Kevin,' she said, with one of those lovely Geordie welcomes. 'What are you doing back here?'

My cover was blown, but at least it was a friendly face rather than a hand being placed on my shoulder. The problem was I didn't know if everybody in the building might be so hospitable and I didn't want to take any chances. I asked if she would mind keeping it quiet and then I took the lift to the top floor. I had rung ahead to say I was on my way. Everyone had been briefed that the operation had to be conducted in complete secrecy and, when I hurried down a corridor, lined with photographs of my old teams, they were waiting for me inside one of the executive lounges. I was in and, apart from one minor scare, Operation KK had been a success. Mission accomplished.

I know how absurd it must sound and, when I think about it properly, what kind of craziness is it that someone with my long emotional history with Newcastle now has to smuggle himself into the ground where the owner used to call me 'King Kev'? But this is an extraordinary club, run by unconventional people, and perhaps the most charitable way I can put it, as Jesus said on the cross, is to 'forgive them for they know not what they do'. These people don't know what a precious club this is. They don't comprehend that football in this big, vibrant city is about self-esteem. They have made a toy out of Newcastle United and, as much as it pains me to say it, I have no desire to be associated with the place for as long as that continues. I will gladly return when they have gone, and I am already looking forward to the day when Newcastle is free of the man who has lurched from one bad decision to another, run an empire of self-harm and handed money and power to people who deserved neither. Until then, however, Ashley and his associates don't need to worry about me making a habit of turning up incognito. I don't want to share my oxygen with these people, trust me.

The only other occasion I have ventured back to St James'

Park was for the unveiling of Alan Shearer's statue but, strictly speaking, that was on public land, rather than the site of the stadium itself, and nobody can stop me walking the streets of Newcastle. That, again, was a bittersweet occasion. The statue, 'Local Hero', was paid for by the family of Freddy Shepherd, one of the directors who stood by my side in happier times. Newcastle didn't put in a penny and it was the city council that found a plot of land in the shadow of the Milburn Stand. It's all so very sad. The statues for Jackie Milburn and Sir Bobby Robson are directly in front of the stadium, but Shearer, Newcastle's all-time leading scorer, has been bumped round the corner because he refuses to be a cheerleader for corporate incompetence. Newcastle didn't even put a few sentences on the club's website and, plainly, it was too arduous for anybody from the club to walk the thirty yards up Barrack Road to attend the unveiling.

Perhaps I shouldn't be surprised when Alan, who is Newcastle through and through, has standards that surpass those of the club's owner, and doesn't feel the need to sugar-coat the truth in his television and media work. I have, after all, experienced the full force of the Mike Ashley regime and, though I won my case against Newcastle for constructive dismissal, you can take my word that it wasn't a pleasant experience being engaged in a legal battle against a man of such power and immense wealth. That it was Newcastle at the centre of this litigation made it an even more harrowing experience. Indeed, the whole thing was so hideous it convinced me I never wanted to work in football again.

It was strange, though, when I returned to Newcastle on that undercover mission, how quickly I felt the place gnawing at my heart again. I had never actually been that high up inside St James' before, and there was something very poignant about seeing the stadium catching its breath, so quiet and still, away from the bedlam of match-day.

The stadium always looked so elegant under lights and, gazing down from one of the corporate suites, I found myself lost in my own thoughts until another of the guests wandered over.

For a few seconds he stood beside me and looked out on the same scene. 'You built this place, you know,' he said quietly. 'None of this would have been possible without you.'

Maybe he had seen a little sadness in my eyes. They were kind words, and later that evening I felt myself drawn to that view again. I didn't often get sentimental about football grounds, but St James' had that effect on a lot of people and, as I looked at that rectangular stretch of grass, all the memories started flooding back. I found myself wondering whether the pitch still had its slant – left to right, as you were standing in the dugouts – and then I looked at the vertiginous stands behind each goal and it struck me that the stadium had grown with the team. The Leazes End, to my left, was now the largest cantilever structure in Europe. On the opposite side, the Gallowgate End, at the side of the ground facing the Tyne, was another magnificent presence on the city's skyline.

Locally, they will tell you this place is their cathedral, made for Saturday worship. Yet my association with Newcastle went back long enough to remember the days when it was two banks of rough, hard-faced terracing behind the goals, with police cells in the corner, four spindly floodlights and barbed wire on the perimeter walls. We didn't have a roof at either end, and it rained so hard that sometimes a puddle the size of a small lagoon would form by the side of the pitch. I can still remember the game against Sunderland when a duck came down to splash around beside the playing surface. Nor have I forgotten when the cranes arrived to start the transformation into what is now a 52,000-capacity stadium and – only in Newcastle – supporters took picnics to Leazes Park, just behind the ground, to watch the new stand going up. They would spend the entire day in their camping chairs with their rugs, their flasks of tea and packed lunches. Then, the following morning, they would be back again.

I have a lifetime of memories from the north-east and I will never allow the way it ended to sway my conviction that Newcastle inspires a culture and devotion that is truly unique in English football. The good times far outweigh the bad ones, and I can happily state that the same applies to the rest of my career, both as a player and manager, now this book has given me cause to reminisce about the fifty years since my debut as a professional footballer.

That was a 3–2 defeat for Scunthorpe United at Peterborough United on 16 September 1968, in the puddles and potholes of the old Fourth Division, and if you had seen my rather nondescript performance that day, I doubt anyone could have imagined that the smallest player on the pitch – seventeen years old, wearing an oversized shirt and playing on the right wing – had so many rich adventures ahead of him.

Frankly, I was just glad to have made it as far as Scunthorpe after all the rejections I suffered growing up in Doncaster, as the smallest kid in my class, and the countless occasions when I was told I was dreaming if I thought I was good enough to make it as a footballer. Nor was there a stampede of clubs rushing to take me away from Scunthorpe and catapult me into the big time. I played well over a hundred times for the Iron before the great Bill Shankly, the man to whom I owe so much, saw something he liked and signed me for Liverpool.

Those fifty years have given me so much that the biggest challenge when it came to writing this book was trying to squeeze everything in. I feel privileged to have led such a life and I cannot have done too badly if, aside from my second spell as Newcastle manager, my only other permanent regrets relate to my various spells with the England team. My playing career as an international footballer can never feel properly fulfilled, coming at a time when the England team was low on quality and achievement, but it was my eighteen months as manager that hurt me deeply. I'm not the only man who has tried, and failed, to restore England's reputation, and it cannot be mere coincidence that football men of the quality of Ron Greenwood, Don Revie, Graham Taylor, Fabio Capello and Roy Hodgson have been obliged to leave with the brand of loser. Yet I am not going to make excuses. It was a step too far for me – and the truth, as hard as it was for me to accept, was that I wasn't up to it.

That apart, how can I harbour any regrets when I consider the way football has enriched my life? I have seen the world, worked with great players, made lifelong friends. For Liverpool, I won just about every trophy attainable and said my goodbyes on a sweet-scented night in Rome for the 1977 European Cup final. At Hamburg, when I took a gigantic leap into the unknown, there was a first Bundesliga title for Der Dino since 1960, and the satisfaction of showing that it was possible, whatever they might tell you, for an English footballer to flourish on foreign soil. Then there were my days at Southampton, where we played so thrillingly for two seasons, and the opportunity to achieve a lifelong ambition when Newcastle first fired their wobbly old cupid's arrow in my direction. Happy days, precious memories.

Everything I have done has been with enthusiasm and passion and, as a player, that ethos not only won me the biggest club prizes in the game, but also European Footballer of the Year awards in 1978 and 1979. It is a unique honour, and when I attend functions now I am often introduced as the only English footballer to win the award twice. Take my word, that beats being ushered in as 'the manager of that great Newcastle team that *nearly* won the league' – at which point I usually stagger on as if I have been punched in the kidneys – though I have to be honest and say, with all due respect, those awards don't mean to me what other people think they should mean.

It was the same at Southampton when I won the Golden Boot for finishing as the top scorer in the country. I felt like saying, hold on, I was a centre-forward for one of the more attacking teams in the First Division. I didn't want to be a spoilsport but, realistically, how many players could win that prize?

Other achievements meant a lot more – my England caps, my winners' medals from Liverpool and Hamburg, and the fact that I made a success of it in Germany when so many people thought I would be back within six months with my tail between my legs.

When it came to the Ballon d'Or, there was none of the pomp and parade in those days that there is now that Cristiano Ronaldo and Lionel Messi have turned it into their private fiefdom. For my first one, a guy wandered onto the pitch – I can't even remember who it was – to hand me the trophy before a game somewhere. I shook his hand, put it in my bag and lugged it home with the rest of my stuff. It never weighed a great deal, like a trophy from a pub darts competition, and it rattles now whenever it is lifted because a bolt has come loose and is floating inside the wooden base. The metal is discoloured and you can even see the glue where the plaque has been fixed on. I had it valued once and the guy took one look before telling me it was worth a tenner. I doubt Cristiano would use it as a doorstop.

It wasn't until many years later that I found out I was also runner-up to Allan Simonsen of Borussia Mönchengladbach for the 1977 award. Nobody bothered telling me at the time, which was probably another measure of how different things were back then, and the truth is that I was never obsessed with personal glory anyway. For me, it was the team medals that counted the most.

Don't get me wrong, though. It is a fabulous honour to win the Ballon d'Or twice and it fills me with even more pride when I look at the names who have lifted the same award – Johan Cruyff and Michel Platini, who both won it three times, George Best, Bobby Charlton, Franz Beckenbauer, Eusébio, Stanley Matthews, Gerd Müller, Alfredo di Stéfano, to name but a few – and realise I was the least naturally talented player on the list. I didn't float like Cruyff, I never had the grace of Pelé or the moves of Maradona. George Best was right – I wasn't fit to lace his boots (or even, to borrow the follow-up quote, to lace his drinks) and, even at Scunthorpe, I wished I had the touch and skill of some of my teammates. But maybe those players didn't have my courage, my dedication and my football intelligence. I had a combination of things and I worked slavishly to maximise them. I wasn't big, but I scored goals with my head. I was fast but I made myself faster, and if I had a weakness I worked on it until it became a strength. I was the mongrel who made it to Crufts, and that was fine by me because, all my life, I had gone by the theory that if I wanted to achieve my targets I would have to work my backside off.

Bill Shankly, as always, put it best. 'A man should always do his best, whatever he attempts,' he used to tell me. 'If you're going to sweep the street then make sure your street is always the cleanest in town.' Shanks had a wonderful way with words and loved to see me causing havoc among opposition defences. He described me as 'a weasel after rats, always biting and snapping at your legs.'

I have been fortunate to win many awards and it was on my watch, just after our promotion to the Premier League in 1993, that Newcastle United were made Honorary Freemen of the City, which apparently gave me all sorts of rights such as being allowed to keep a cow on Town Moor. It doesn't get much better than that! Alan Shearer was honoured the same way a few years later and I have told my former player he can put two cows on there if he likes because I am not using mine. It was a lovely honour, and recognition of how hard we worked to put a smile on the faces of the thousands who flocked to St James' Park. All the same, I would have swapped it in a shot for the elusive trophy that Newcastle have been chasing for longer than they probably wish to remember.

It was the same at the 1982 World Cup, when I found out I was to receive an OBE and, truthfully, all I really wanted was for the back injury that was wrecking my tournament to clear up. The other England lads reckoned OBE must be an abbreviation of Other Buggers' Efforts, because I was consigned to my sick bed when I heard the news. I reminded them it was actually Order of the British Empire, but there has never been a point in my life when my ego has felt it necessary to put those three initials after my name.

I did go down to Buckingham Palace, however, to accept the

award, and even tried a little bit of Keegan humour with Her Majesty. As she passed down the line, the Queen's first words when she reached me were, 'Oh, you've been around a long time, haven't you?' I gave a little bow and tried my best to make her laugh. 'Yes, Ma'am, some people think possibly too long.' At which point she peered at me inquisitively. 'Is it possible for one to be around too long?' she asked, then moved off without waiting for an answer.

Well, I stuck around for another quarter of a century before deciding my time in football was over. The only pity, I suppose, is that the one thing you are never guaranteed in this profession is a happy ending. I would have dearly loved to have reminded everyone that it was possible for Newcastle to thrive in a hard world inhabited by serial winners such as Manchester United, Liverpool and Chelsea. Sadly, it wasn't to be. My last job ended in rancour and recriminations and my final game as a manager was a 3–0 defeat at Arsenal in September 2008 that will probably always be remembered for the television cameras picking out Mike Ashley in the away end, where he proceeded to down a pint in roughly the same amount of time it has taken you to read this sentence.

It wasn't Mike's beer-guzzling that upset me that day. It was the fact Tony Jimenez, the executive who had been put in charge of Newcastle's transfer business, had informed me we were spending £5.7 million on a Spanish player called Xisco whom nobody from the club had ever seen play.

On the same day the Xisco bombshell was dropped, I had also found out a Uruguayan by the name of Ignacio González was joining us as a 'favour' for two South American agents. Evidently, Ashley and his associates didn't seem to think there was anything wrong in spending millions of pounds, making a number of people very wealthy in the process, while telling me to 'park' this player. That is still only a fraction of the story, but I find it mystifying that the football authorities did not think it worthy of investigating.

Life moves on. I have far too much in my favour to be engulfed by bitterness, and my affections for Newcastle aren't diminished just because of the unpleasantness with Mike Ashley, Tony Jimenez, Dennis Wise, Derek Llambias and assorted others. Would I be tempted back for a fourth spell at the club – Keegan IV, if you like – if a takeover meant new owners and a club no longer powered by the theory of chaos? No, that ship has sailed, but I do retain an exhilarating vision of what could happen if Newcastle were reignited in the way that happened during the 1990s.

In my case, unfortunately, that involved burning out a twelve-point lead at the top of the Premier League and the anguish of seeing Manchester United release our grip, finger by finger, from the championship trophy before carrying it off to Old Trafford. It was like watching a beautiful painting being ripped apart in front of your eyes. After all this time, I'm still acutely aware I will never be allowed to forget that infamous interview on Sky Sports when I squared up to Alex Ferguson, the manager of our rivals, and made it absolutely clear I would love it if they blew up in the final week of the season.

Strangers shout the critical two words to me from car windows. Autograph hunters tell me they would 'love it' if I could sign their pieces of paper. One family friend had 'love it' as his ringtone, and when I go to charity events I am often asked to sign photographs showing me in that classic pose: headphones on, finger jabbing, blazing eyes. Strangely enough, those pictures tend to be auctioned for a lot more money than the ones where I am playing for England or any of my clubs. I've heard all the gags a thousand times and, for the generations who aren't old enough to remember me as a player, that is probably what they know me for: The Rant. That's life, and I am comfortable enough in my own skin to see the funny side. It is even part of my routine when I am giving speeches because, heck, if you cannot laugh at yourself, who can you laugh at?

History will remember us kindly, too. The Geordies loved to

see a good game. They didn't want to see their team playing boring football, and it was my job to put on the pitch what they wanted. I wasn't going to change that philosophy for anyone and, though we might have come up short in the end, we had a lot of fun seeing how far it would take us.

Somewhere, in the old filing cabinets at St James' Park, they might still have the fax that Sepp Blatter, the president of FIFA, sent me after our never-forgotten 4–3 defeat at Anfield during the 1995–6 championship chase – a bona fide seven-goal thriller between two famous teams playing at full pelt – to commend us for our devotion to attacking football, our sporting behaviour, and the way in defeat we never sought to blame match officials.

Maybe Sepp should have bought a season ticket, because going to St James' Park in those days was like going to a carnival. There was a reason why children all over the country were asking their parents to buy them Newcastle shirts – and their mums and dads were agreeing to it – and it wasn't because we were collecting trophies like Manchester United. It was because of our style of play and the way I always tended to focus on the goals we could score rather than the ones we might let in. A lot of my time as a football manager was taken up with thinking adventurously and, with Newcastle in particular, if it came to a toss-up between a really skilful player who would bewitch the crowd, or one who would do a steady job, I always preferred the exciting option, whatever the risks. That was my way and I made no apologies for it – then or now.

I have already mentioned how FIFA's top official felt compelled to put his admiration in writing, but it would need several books to cover how far and wide the Newcastle fan club spread. I think of the time, for example, when Manchester United came to St James' as champions in the season after our title collapse and encountered a team desperate for revenge. We won 5–0 and our chairman, Sir John Hall, was so emboldened by what he had seen, he came into the press conference. 'Gentlemen,' he

said, 'you've seen the next champions of England here today.'
Too right, chairman – though sadly, it was Manchester United,
yet again, who finished the season with another title for their
collection.

On that occasion, however, Alex Ferguson's team couldn't get
near us. Nothing could make up for what had happened the previous season, but we did at least give the Manchester United
players something to think about. I always remember standing at
the top of the steps as they left the ground. One by one, they filed
past, ashen-faced: Peter Schmeichel, Gary Neville, Denis Irwin,
Gary Pallister, David Beckham, Paul Scholes, Nicky Butt and all
the rest. The last one out stopped to look me in the eye, and I
learned in those moments that Eric Cantona spoke better English
than I had realised. 'Fucking good team you have here,' he said.
Six words, and then he was gone.

I would have to say Old Trafford's *enfant terrible* was a fine
judge. That was an astonishing era for Newcastle, and English
football as a whole, and it didn't start with a team known as the
'Entertainers'. It started with a very average bunch of players who
were second bottom of the old Second Division and a rookie
manager who had spent the previous seven years in Marbella
trying to master how to swing a golf club.

The critics said it would never work, questioning how I could
spare Newcastle from relegation when I had been parachuted in
without even knowing the names of the players. Well, it was a
close-run thing but we did stay up, and when we went up as
champions the following year, we did it by playing beautiful football rather than, as we were told, by trying to kick our way to
promotion. My favourite saying to the press was, 'watch this
space'. Then, in the Premier League, we were told we wouldn't get
anywhere unless we ditched our obsession with attacking perfec-
tion. We ended up within a whisker of winning the title, and I
kept to my promise that we would become a better side than
Liverpool. I just hadn't figured on Manchester United.

After all these years and everything I have done in my career, it never ceases to amaze me how many people seem to think my lifetime's achievements have nothing to do with football and consist of, in rough order: the time I crashed off my bike on television's *Superstars*, my perm, and my top-40 record with 'Head over Heels in Love'.

Not everyone, though. Liverpool fans of a certain age tend to ask why I ever wanted to leave Anfield, or if it was true, as many people genuinely seemed to believe, that I had telepathic powers with my strike partner John Toshack. Others mention the night in Rome when Liverpool won their first European Cup, or all those intoxicating occasions under Anfield's floodlights against Club Brugge, Saint-Étienne and many others. For Hamburg, there was another European Cup final, and it was in Germany that I was twice pronounced the best player in Europe. Southampton's fans, I hope, will not be short of their own memories from my two seasons at the Dell and, from my managerial years, I would like to think there are also supporters of Manchester City and Fulham who remember my spells with their clubs with fondness.

Mostly, though, people want to talk to me about Newcastle and to reminisce about a time when, briefly, anything seemed possible. Were we exciting? I couldn't even begin to remember how many times we were clapped off at opposition grounds, including Elland Road, Upton Park and various other places where away sides didn't generally have petals thrown at their feet. We were the new kids on the block – a bit cheeky, but popular with it. We didn't seem to rile fans of other clubs in the way Manchester United did and, even now, over twenty years on, people still tell me how our 1995–6 side became their 'second' team from one of the more memorable seasons in living memory.

Unfortunately, that didn't mean filling the space in a chronically under-used trophy cabinet, and nothing changes the fact that Newcastle have not won any notable form of silver since the year – 1969 – that man first set foot on the moon. That doesn't mean to say, however, that it was the wrong way to play football.

I did the same wherever I went, and it gives me a lot of satisfaction to know that all the clubs I managed, not just Newcastle, were in far healthier positions when I left than when I arrived.

With City, we were promoted to the Premier League with ninety-nine points and 108 goals; to put that into context, it was three points and sixteen more goals than the Newcastle side I took up. Those times in Manchester have been eclipsed now the Abu Dhabi royal family has assembled the most expensive team in English football history. Yet we had a lot of fun during my four years in the north-west, and perhaps we could have gone even further if the club had been in a position to back me, once we had gone up, in the way Sir John Hall did for Newcastle.

As for Fulham, I wonder if I would have been happier staying at Craven Cottage rather than leaving the club, after two seasons, to take the role of England manager. I started at Fulham as chief operating officer, but when my circumstances changed and I returned to the dugout, I went by exactly the same principles as usual. If I was going to coach a team I wanted to make sure everyone, including myself, enjoyed watching us play. I took little pleasure out of a 0–0 draw, no matter who it was against, and now I am a spectator, not a manager, I find it difficult to watch some of the modern teams when the tactic – 'parking the bus,' to use today's parlance – is to suffocate the life out of what should be entertaining football matches.

Too many managers put on the handbrake and, worse, I have seen it described as a tactical masterclass, even if the teams in question feature some of the best attacking players in the land. It's not for me, and if I had been asked to try it even once as a manager, it would have left me hugely dissatisfied. My strength was attacking, working with the midfielders, particularly the forward-thinking ones, the wingers and the strikers. We attacked, we had pace, we used the wings, we scored goals, we brought the crowd to its feet.

Were we too gung-ho at Newcastle sometimes? Yes! But that was what we built and, contrary to what you might have heard, we were no mugs at the back. 'Emotion, excitement, passion, free with every seat' – that was the promise from the box office. There was nowhere else like it, and if you can find anyone who thought our approach was bad for the game, I would be interested to meet that person. You had to see us. That wasn't me talking, it was everyone. And if that is how I am remembered, that, ultimately, will be fine with me.

2

GOALS AND GROCERIES

Although I have no intentions of returning to the Grey Hair Club, otherwise known as football management, I am on my way to having a five-a-side team that is already keeping me busy enough. My count of grandchildren is up to four now, and I have already bought Zabian, the eldest boy, a Manchester City kit to counter his father Dominic's attempts to bring him up as a fan of Manchester United. Sadly, it doesn't seem to have done the trick, and Zabian, who is four, gave me a stirring rendition of 'United are magic, City are tragic' at the last family get-together. Perhaps I will have better luck with his sister, Myla, or maybe their little brother, Harlow. Then there is Jack, the newest arrival, who has also brought so much happiness into our lives.

I hope they can read this book one day to learn a bit more about their grandfather, just as I would have liked to have known more about my own, and it is a pity, perhaps, that if they ever want to see the football ground where it all started for Joseph Kevin Keegan, I will have to tell them it is now a place where people buy their weekly groceries.

The Old Showground, where I began my professional career with Scunthorpe United, was consigned to history thirty years ago, bulldozed to make way for a Kwik Save supermarket, with a plaque at the delicatessen counter to mark what was previously the centre-spot. It is a Sainsbury's now, and I wonder if there is another player in the country who can beat my goals total from England's lost football grounds. I reckon I have at least a dozen from sites now occupied by Sainsbury's, Tesco and Waitrose. I will have to check if I ever scored at B&Q in Huddersfield, previously the old Leeds Road ground. But I know I got a couple at what was until recently Toys R Us, its Brighton branch, known to my generation as the Goldstone Ground.

I can laugh about it now, but I know from experience it is a tremendous wrench for supporters to see their football grounds sliding into history. It was on my watch at Manchester City that the Etihad Stadium, as it is now known, was built. Maine Road was a wonderful old place and a vital part of the city's life, but the new stadium has been crucial for the club's growth. If that had never happened, City would never have attracted the wealth from Abu Dhabi that has transformed the club since I left in 2005.

I do find it sad, though, that so many of the grounds where I have treasured memories have been lost to history. The Dell, formerly the home of Southampton, is another one. That was another terrific place to play football – a tight, compact ground, jammed to the rafters every other week with 23,000 fans. But it is long gone now and, like Maine Road, my memories are buried in the clay of a new housing estate.

At least St James' Park is still rising proudly against the Newcastle skyline, and Anfield remains an iconic part of Liverpool's landscape. Those, however, are my only two 'home' grounds that are still intact. Wembley is a completely different stadium from the one I knew during my ten years as an England player and the eighteen months I spent, unhappily, as manager of the national team. The whole place was rebuilt a few years ago and they did something similar with Hamburg's Volksparkstadion twenty years after I left the Bundesliga, knocking it down to put up a brand-new stadium.

I had another jolt on the last occasion I was in Scunthorpe and decided to take a trip down memory lane to visit some of the places we used to go after training. My favourite cafe, Monte Carlo, where I used to spend hours on the pinball machine, was now a fast-food takeaway called Kebabish, and another of my old haunts, the Buccaneer bar, with its bottle-green facade in Oswald Street, was a boarded-up eyesore. I remembered the Buccaneer being one of the best places in town. It was sad to see it in such a state, awaiting demolition after standing derelict for the previous decade, but perhaps I shouldn't have been too surprised, bearing in mind half a century had passed since us Scunny lads used to gather inside for a coffee and a slice of toast. Feeling nostalgic, I still had my photograph taken outside both places, for old times' sake.

The house where I grew up in Doncaster, at 25 Spring Gardens, was knocked down in the 1960s because they were rebuilding the town centre. It is a shopping precinct now, and an ABC cinema, with a multi-storey car park, went on the strip of grass at the back where I first learned to control a football, making believe I was Billy Wright in the gold and black of the famous Wolverhampton Wanderers.

As for Belle Vue, where I used to watch Doncaster Rovers grubbing around for points in the old Fourth Division, the club abandoned its home of eighty-five years to move to the Keepmoat Stadium in 2007. A gas explosion then ripped through the old place, blowing the main stand to smithereens. It is another housing estate now, but I will always have fond memories from the days when it felt like the centre of my football universe and Alick Jeffrey, the original boy wonder, was the local hero, still thrilling the crowds despite the appalling misfortune that cost him a move to Manchester United in the mid-1950s.

Jeffrey, a legend in Doncaster, was once revered in the same way as Duncan Edwards, with the potential to be one of the greatest English players who ever lived, but that was wrecked at the age of seventeen when he broke his leg playing for England's under-23s just before he was due to sign for Sir Matt Busby, creator of the 'Busby Babes' at Old Trafford.

How good was he? Jimmy Murphy, Busby's assistant, reckoned Jeffrey could have been the 'English Pelé.' Jeffrey was the youngest player to appear in the league since the Second World War, aged fifteen years and 229 days when he made his debut for Doncaster, and Jackie Milburn described him as the best young player he had ever seen. Stanley Matthews had also witnessed what the teenage Jeffrey could do. 'I predict he can become one of the greatest inside-forwards in the game,' Matthews said. 'His play bears the stamp of genius.'

Unfortunately, a broken leg in those days, without the medical expertise we have now, could wreck careers. Alick was in his second spell at Doncaster when I started watching him, and he had done well even to get back on a football pitch, bearing in mind he suffered another fracture trying to revive his career at Skegness Town. He had put on weight, as someone who was fond of a few drinks, and lost his speed and agility. He had also been to Australia to get his career going again, but he still had a deft touch and a phenomenal shot. He was light years ahead of everyone else, even when he was supposedly finished, and the main attraction for my little group of friends when we took our place on the old Rossington End terrace.

Three or four of us would go to every home game and, kids being kids, we never used to pay to go through the rusty old turnstiles. Why would we, when the alternative was to make a detour behind the ground and use our ingenuity to sneak in at the back of the stand? We used to stack up a pile of bricks to give us a leg-up, and then we would climb over a fence. Someone even took the trouble to dig a hole beneath the fence and we squeezed through that way. We were caught a few times and sent on our way, but we were a resourceful lot and invariably found another opportunity to get back in. It was all part of the fun of a Saturday afternoon watching our local team. Doncaster were known for having the biggest pitch in the country, and I spent a lot of time wondering whether I might get my chance to play on it one day.

At that age, I wanted to be a goalkeeper, and I stubbornly held on to that dream until Mr Teanby, the history teacher who looked after the football team at my secondary school, St Peter's in Cantley, broke the news that he was replacing me with a boy called Arthur Cadman who could actually reach the crossbar.

It was true that the goalposts had grown and I hadn't, standing not even five feet tall, but it was still a shattering development. I used to love throwing myself around a muddy goalmouth, coming home 'sludged up to the eyeballs', as my mum used to say, and I even had a cloth cap like the one I had seen Egon Loy, the Eintracht Frankfurt goalkeeper, wearing on television in that classic 1960 European Cup final against Real Madrid at Hampden Park. Willie Nimmo was Doncaster's goalkeeper, and I used to make sure I always had a spot behind the goal so I could study his pre-match routine. It was the same every match: he would jump to touch the crossbar then run to the posts, kick his boots against each upright and give them a little push. I was fascinated. Willie was one of the guests when Eamonn Andrews leapt out of a huge cake, at a party for my daughter Laura's christening, to inform me that I was on *This Is Your Life* in 1979. I was also introduced to Alick Jeffrey when I was playing for Liverpool. Alick was running the Black Bull pub in Doncaster. He brought me one of his England under-23 caps and I gave him one of mine.

My other heroes tended to be players from the Wolves side that was at the forefront of English football in the 1950s. I idolised Billy Wright in particular, especially when I found out England's captain and centre-half was relatively small, at only five feet nine, and had never let his lack of inches handicap his career. That was my intention, too, and it was always a treat to visit my friend Maurice Freedman and take advantage of the fact that his family were rich enough, unlike mine, to have electricity and, joy of joys, a television set. It was at Maurice's that I learned about Bill and Ben, the Flowerpot Men, and other characters such as Torchy, the little battery boy. More importantly, it was there I saw my first flickering images of professional football, watching Wolves capture the nation's imagination with the famous 'floodlight friendlies' against the cream of Europe. Everyone remembers the game against Honvéd, but the one that enthralled me was a

European Cup tie against Red Star Belgrade in 1959. My first kit was a Wolves one and my enthusiasm for the team from Molineux increased when Barry Stobart, another Donny lad, played for them in the 1960 FA Cup final against Blackburn Rovers.

My dad, Joe, was from the north-east and a typical miner. He knew all about hard graft. He loved a pint of beer, he smoked his Woodbines and he liked to go to the betting shop on Saturday morning to have a flutter, often taking me with him to hear about the 'gee-gees'. He would talk to me about Newcastle legends such as Hughie Gallagher and Jackie Milburn and I found out many years later that he used to write to 'Wor Jackie' when I was playing for Liverpool. Jackie could be located in the press box at St James' Park by that stage, as a football journalist for the *News of the World*, and Dad used to send him letters to say how proud he was of his son.

Dad was not a sportsman himself, but I had the football bug from a very early age. My first ball was a present from my uncle Frank, with his initials, FK, inscribed in the brown leather from when it belonged to him, and a win on the horses helped Dad pay for my first pair of boots – second-hand Winits from Harrison's sports shop, run by the former Doncaster centre-forward Ray Harrison.

Apart from war service in Burma, Dad had spent a lifetime down the pits, and he paid the price for it, as many did in an era when miners did not have to wear masks or suitable protective clothing. Dad had to endure severe bronchitis, silicosis and, ultimately, cancer. His skin was pitted from the coalface and, though he was proud to belong to the mining community, he always used to tell me not to follow him down the pits. He did not want me to suffer the way he had done, with the awful, hacking cough I used to hear first thing every morning, and the time, when I was nine, that he was so ill he took my sister, Mary, and went to convalesce at an aunt's house in Llandudno.

Dad eventually had to come out of the pits when he was fifty-eight. He found another job, working in the boiler room of the

local International Harvester plant, but when he went for his pit pension, the tests showed traces of malaria in his system, something he had picked up in the jungles of Burma, and that meant neither he, nor later my mother, Doris, was entitled to the full amount.

He did well to make it to the age of seventy-one and, though it was always a regret he never saw me play for Newcastle, I am glad he lived long enough to share some of my proudest moments. Dad used to keep pictures of me in his pocket when I was at Liverpool. I would go to the Liberal Club in Doncaster with him for a drink sometimes. Someone would ask for an autograph and, quick as a flash, Dad would reach into his pocket. 'Here,' he'd say, 'have a picture too.'

It could be embarrassing sometimes. 'Please, Dad,' I'd say, 'don't bring the bloody pictures out.' I feel bad about that now because he was obviously chuffed to bits that I had made it as a professional footballer. Dad used to tell me when I was a kid that 'a good big 'un will always beat a good little 'un.' I had set out to show him that size didn't matter. I managed it in the end and I know how proud he was.

John Roberts, the old Fleet Street sports writer, used to tell a story about spending a day with the old man when a family friend, Harry Wadsley, called in, as he often did, to drive them to a pub they liked on the outskirts of Rotherham. On the way Harry played a cassette recording of the 1974 FA Cup final to listen to the commentary. Harry and my dad knew that commentary off by heart and, according to John, their excitement built to fever pitch as the tape went on. John sat in the back, lapping it all up. 'I was convinced that they expected Liverpool to win by a wider margin than 3–0 and that Kevin would at least score a double hat-trick,' he recalled. It was a lovely story.

Nobody apart from me on my side of the family could drive, but Harry was a willing chauffeur and used to transport Dad to all the games at Anfield. I would fix them up with a couple of tickets. What Dad really loved was that the chairman, John

Smith, would fetch him a whisky before every game. Dad would take his seat and, regular as clockwork, John would appear with a drink in his hand. 'Here you go, Joe,' the chairman would say, 'there's your medicine for the week.' That, for my dad, made him feel like a king.

He was desperately ill by that stage. Mum used to say she was convinced it was watching me play every other Saturday that kept him going. Dad would be in bed most of the week. Then he would get up on Thursday for a shave. On Friday he might get a bit of fresh air, and when Harry picked him up on Saturday morning, Dad was like a new man, batteries recharged. When he came back home again he was absolutely drained. All his energy had been used up.

One day I found him running his finger behind his ear. 'Feel that, son,' he said. It felt like a hard pea beneath his skin and I told him he should probably get it checked by a doctor. He never did, though, and eventually that growth started to spread across his face. In the end, it was turning his mouth and even affecting his tongue. His health was always poor, but I knew it was really serious when we went to the pub one night and he asked for a half pint. Dad loved a pint of beer and it used to drive him mad when I insisted on having a half.

We were wired differently that way. While he was a smoker, I have never had a drag of a cigarette in my life. Drinking a pint never appealed to me. I would rather have two halves and, truth be told, I was just as happy with a lime and lemonade. Dad understood in the end but, for a long time, he would refuse to go to the bar on my behalf. 'I'm not getting you a bloody half,' he'd grizzle.

Now he was sipping from a half-pint glass himself, and that, more than anything, made me fear the worst. I went back to Mum and I must have been pretty worried because I told her I did not think he had long left. Then we had a game at Ipswich on 4 December 1976, and I sensed something was wrong when my brother, Mike, who was supposed to be getting a lift from Harry

Wadsley, did not show up. It was first against second at the top of the First Division that day and we lost 1–0. All I really remember is the manager, Bob Paisley, breaking the news. 'You're going to have to go home, son, your dad's passed away' – as blunt as that.

I knew it had been coming, but the drive back to Doncaster was purgatory. I thought that journey would never end and my mind was filled with all the thoughts of Dad. The last time I had seen him I had trimmed his hair and told him he was getting too trendy. Apparently Dad had asked Mum for the final score while he was lying on his deathbed. 'I know they lost,' he said. 'No,' Mum told him. 'They won 2–0 with goals from Toshack and Keegan.'

I thought the world of him and, in my imagination, I can still see him now, with his white hair, streaked by nicotine because of the way he held his cigarettes. As a kid, I used to climb into bed with him and listen to his stories about fighting the Japanese. He would sing all the old wartime songs and teach me the verses. Even now, I still know the words to 'White Cliffs of Dover' and 'Lay Down Your Arms'. My eyes water when I hear those songs.

He used to tell me my grandfather, Frank, was a hero because he had rescued a lot of people from an underground disaster. At that age, it just felt like a childhood story, a fantasy from another time, and I didn't really understand the magnitude of what had happened until I joined Newcastle as a player in 1984 and mentioned my family had Geordie links. One of the supporters got in touch to ask whether there was any association with Frank Keegan or if the surname was mere coincidence. The newspapers picked up the story, and when people started sending in old cuttings and letters, the story began to take shape about that fateful day, 16 February 1909, when there had been a devastating explosion at West Stanley Colliery.

My grandfather was the mine inspector. Having been rescued himself, he went back into the inferno, time and again, to get others out. It was largely due to him that thirty people were rescued. There were no paramedics, no emergency equipment, it was just left to whoever was there, forming search parties and risking their own lives amid the flames and noxious gases.

One hundred and sixty-eight people died in the disaster; twenty-one were under the age of sixteen. The ages of the dead ranged from thirteen years old to sixty-two. Two of the men were unaccounted for until 1933, almost a quarter of a century later, when their skeletons were finally discovered.

On the day of the explosion, my grandfather and the other rescuers didn't have a clue who was down there, or how many people had died. The only way to get some sort of idea was by checking whose helmets were missing. It was that tragedy that led to the mining authorities bringing in a 'tally' system to monitor miners underground. From that point onwards, each miner took a number, or tally, as he went into the mine, which he had to hand back on his return.

I still keep an old sepia-tinted photograph of my grandfather in his pit gear and flat cap, lined up with the survivors. Their names are written at the bottom, and beneath my grandfather it says: 'Frank Keegan, to whom many people owed their lives.' There was even a poem written about his heroism.

> *Although just rescued from that mine,*
> *Frank Keegan turned again – a rescuer.*
> *He thought not of his own escape from that fiery hell,*
> *But of his fellow hewer,*
> *Was such duty ever nobler done?*
> *Was the VC ever nobler won?*

My ancestors had arrived in Newcastle from Ireland, but Dad eventually decided to leave for South Yorkshire because work was so scarce on the Durham seams. He had an offer of employment at Markham Main Colliery in Armthorpe, but it wasn't exactly a life of luxury in our little terraced house. We had a detached outhouse where we washed. Our bath was an old zinc tub and the toilet was at the foot of the garden. It used to take an age to fill the bath by boiling water on gas rings, and we never had electricity until I was ten and we moved into a council house in Balby, the suburb of Doncaster where they filmed *Open All Hours* at a shop – a hairdresser's salon, believe it or not – in Lister Street. I was actually born at my aunt Nellie's house, at 32 Elm Place in Armthorpe, on Valentine's Day 1951, because she had electricity and that made it safer for childbirth. I was christened Joseph – named after my father, in a family tradition, though I never heard anyone call me that until the register was read out on my first day at school. I had no idea it was me and assumed it must be another boy with the same surname.

Dad never drank at home and we didn't keep beer in the house, but he loved to pop down to the Liberal Club. Mum would join him on Saturdays to play bingo and Doncaster, a horse-racing town, did have its occasional highlights. When I was older, I saw the Four Tops at the Co-op Emporium and the town came alive when it was St Leger Festival Week. It was such a big week for Doncaster, they even closed the pits. There was free entry to the course if you were from a mining family and, for a kid, there was hardly anything more thrilling than running over to the rails to see the horses flashing by, with the incredible noise they made and the blur of colours and numbers. A fairground was next door, and it was on the waltzers in September 1970, around the same time Lester Piggott and Nijinsky were completing the Triple Crown, that I met Jean, my future wife.

Bobby Thompson, otherwise known as the Little Waster, was one of the top comedians in the country, with his stripy jumper, his flat cap and harmonica, and used to come down from the north-east to play in Doncaster. Bobby and his two sons would sleep in a caravan behind the Leopard pub in West Street. Dad found out and offered to put the boys up at our place.

Most of the time, though, the routine was fairly simple. Dad was a creature of habit, addicted to his Woodbines, and never had a bank account as long as he lived. Instead he would come home on payday and place his wages on the table for Mary and me to count out. When he was too poorly to work one year, Mum took all kinds of jobs, including cleaning in a pub. Money was tight but Dad kept to his principles, even when he was offered £20, a considerable sum in those days, to let the local Conservative Association use our home, right in the centre of town, as a canvassing centre during the election. Dad was staunch Labour, like just about every miner in the area, and horrified by the idea. 'Bloody Conservatives!'

That stubborn streak was passed down to me. If Dad thought he was in the right, he was in the right. His word was his bond and Mum always used to laugh about the night he was walking home from the pub and saw a man and woman fighting in the street. Dad had come out of the Scarborough Arms and, with his acute sense of right and wrong, felt compelled to go over. He got hold of the fella to ask him what the hell he was doing and, bang, the woman gave him a right hook. 'Mind your own business!' They had to pick Dad off the floor. There was a lesson to be learned from that story, but I liked the fact that he was trying to do the right thing.

Mum also knew the importance of hard work. She had left school at the age of fourteen and took jobs in various factories before Mary, who was two years older than me, came along. Mum spent so long standing on those concrete factory floors that she suffered terribly with varicose veins, and one of my childhood jobs was to let her rest her legs on me. She was told her veins were so bad there was nothing they could do to help her, but that wasn't good enough for me when I was old enough to do something about it. I went to see a specialist who said he could help, and so Mum had an operation in London. We were very close, my mum and me, and it meant a lot to me that she was pain-free.

Mum used to make rag-rugs to sell locally. She loved to laugh, and I can still picture the way she used to cross her legs when she was in fits of giggles. She also had a mischievous side and landed herself in trouble when she was working at Pilkington's Glass by putting some itching powder in one of the other factory worker's clothes. Mum thought it was hilarious. Her colleague wasn't quite so amused, just as Dad wasn't the time he turned up after a few too many drinks one night and Mum decided to teach him a lesson. Dad's hair had been white since he was twenty-one, something he blamed on the soap at the mine, but when he woke from his drunken slumber it had been smeared with black boot polish. Mum did at least leave his moustache its usual snowy white.

In those days we lived opposite the Co-op Funeral Services and, when I was old enough to start kicking a ball around, my friends and I used the mortuary doors at the back as our goal. We would also sneak inside to peer at the dead bodies if the owner, Mr Anderson, was out and his son, David, one of my pals, knew where to locate the keys. We thought nothing of walking around the different corpses, making up stories about how all these people might have met their ends, though it did backfire one day when David, who was three years older than me, rushed over to break the news that Father Christmas was dead.

I was six at the time and had just started to wonder about this bearded old man, riding a sleigh, who would come down the chimney with a sack full of presents if we were good little boys and girls. Was there such a person? I had come to the conclusion that, yes, there was – and now I was being told he was lying across the street, stone-cold dead. I went over to see for myself and, sure enough, there was a big fellow in one of the coffins with a long white beard, who looked very much like the Father Christmas my mum had taken me to see in one of the town's big stores. How can you take in such devastating news? It was a tragedy, not least because Christmas was only a few weeks away. Who was going to put the tin soldiers in my stocking?

At that age, we already had our own money-making schemes. I cleaned cars with David and Maurice at the Glasgow Paddocks, where hundreds of horses were kept in stables, and some of the racegoers who were staying at the Danum Hotel were wealthy enough to reward us with a shilling or even a half-crown. It was too good to last, sadly, and when it was decided the Paddocks would be knocked down, the local newspaper, the *Doncaster Free Press*, heard about our plight and printed a picture of us sitting disconsolately on our buckets.

Our other enterprise was to take trolleys down to the market-place, collect the discarded wooden crates and break them up to make bundles of firewood. We would sell them round the block for twopence, or even a threepenny bit, and the money went towards the family's income. As with the car-washing venture, I would pass all the profits to my mother.

Sadly, my attempts at the age of seven to get a newspaper round led to nothing other than my pride being hurt. Dad took me to the local newsagent's to see if there were any vacancies, but I was knee-high to a grasshopper, and when the shop owner peered over the counter to look me up and down she tried to explain, as gently as she could, that it might be tricky giving me a job when I could not reach the letterboxes. She walked me down the road for a trial and she must have chosen the most awkward letterbox in Doncaster because, even on tiptoes, I could not get close. 'I'll carry a box around with me,' I pleaded. But the best she could offer was a job in a few years' time and a sympathetic pat on the head.

That was not the first time my size had been used against me and it could be disheartening sometimes, being told I was too small or not strong enough. I eventually shot up to five feet seven, but I was a late developer. I wish more people had shown the kind of support I received from Sister Mary Oliver when I was sent to Saint Francis Xavier Catholic primary school at Balby Bridge, where she was in charge of the football team.

Not many footballers have a nun as their first mentor, and Sister Mary was certainly quite a sight as she refereed with her crucifix flying around and her habit whipping round her knees. But I would go as far as to say she had the same influence on me at school as Bill Shankly did later on at Liverpool. 'Kevin's football must be encouraged,' she wrote in my school report in 1961, and I never forgot the way she gave me something to believe in.

A world of change has taken place in my life since then, but I have always wanted to encourage others in the way Sister Mary did with me. I always wanted people to believe they could achieve what they wanted to achieve. She was a huge influence on my life and I still have photographs of the two of us when the newspapers arranged a reunion many years later. It gave me a chance to say thank you and we kept in touch over the following years. She was like an angel, so full of kindness and warmth, and in the last years of her life I hope it gave her some happiness when I visited. She used to call herself 'STS' – 'Soccer Talent Spotter'.

Not all my teachers were so enamoured with me. 'He is an exhibitionist and will do much better when he loses this trait,' read the report from Mrs Wrennall, my form mistress. I passed my eleven-plus, but I did have a tendency to clown around, and it was the same when I moved to St Peter's. It was a strict school, but I had a habit of fooling around, even though there were teachers who could terrify me. My studies suffered and I cannot even remember how many times I was caned for daft little things such as writing on blackboards or playing practical jokes. One teacher rapped my knuckles so hard with the wooden part of the blackboard eraser that my whole hand was red and swollen. The nuns used to hit you with their belts. That was bearable, but the cane was agony. The first blow was the worst because, after that, you could hardly feel your fingers anyway. If you lowered your hand or pulled it away, the punishment would start again. It was quite common to have your backside tanned, too. I tried the old trick of sneaking a book down my trousers to absorb the blow, but the teachers realised what I had done. Looking back, it was never likely to work.

Some people might assume that I didn't study harder because all I cared about was football. I would say I was just a bit daft and immature and intent on enjoying myself. Yet I would certainly have done better at school without football being such a distraction. Even at junior-school age, I would often walk a mile and a half on my own to Hyde Park, where there always seemed to be a game going on, and when Mike was born I would wheel his pushchair with me. If Mum was working, Mary had the responsibility of looking after the house, and it was my job to look after my baby brother. I used to take him everywhere, but Mum wasn't too pleased when she found out he had been whacked flush in the face with a stray shot. We were using his pushchair, with Mike in it, as one of the goalposts at the time. 'That's why I'm such a good header of the ball,' he used to say years later.

There was always something going on and I can still hear our next-door neighbour, Mr Gibbons, bellowing with anger because he was sick of the noise of my ball banging against his wall. I used to think he was a ferocious moaner, but I think that constant thud, thud, thud would have driven anyone to distraction. Nor did it improve neighbourly relations when I accidentally threw a stone through his window while trying to get a balloon down from a tree. I doubt 'Old Gibby' missed us too much when we moved to Balby.

Our new place at 36 Waverley Avenue was an unpretentious 1930s council house and a dream for me, because it was directly across the road from a big, grassy godsend known as the 'Bull-ring'. It was luxury compared to Spring Gardens, with three bedrooms, electricity and an indoor lavatory. The back garden was pretty small, but having a playing field right on the doorstep more than made up for that. The only problem was ingratiating ourselves with our new neighbours, and we probably could have made a better first impression. As we were carrying in our sofa, a dead mouse fell out in front of everyone.

I was lucky even to be playing sport, bearing in mind I had such a weak chest as a toddler. I suffered from bronchitis and croup, and the doctors once told my parents I would not be able to take part in physical activity. It was a misdiagnosis, fortunately, but any chance of a career in football might have been dramatically ended one day at Hyde Park when one of my friends was showing off a new bow and arrow. He fired it in the air and, when I looked up to see where it had gone, I lost it in the clouds. I still had my face turned to the sky as it came down and hit me just beneath my right eye. I could have lost my eye if the impact had been a few millimetres higher, and it left a little black scar where part of the arrowhead had broken off beneath my skin. It was there for twenty years, and I expected it to be forever, until I moved to Germany to play for Hamburg and invited one of the neighbours around. It turned out he was a cosmetic surgeon, and he arranged to have the little flecks from that arrowhead removed. There is still a tiny scar but you can barely see it now.

The Bullring was my hallowed turf, come wind, rain or shine, and the scene of some epic matches, with jumpers down for goalposts and countless arguments about whether the ball had scraped inside or gone wide, especially if someone had left a sleeve dangling free. It was here that I first tried to knock a ball to one side of an opponent and run round the other way to meet it. It worked, leaving me feeling very pleased with myself, though I didn't realise at the time that in years to come I would be trying that trick on some of the best defenders in the business.

By the age of twelve, I could head the ball against a wall nearly fifty times without letting it touch the floor. The reality, however, was that I was not even good enough to get into the Doncaster Boys team. I was a decent footballer for my school side, certainly better than average, and my classmates were convinced I would make the cut. They were wrong. Instead they chose a boy called Kevin Johnson from West End Bentley School, a left-footed player who went on to join Sheffield Wednesday. Two other boys from St Peter's made it, but not me.

Another time, Dad came home from the pub to announce he had been drinking with someone who had a contact at Doncaster Rovers and had fixed up a trial for me. All I had to do was turn up at Belle Vue at half past six the following evening and my name would be down. 'Go looking smart,' he said. Hallelujah! It was my schoolboy dream to play for Doncaster, but when I turned up the place was deserted. Apparently, all the other boys had arrived much earlier and gone off somewhere for the trials. Either my dad had given me the wrong time or it was duff information from whoever he was having a pint with. Whatever the mix-up, I was devastated – and there was no invitation back.

Then there was the time I spent a weekend at my uncle Frank's, who lived near Nuneaton, and he arranged for me to have a trial at Coventry City. There must have been 200 other boys in the same position, but when the numbers were whittled down it was myself and a lad called Brian Joy who were invited back for an extended trial, this time lasting six weeks. That meant getting time off school. The sports master, Mr Gormley, a disciplinarian who had previously taught at a borstal, made it absolutely clear I was wasting everyone's time. Fortunately, the headmaster, Mr Smith, took a more sympathetic view, and I headed down to the Midlands in the hope that it was going to be my big break.

Coventry were going for promotion from the Second Division at the time and their manager, Jimmy Hill, was one of the more forward-thinking people in the sport. They also had a player, Willie Carr, who was already in their first-team squad despite being only thirteen months older than me. Willie was another 'little 'un', already being spoken about as a Scotland international; he became famous for his improvisational 'donkey kick' against Everton in 1970, when he took a free kick by gripping the ball between his ankles and flicking it up for Ernie Hunt to volley in – an impudent trick that was subsequently banned by the authorities. He was an inspiration to me and I dreamed that one day we would share the same team. But I was kidding myself. Approaching the end of the six weeks, I was brought in and given the news. They liked the look of me, but I was too small, again, and they had decided to take on Brian instead.

Rejection, I always say, can be a good thing if it increases your resolve. But it can also hurt like hell. I was distraught on the train back to Doncaster. I felt like a complete failure, and when

I returned to St Peter's not everyone was as supportive as Sister Mary Oliver had been at my previous school. 'Get it into your thick skull,' one of the teachers said to me, 'you're never going to be a footballer.' And, for the first time, I started to think the same myself. I knew I was not that far away in terms of ability, and I was determined not to give up, but when every door was being slammed in my face I had to accept it was time to think about getting a proper job.

The problem was I had gone from being a bright pupil, often finishing top of my class in junior school, to being overtaken by the other children. I was sports mad, and it was not just football that dominated my life. I was the school one-mile champion and ran in cross-country championships. I played rugby and I was captain of the school cricket team, including the less than heroic day we were dismissed for a grand total of twelve runs against Thorne Grammar. I had lost myself in sport and, without necessarily realising it, given up on my grades. All I had when I finished St Peter's were two O-levels in art and history and that, frankly, was never going to get me very far.

That is how, in July 1966, with the country basking in the glory of England's World Cup triumph, I started work at Peglers Brass Works in Doncaster, still only fifteen and trying not to think of all the adventures Brian Joy must be having at Coventry. I was supposed to be an office clerk in their central stores. In reality, I was the tea boy and messenger, and it was certainly an eye-opener for a naive kid straight out of school to listen to the factory girls when they started gossiping and, worst of all, plotting my initiation ceremony. 'Wait until Christmas,' they kept saying. I asked the men in the office what that meant. 'Be careful,' came the reply. 'At Christmas, they'll get you, strip you and grease you all over.'

It wasn't how I had envisaged my life panning out. The only games I was getting at that time were for a local youth club, Enfield House, on Saturday afternoons, and for the Lonsdale Hotel, a pub team in Doncaster's Sunday league, paying my subs and breathing in the stale alcohol fumes from the players who had been out the night before and, unlike me, were old enough to go into the hostelry that gave the team its name.

My dream of playing professional football looked shot, and when one of my new colleagues, Harry Holland, asked if I fancied having a go with the Peglers works side on Saturday mornings, it wasn't even their first team. It was the reserves on a sports ground that was about as flat as a links golf course. I was given a tatty number ten shirt, which was about three sizes too big for me, and though I did have a couple of run-outs for the first team, that was only when somebody was injured. It was always made clear I would be straight back in the reserves once everyone was fit again.

Brian Joy did not actually play a game for Coventry. He did, however, have a fifteen-year playing career ahead of him and, checking into my office job every morning, I could only imagine the glories he might encounter. My own football career, in contrast, was beginning to feel like a distant ambition. My instinct was not to give up. But it hardly filled me with optimism if even Peglers Brass Works, of the Bentley & District Football League, did not think I was up to scratch.

3

THE FIRST RUNG

My lucky break came for my pub team, Lonsdale Hotel, one Sunday morning in 1966, when we were playing a side called Woodfield Social and I was fortunate enough to be marked by a guy named Bob Nellis. Bob had once had trials for Doncaster Rovers, but he was in his late thirties by the time he came up against me and had piled on a few pounds since those days. He was too slow to keep up with me, and when he came over afterwards to shake my hand he told me he had never been given the run-around like that before.

Bob explained he had some contacts at Scunthorpe United, and asked if I would be willing to go for a trial. Bob had a deal in place with the club that they would make it worth his while if he could find them a player who was talented enough to sign apprentice forms. His prize? Ten balls and some free kit for the junior team he coached on Saturday mornings.

I didn't need to be asked twice. Bob even took the trouble to drive me to Scunthorpe in his van. After a series of trial matches, a cross-country run with the first-team squad and a car-park game outside the Old Showground, I was summoned by the manager, Ron Ashman, and given the news that changed my life. Bob got his free balls and, having spent the previous three months at Peglers Brass Works learning about the world of taps, ballcocks and toilet fittings, I handed in my resignation to climb the first rung of the football ladder, as an apprentice professional.

It didn't even matter that my weekly wage, four pounds and

ten shillings, was less than I had been earning at Peglers. Why would that bother me? I was a footballer, at last, and nothing else mattered, even if Fred Leatherland, the factory-floor boss, made it clear he thought I was making a terrible mistake. Fred told me, as blunt as you like, that 'you'll not make the grade, lad', and followed up that confidence-booster by saying I shouldn't waste my breath asking for my job back when it all went wrong.

It was twenty-four miles to Scunthorpe and, without a car of my own and no Bob Nellis to give me a ride, I had to improvise. My routine was a 6 a.m. rise, out of the house by 7 a.m., and then a walk across Doncaster to catch the Thorne bus. If I had time I might drop into Cooplands Cafe, where I would get a drink and put one of my favourite Motown records on the jukebox – 'The Dock of the Bay' by Otis Redding, usually. There was no direct bus, but I could jump off a few miles outside Scunthorpe and then I would hitch-hike the rest of the way. Nobody would dream of doing the same now, but that was the norm in those days. It was never long before a milk van or lorry picked me up, and when I was able to afford my own car I always felt I should do the same if I saw anyone 'thumbing it'. Or at least I did until I had a bad experience with a couple of lads near Keadby Bridge. One of them started smoking and put his feet on the dashboard. They started getting aggressive, and I was relieved to get rid of them without it getting really unpleasant. That experience put me off picking up strangers again.

Eventually I moved out of Doncaster when Scunthorpe provided me with a small allowance for digs, and I started lodging with Mrs Duce in King Edward Street. Mel Blyth, who went on to play for Southampton in the 1976 FA Cup final against Manchester United, was next door with another of the players, Steve Deere, at Mrs Baker's house. We still had to buy our own boots, but the club gave us a 'chitty' to get a fifty per cent discount from Sugg Sports. It might not mean much to the modern player but, for us lads at Scunthorpe, what a treat to get a pair of football boots half price. I used to feel a million dollars carrying my 'chitty' into Sugg's.

Not that we were always required to wear our football boots as apprentice professionals. There were times at Scunthorpe when it felt as though football was secondary, and I can still remember the outrage of the first-team trainer, the legendary Jack Brownsword, when he found me playing head-tennis one day with Keith Burkinshaw and some of the other senior players. Jack, an ex-miner, was a one-club man, with almost 800 appearances for Scunthorpe, and such a loyal servant to the club that the approach road into Glanford Park, their home since the Old Showground was knocked down in 1988, was named in his honour. I liked him from the first day I arrived in Scunthorpe, but he was an incredibly hard taskmaster. 'What the hell are you doing?' were his precise words. 'You're supposed to be doing your jobs. You're not here to play football!'

Not here to play football? That wasn't how I necessarily saw it, but it did feel that way sometimes. As apprentices, we were expected to turn our hands to virtually everything, whether it be painting the ground, cutting the grass, cleaning the boots, laying out the kits, scrubbing the dressing rooms or running the baths for the players. Jack even had me scaling the floodlights to give them a polish one day, dangling off the metal frame eighty feet in the air, and when we did put on our boots, the cross-country runs he organised on the edge of Scunthorpe were a form of torture.

Jack would take us to a steep, unforgiving hill at Atkinson's Warren, or 'Ackie's Warren', then split us into groups and make us run to the top and back half a dozen times. From the top, you could see Doncaster on a clear day and, trust me, there were times when I wished I was back there. The gradient was so steep that when you ran downhill it was difficult to stop yourself going head over heels. Uphill was even worse, with a stretch of sand that would sap the energy from your legs, and once we had completed that course we would have to set off on a cross-country run around Flixborough. One lad, after three climbs at Ackie's, simply found his legs were no longer willing to respond and collapsed into a bush. Some would be physically sick. Others used to cheat on the Flixborough circuits by thumbing lifts or taking shortcuts across the fields. What they did not realise was Jack, the wily old so-and-so, had a pair of binoculars. He caught four of them red-handed on one occasion and gave everyone a tongue-lashing, making us all do it again as punishment.

Jack had to be hard because it was tough at that end of football. Scunthorpe finished eighteenth in the old Third Division in my first season with the apprentices, 1966–7. The next year, the club were relegated in bottom spot, with eight wins from forty-six games. I made my first-team debut in September 1968, at the age of seventeen, and we finished sixteenth before rising to the dizzy heights of twelfth the following year, then falling back again to seventeenth in my final season. Scunthorpe were one of the few full-time teams in the Fourth Division, but it was a hand-to-mouth existence. The standard of football wasn't much better than what I was already used to, and I had never realised, as one of the trainees who had passed his driving test, that myself and another player, Nigel Jackson, would have to take turns behind the wheel of the minibus for some of our away matches. For one at Newcastle, we were so short of players we had to borrow two of theirs for the game to go ahead. We took a heavy beating and, to add to our shame, both of our goals were scored by the north-east boys we had on loan.

We hardly set the world alight when I progressed to the first team, either, though if you were familiar with our training ground you might have a better understanding of why some of our shots were a little wayward when it came to Saturday afternoons. Quibell Park had two pitches, one for rugby and one for hockey. What it didn't have were football nets. We used the rugby posts instead, with a crossbar almost ten feet off the ground, and with that as my target I always used to chip the goalkeeper, Geoff Barnard. What was the point of blasting it when the crossbar was nearly two feet taller than usual? It used to drive Geoff mad, though I was never sure it was the best way to prepare for games. We must have been the only footballers in the country who never saw a set of orthodox goalposts until we played a proper match.

It certainly wasn't usual to practise that way, and the same applied to our five-a-side matches on the rough expanse of concrete that passed as the Old Showground car park. Injuries were inevitable, and if you did break a bone or gash your head open, our physiotherapist, Charlie Strong, was often unavailable. Scunthorpe were too hard up to take him on full-time, and if he had a 'PP' – a private patient – you had to wait outside his room until a red light flashed above the door to indicate he was free. It could take three hours sometimes before all the players had their turn.

The rather haphazard way Scunthorpe were run was all part of the charm, and I have fond memories from my time at the Old Showground. It was also vital to my development, not just as a footballer but as a person. It was the bottom rung of football, or it certainly felt that way sometimes, but what a grounding for a budding professional who was not just learning about what it took to be a proper footballer but also about life in general.

It was my first experience of playing in front of a proper crowd and, though we lost more than we won, I was also given an early taste of elite football when Arsenal visited the Old Showground in the League Cup. We lost 6–1 but it was a thrill to play in front of more than 17,000 people, roughly five times our usual crowd, and it was the same in the FA Cup the following season, when we had a money-spinning tie at Sheffield Wednesday. They were a First Division club at the time, but we beat them 2–1 to reach the fifth round for only the second time in Scunthorpe's history. Swindon Town knocked us out on the wettest, muddiest pitch I have ever seen in my life, but that win at Hillsborough was one of the giant-killing feats of the season.

I was being paid such a pittance at Scunthope that I couldn't even afford to run my first car, a Morris 1100, when my summer wages went down from £15 a week to £10. I even found a temporary job plate-laying at Appleby Frodingham Steelworks and, later, boosted my income as the head porter of a mental hospital in Doncaster. I always resented the way our footballer salaries came down in the summer, and it brought to mind the famous story about Stan Mortensen finding out Stanley Matthews was on more money than him at Blackpool. Blackpool's explanation was that Matthews was the better player. 'Not in the summer, he's not,' Mortensen pointed out.

I did become a bit disillusioned in my final season at Scunthorpe, mostly because I could see other players leaving for bigger clubs and wondered why nobody was coming in for me, but they were happy times overall, and Ron Ashman did so much for me that when he started up a travel agency many years later I went back to open it for him. Ron, like Jack, had spent his playing career as a one-club man, making a record number of appearances for Norwich City and captaining them, as a Third Division side, when they beat Manchester United and Tottenham Hotspur to reach the 1959 FA Cup semi-finals. He was an honourable, straight-talking man who was liked and respected by everyone, and never seemed to get too upset with the players after our frequent poor performances.

That said, I have never forgotten the lecture I received when five of us – Nigel Jackson, Jimmy Coyne, Alan Olbison, Steve Hibbotson and me – decided it would be fun one day to build a track around the back of the stand and arrange a rally on the club's ancient tractor. We even borrowed Jack's stopwatch, without him knowing, and when it was my turn on these unofficial time trials, I went so fast over one bump that the impact of the landing forced the axle up through the engine and the front of the tractor collapsed in a heap of steaming metal. That tractor was at least thirty years old. It must have cost a fortune to fix, and it was money Scunthorpe couldn't afford. It was a hell of a rollicking we received, first from Jack and then Ron, and a lesson that it was time to start behaving more responsibly.

Not that I completely lost my enthusiasm for joking around

once I was a regular part of the first team. On the bus to away games, we used to have a running joke where I would sit on the journalist Tom Taylor's knee and he would bounce me up and down while we pretended I was a ventriloquist's dummy. Tom was the father of Graham Taylor, then a player for Grimsby Town, and covered Scunthorpe as the sports correspondent for the *Scunthorpe Evening Telegraph*, going by the pseudonym of 'The Poacher.' He was a big man and, me being so small, we made quite a double act with that 'gootle-o'-geer' routine on our long treks across the country. There was no such thing as an overnight stay for a club with Scunthorpe's means, and we had to make our own entertainment, playing endless hands of whist and other card games. On one trip to Exeter it took the entire night to get home, arriving back around the same time the milk was being delivered. We didn't even have a toilet on the bus.

As a teenager breaking into the first team, I was also expected to turn out for the reserves in the old Midland League, facing teams such as Long Eaton, Matlock and Grantham, and various other opponents who thought nothing about using their boots, elbows, kneecaps, craniums and the odd tooth to get their message across. That was tough. All the other teams were part-timers, often including battle-hardened miners straight up from the coalface. A lot of those players wanted to be where we were but, for whatever reason, had fallen short – and despised us because of it. The irony was that they were often earning better wages than we were, but that didn't stop them wanting to kick the living daylights out of us.

Intimidation was the norm – 'You go past me, son, you'll be spending the night in hospital' was as polite as it ever got – and the brutes staring me up and down, often ten to fifteen years older than me, gave me the impression that they meant every word. We used to have iron railings around the side of the pitch and the opposition defenders saw it as a personal challenge to put irritating kids like me into those metal stanchions. I was never seriously injured, but I did see George Kerr's leg being broken in a reserve game against Gainsborough Trinity. George was a tough, experienced Scot and knew how to handle himself. It was a diabolical challenge. I was the nearest teammate to him and heard the crack before seeing his bone jutting out of his sock. It was horrendous, the worst thing I had ever seen on a football pitch.

Fortunately, I was quick enough for the most part to avoid too much of a battering and, though I was often sent spinning, I was generally too fast for my opponents. A lot of that was because of Jack's hard-line training regime, but I also had a head start, fitness-wise, because of my long-distance running at school and a masochistic attempt, aged fifteen, to take on a fifty-mile run from Manchester to Doncaster and the equivalent, very nearly, of back-to-back marathons.

There were seven of us who set off from Piccadilly railway station and, looking back, it was a ridiculous undertaking to expect us to make it across the Peak District. If you know Wood-head Pass, it is hills all the way and, however hard we trained, it was nothing compared to the agonies we suffered on those long, steep gradients. The first drop-outs came at sixteen miles, and Dave Brown, the guy who had come up with the idea, hit the deck somewhere near Penistone. That left me alone. I was desperate to finish because the mayor was supposed to be putting on a reception when we arrived in Doncaster. But it was lunacy. I struggled on past the thirty-mile mark, up and down those brutal hills, until my legs buckled and I started staggering around as if Cassius Clay had landed a right hook on my chin.

Most people would have been satisfied to make it that far, especially as we had raised a few bob for charity, but we were determined not to be beaten. We decided to try another fifty-mile run, but this time from Nottingham to Doncaster over a much flatter route. Billy Gray, the Notts County manager, started us off outside Nottingham railway station and three of us – myself, Dave and another friend called Alan Dykes – made the full distance. We arrived in Doncaster in style, with a police escort taking us to the mayor's parlour. Of all the things I have done in my life, I will always consider that one of my prouder achievements.

After that, I never lost my fitness. Jack Brownsword used to make us run from Quibell Park to the ground sometimes, if the minibus was full of equipment. It was uphill and the other lads dreaded it, whereas I thought it was a piece of cake. I was out-standingly fit, and that gave me an edge in matches, because I knew whoever I was running against would have to be excep-tional to keep up with me. Bill Shankly couldn't get over it when I moved to Liverpool. 'Slow down, son,' he'd say. 'You don't have to win every race.' Tommy Smith, in particular, didn't appreciate this young whippersnapper haring past him in training.

Jack was so dedicated to his profession that when he came out of Bentley Colliery to make it as a footballer, joining the club when it was known as Scunthorpe & Lindsey, he soldiered on until the age of forty-two. 'The thing that impresses me most about you is that you are a hundred per center,' he used to tell me. 'Every time you run, whether it be twice round the rugby pitch, four times round the ground, or on a cross-country, you always want to be first. Never lose that because it's the biggest thing you've got going for you.'

That, for me, was the ultimate compliment, and remains that way to this day. Scunthorpe used to have the first cantilever stand in the country and it fascinated me to see Derek Hemstead, a full-back with a tremendous physique, holding a dumbbell in each hand and running up and down the steps, over and again. I used to stare at Derek's bulging calf muscles with a mix of awe and envy, especially when I looked down at my own skinny legs. Soon, I was getting two weights from the gymnasium to join him on those drills, two afternoons a week. It did me the power of good.

It was after a year or so in the first team that I began to attract the attention of some scouts from other clubs, who started coming to watch me. I started twenty-nine games in that first season and appeared as a substitute four times. The next season, 1969–70, I played every match and, having established myself in the team, I missed only one game the following year.

Gerald Sinstadt came from Granada TV to interview the promising whelp beside our rugby-cum-football training pitch at Quibell Park. It was my first television interview and he asked how I was finding professional football. I was eighteen and my accent was a lot broader, pure Doncaster, in those days. 'At first very tough. Couldn't do much right, to be honest. But the more I've played, easier it's come, y'know.' That clip has found its way on to YouTube and, plainly, I didn't want to sound bigheaded about my prospects of moving to a bigger club. 'I'm getting first-team football here. Should think if I went First Division, I'd struggle a bit . . .'

As time went on, however, I was beginning to feel impatient. Scunthorpe had given me my chance in professional football and I was eternally grateful. They must have rated me because, at the age of eighteen, I was a mandatory first-team pick and even nominated as our regular penalty-taker. But I had played almost 150 games in their colours and I was starting to wonder whether any team from the higher divisions would ever take a chance on me. Nigel Cassidy had been sold to Oxford United two leagues above. Mel Blyth had been snapped up by Crystal Palace in the top division, and it felt as if I was being left behind. I didn't want to be a Scunthorpe player all my life, and at one point I even told Jack Brownsword that, as much as I appreciated everything the club had done for me, I might pack it in at the end of the season. I was young, and I had that streak in me.

Jack told me to stick it out and promised that I would be in the First Division within two months. He also told me that Don Revie, the manager of Leeds United, was constantly pestering him about me on the telephone and that at least gave me hope. Don told me years later it wasn't true. It was Jack calling him, rather than the other way around, and Don wasn't sure I was a risk worth taking. Arsenal asked me to go on tour at one stage with their youth team, but the Football Association's rules would not allow it. Preston North End, on their way to the Third Division championship, were supposed to be interested, but so were a lot of clubs, including Millwall, Notts County and Birmingham City. Nothing had materialised, though, and the longer it went on the more I felt I was in danger of stagnating.

What I didn't realise was that Liverpool were already putting together a dossier on me. The scouting operation at Anfield back then was run by Andy Beattie, whom Bill Shankly had once assisted as manager at Huddersfield Town, and Geoff Twentyman, an ex-wrestler who used to drive up and down the country in search of talented up-and-coming players. Shankly's staff came to watch me when we played Tranmere Rovers in an FA Cup second replay on neutral ground at Everton's Goodison Park and, though I have heard various accounts about exactly how the deal came together, apparently Bob Paisley, his right-hand man, had also given me a solid recommendation.

Unbeknown to me, Shankly's scouts had already been banging the drum on my behalf, and apparently it helped as well that Peter Robinson, Liverpool's club secretary, once worked in the same role for Scunthorpe. Liverpool had already used that link to help them sign Ray Clemence, a future England international goalkeeper, and the story goes that Jack Brownsword rang Peter one day to ask, as clubs often did, for tickets to a game at Anfield. Shankly was in the background and asked to be put on the line because, though he did not know Jack, he was impressed by the way our trainer had played into his forties and wanted to introduce himself. Peter put them on the line and it was in the following conversation that Jack mentioned Liverpool should pay attention to the young lad wearing Scunthorpe's number eight.

Not that I knew any of this. As far as I was concerned, I was going to be stuck at Scunthorpe for a long time to come and I was still feeling a bit sorry for myself, impatiently of the view that my chance might have passed me by, when Ron Ashman took me to one side to say he had an important question for me.

What he said came totally out of the blue. 'Have you got a good suit?'

The honest answer was that, no, I hadn't.

'Well, you're going to need one,' he said. 'Where you're heading, you're going to need to look smart.'

4

THIS IS ANFIELD

I will never forget the first time I played in front of the Liverpool fans and the way they used to funnel all their colossal passion into ninety minutes on a Saturday afternoon. The only thing I used to fear was missing an open goal in front of the Kop – I think I would have died on the spot – and it used to make my eyes water when the crowd started singing 'You'll Never Walk Alone'. Even now, it can still make me emotional to hear that famous anthem. I've actually cried during games listening to it reverberate through the stands.

My debut came against Nottingham Forest on 14 August 1971, though if you ever see the five-pence 'Anfield Review', Liverpool's match-day programme, from that game, you could be forgiven for suspecting I might have my dates mixed up. Someone sent me a copy some years later and it amused me to realise my transfer from Scunthorpe, for the princely sum of £33,000, had not merited a single sentence. I didn't even feature in the list of first-team players or the statistics page, 'Just for the Record', that was described in the chairman Eric Roberts's column as being as 'detailed as any in the country'. There was, as we Yorkshiremen say, nowt about me – though, in fairness, who could possibly have imagined the mighty Liverpool would start the 1971–2 season with me in their team? I certainly didn't. I doubt the Nottingham Forest players had ever heard of me, and the thought did occur when I ran on to the pitch, with 23,000 Liverpool fans swaying like human blancmange on the Kop, that there must have been a few of our own supporters wondering who this little imposter with the long hair was.

I couldn't blame them either, because it was virtually unheard of for a player to go from the wilderness of the Fourth Division straight into the first team of a club Liverpool's size. I was as surprised as anybody and – demonstrating why my teammates would later give me the nickname of 'Andy McDaft' – I shudder to think how close I was to dropping the biggest rick of my life.

The problem was my lack of local knowledge. My digs were on Lilley Road, in Liverpool's Fairfield district, under the care of my new landlady, Mrs Lindholme, and on a normal day I had worked out it would take five to ten minutes to get to Anfield. Stupidly, though, I had forgotten to take into account it was the first weekend of a new football season and that, amazingly enough, the traffic for a Liverpool match watched by 50,000-plus people might be a little heavier than the roads around the Old Showground, Scunthorpe, on an average Saturday afternoon. I had been told to be at Anfield by 2 p.m. I didn't set off until 1.45 p.m., with Jean, Mum, Dad and Mike in my Ford Cortina and, after inching through the choked streets, when we came to a police roadblock half a mile from the ground I was starting to fear the worst. I leant out of my window and tried to explain to the policeman that I had just left Scunthorpe United in the Fourth Division and was meant to be playing for Liverpool that afternoon. But he had heard it all before. 'Of course you are, son,' he laughed. 'You don't think I do this for a living, do you? Twenty minutes more of this, lad, then I've got to get my kit on, too. Now, go round the other way like everybody else.'

I couldn't blame him for thinking I was trying it on, and I was just glad the stewards let me through when I finally made it to the ground. I'm not sure they recognised this anonymous kid with a Yorkshire accent either. Nobody really had a clue who I was and I have to confess I felt a bit of a fraud when we ran out of the tunnel that day, into the most incredible din I had ever heard in my life, and my teammates took the crowd's acclaim by clapping each side of the ground. I didn't know this routine but I tried my best to make it look as if I knew what I was doing, and when we turned to face the Kop, with all the red and white scarves and banners being held aloft, the reception was something special.

In those days it was customary for a new player to be welcomed by a representative of the Kop. Suddenly an old chap appeared on the pitch to give me a stubbly peck on the cheek. He had enough booze on his breath to knock me out! Then he knelt down to kiss the grass before rejoining his mates in that vast, heaving terrace. The noise was deafening and, in a strange way, maybe it worked in my favour that I had been delayed on the drive to Anfield. I had to get changed in such a rush that there was no time to feel nervous or start fretting that perhaps the crowd were expecting Ian Callaghan to be wearing Liverpool's number seven. Then the game kicked off. I played, I scored, and my life was never the same again.

Everything had happened so quickly since Ron Ashman, my manager at Scunthorpe, had driven me across Woodhead Pass and the East Lancs Road (the M62 not being open at that stage) at the end of the previous season to complete my transfer and have my first audience with Bill Shankly. I had bought a new suit, following Ron's advice, and matched it with a red kipper tie. It turned out I looked a good deal smarter than Anfield, where the main stand was being rebuilt and Mr Shankly, as I addressed him, was doing his business from a temporary office to the side of the ground. As I waited for him outside, there was nowhere to sit apart from on an upturned dustbin, so I perched on the top, making chitchat with Ron until the manager of Liverpool made an appearance.

Fortunately, Shanks didn't hold it against me when I was late for my debut and, deep down, I think he admired the way I stood up for myself in our first meeting, when he offered me £45 a week and, cheeky whippersnapper that I was, I told him I had been expecting more. I can imagine Ron saw Scunthorpe's £33,000 floating away when I started haggling for a better deal, and he gave me an ear-bashing on the drive home for claiming, with maybe a touch of exaggeration, that I was actually earning close to £45 a week in the Fourth Division. Equally, I had to get a good deal for myself. Dad's last words to me when I left the house were, 'Don't sell yourself cheap, son.' Shanks knocked my wages up to £50 a week and passed me the pen to sign. 'If you do it for me, son, you will never have to ask for a rise again.' And I never did. Shanks, as always, was true to his word.

It certainly isn't easy to convey the respect I had for that man, other than to say it was one of the defining relationships of my life. He just had a special aura, with all that worldly knowledge and a rare, precious gift to express himself with wit and eloquence. Add to that an obsession with excellence and an acute understanding of what made a man tick. I will never meet anyone like him again. I loved him to bits and he was, without doubt, the most important influence on my playing career. He signed me, he opened my eyes, he turned me into a high-achieving striker and he was there at the point of my life when I needed someone to believe in me. 'Jesus Christ,' he was always saying, 'you're a great player. You're not just a great player, you're one of *the* great players.' That was exactly what I wanted to hear.

In a football sense, it felt as if he adopted me. We were miners' sons and maybe he saw something of his younger self in me. 'Son, just go out there and drop some hand grenades,' he told me before that first game against Nottingham Forest. I knew exactly what that meant: he wanted me to cause problems for the opposition all over the pitch. That was precisely what I wanted to do, too. But nobody had ever let me play that way before.

I have spent many hours talking with Shankly, and those times rank among the highlights of my life. It was a privilege to know him. It was because of Shanks and the way he could motivate and instil belief in his players that my career went on its sharp upward trajectory. Shanks told me I would play for England and, within eighteen months, I was. It was difficult at first to adjust to international football, but it was Shanks, again, who soothed my mind. 'They don't know how to play you,' he'd say. 'They don't know what your position is. Don't they ever come to watch you play for Liverpool to see what you can do? Don't they want to know how to get the best out of you?' Suddenly, like a conjuror waving his wand, he had made it England's fault, not my fault. That was Shanks – he always seemed to say the right thing at the right time.

My six years at Liverpool completely changed my life, given that the sum total of my football achievements until that point was a medal from my days in Doncaster junior league football and a silver nut dish when Scunthorpe were runners-up in the Lincolnshire Senior Cup.

By the end of my second season at Anfield, I had a league championship medal, a UEFA Cup winner's medal and all sorts of personal prizes to fit in a cabinet at my parents' house. Liverpool had never won a European trophy before, but we repeated that league and UEFA Cup double in 1976, after Bob Paisley had taken over from Shanks. Then the following season we went one better, winning the First Division again, plus the big one, the European Cup, in my final game for the club. Add to that the 1974 FA Cup final against Newcastle, which had an almost dreamlike quality, and I could never have imagined that football would bring so many joys, one after another, after another.

It was a fairy tale, and perhaps the best way to describe those years is that I can remember wanting each game to come quicker than the last one. Shanks made Liverpool great. Bob, to give him his due, made us even greater. I could never get as close to Bob, but in his quiet, understated way he proved to all the doubters, myself included, that it wasn't true that nobody could follow the great Shanks. Bob's knowledge of football was terrific. We just didn't appreciate it straight away because it had been concealed for so long under Shanks's brilliance.

There are so many great memories and, despite my humble beginnings at Scunthorpe, I cannot recall a single occasion when

I felt overawed. I joined in the week Liverpool were playing Arsenal in the 1971 FA Cup final, and I was invited to stay with the directors and players' families at the Waldorf Hotel in London. I had never been anywhere so posh in my life. Yet when I went to bed that night I told myself I was there because I deserved to be, and the following day, as Charlie George scored the winning goal for Arsenal and lay flat out on the Wembley pitch to celebrate, I was gripped by the feeling that if I had been playing I could have held my own. All the people sitting around me were telling me what they thought I wanted to hear, saying that if I knuckled down I might break into the team in a year or two. I didn't say it but, deep down, all I could think was that I might just shock a few people. I didn't feel a flicker of self-doubt and once I was given the chance to prove myself, I never looked back. I didn't know how, or why, I found it so easy to adjust. I just did.

It helped that I got off to a flying start by scoring twelve minutes into my debut against Forest and, of course, it quickly became clear that Shanks was ideal for me. I had heard of Bill Shankly when I was at Scunthorpe, but I didn't realise he had such an aura until that first meeting when he drove me to the medical examination and, sitting behind the wheel of his Ford Capri, off he went, half concentrating on the road, half looking at me. 'You'll like this place, son. Great supporters, you know. The best in the land. Tremendous to play for. Have you seen the Kop? No, I don't suppose you have.'

I knew my place. I didn't say a great deal, I just listened and soaked it all in. 'We've got some great players here, son. Emlyn Hughes, great player. Chris Lawler, great player. Tommy Smith, hard boy. Hard boy is Tommy . . . great player. Roger Hunt is gone now, but never forgotten. Ian St John, another great player. Aye, you'll like it here, son. There is a future here if you knuckle down and play.'

I got the impression straight away that he had warmed to me. I was twenty years of age, with little more than potential, but his eyes widened when I took off my shirt for the medical examination. Shanks wanted to know if I had ever considered boxing as an alternative career and, back at the club's offices, I overheard him making the same point to the staff, deliberately loud enough for me to hear every word. 'He looks nothing dressed, but you should see him stripped off. The boy's built like a tank.'

What really helped me settle in was an end-of-season tour to Scandinavia when I was one of the sixteen players chosen. It gave me the chance to get to know everyone and, while the senior players seemed to be treating it as a bit of a jolly, I was determined to make a favourable impression. We lost the first game 3–2 against Aarhus, but when we moved on to Luleå for our second game we won 5–0 and, as well as scoring my first goal in a Liverpool shirt, I was presented with a bronze statuette for winning the man-of-the-match award. I could tell from the attitude of the other players that they were beginning to think I could play, and even more so when I followed that up with another goal and man-of-the-match award in our final game of the tour in Sundsvall.

When we came back for pre-season training I was raring to go, but there was still no inkling that I was going to be fast-tracked into the first team, and I wasn't even included when Shanks put up the list for a tour of Holland and Germany.

Instead I stayed behind to play for the reserves against Tranmere Rovers, and was given my first lecture as a Liverpool player. The club had signed me as a midfielder and wanted me to play with positional discipline, not just trying to get behind the opposition defence, but also taking care not to stray too far from my own back four. I saw myself as an attacker. I thought it was a waste to put on the defensive shackles and Ronnie Moran, who was in charge of the reserves, didn't appreciate the way I kept bombing forward. 'What the hell do you think you're doing?' he started shouting at half-time. 'You're not playing like a Liverpool player.'

I thought I had been playing quite well and I felt myself shrinking in my seat. 'You're far too free and easy,' he continued. 'You're charging about the midfield, nearly playing up front.

You're a midfield player – you've got responsibilities defensively as well as in attack.'

I have to admit it knocked the wind out of my sails and, for a while, I genuinely thought Ronnie had it in for me. That was silly of me. Ronnie knew the game inside out and I suspect he explained to Bill Shankly what had happened, because when we had another reserve game shortly afterwards at Southport, I was moved into attack. Shanks was back from Germany and came to watch as I scored both our goals in a 2–1 win.

A few days later we had a game at Melwood, Liverpool's training ground, of red shirts against white shirts – first team against the reserves – and I was chosen ahead of Bobby Graham and Alun Evans to play up front with John Toshack in the first-choice XI. I didn't feel too much pressure because, in my view, it was probably the gaffer giving the others a kick up the backside after some iffy performances on tour. I was, however, absolutely determined to make Ronnie eat his words. We won 7–0 and I scored four. Everything I tried that day – overhead kicks, volleys from the edge of the area – came off, and Ian Ross, the defender I was up against, told me afterwards I should expect to start against Forest that coming Saturday.

Nobody from the coaching staff said anything, however, until two days before the game, when Shanks ambled over and asked me how I was finding my first summer as a Liverpool player.

I told him it had been brilliant.

'Do you feel fit?'

'Absolutely.'

'Where do you want to play on Saturday – for the first team or the reserves?'

That was the question I had been waiting to hear. 'I haven't come to Liverpool to play in the reserve team,' I replied.

'Good, good, off you go and get yourself a cup of tea, son.'

I telephoned Dad straight away and explained that he might want to start making travel plans. I didn't want to be too presumptuous but, sure enough, when the typewritten team-sheet, signed by Shanks, went up in the dressing room the following day, there it was: 'Liverpool v Nottingham Forest . . . 7 – Keegan.'

I hadn't even played a single reserve game, and it was a strange feeling to see my name up there. Ray Clemence, Chris Lawler, Alec Lindsay, Tommy Smith, Larry Lloyd, Emlyn Hughes, Kevin Keegan . . . wow . . . Peter Thompson, Steve Heighway, John Toshack, John McLaughlin. Yet I genuinely believed I deserved to be there, and my only problem, as it turned out, was my lack of Liverpudlian knowledge that meant turning up twenty-five minutes late on match-day.

Shanks did growl at me when I bolted in. He had been pacing the corridors, waiting for me, and there were a few wisecracks from the other players. But I was ready. The dressing room was pristine and my kit had been laid out neatly, with my boots beneath the bench. 'Go out and enjoy it,' Shanks told me. And then I was on the pitch, trying to take in all the colour and noise. The Kop was every bit as loud and magical as I had been told, and when Tosh picked me out for my first chance inside the penalty area, I fully intended to leather the ball as hard as I could and, if possible, put a hole in the roof of the net.

I mishit it and, inwardly, there was a split second where I cursed myself for snatching at the shot. Then I looked up and saw the ball bobbling past Jim Barron, Forest's goalkeeper, and the two nearest defenders. It was the scruffiest, most beautiful goal I had ever scored, directly in front of the Kop. We won 3–1 and at some point I became aware of a deep, booming noise I had never heard before. It was the crowd chanting my name. 'Ke-vin Kee-gan . . . Ke-vin Kee-gan.' It was surreal and could not have been more different from Scunthorpe, where you could hear the fans' individual shouts, and often a holler suggesting that such-and-such a player should have stayed out of the pub the previous night. I was soon knocking the ball one side of a Forest player and running round the other way to meet it, just as I had done on the Bullring all those years before. I was a Liverpool player and everything had fallen into place. It was some feeling.

After that game, I was a fixture in the team, and my life changed very quickly. Alf Ramsey selected me for my first England under-23 cap the following February. Liverpool finished third in my first season, though only a point behind the champions Derby, and I was voted as the Football League Review's Young Footballer of the Year, Granada TV's Player of the Year and Bargain Buy of the Year and Merseyside Footballer of the Year.

George Best was still bewitching the crowds at Manchester United, but the media wanted another player who could be built into a superstar. I ticked all the boxes, I suppose, but it was a completely new world to me. I had scarcely been asked for an autograph in all my time at Scunthorpe, and it felt weird that suddenly fans were queueing up for one. I used to sign my name as 'JK Keegan' but, now people actually wanted me to write it down for them, it didn't feel right to confuse everyone with the fact I was christened Joseph. Dad thought the same and suggested I started squiggling down some different ideas until I had perfected a new signature.

I had always enjoyed meeting people, and I knew from experience that it should be taken seriously. As a youngster, I once waited two hours outside Belle Vue in the hope of getting the autograph of one of my favourite Doncaster players. The car park was virtually deserted by the time he came out. There was nobody else around and he was walking to his car when I held out a pen and asked if he could please sign my book. He could have sent me home as the happiest child in the world but he didn't break stride. 'Sorry, son, bit too busy today.' It broke my heart. What he meant was, 'I'm too important for this, pal – now get lost, buzz off.' I won't mention his name, but it taught me a lesson that I never forgot. I would always devote time, no matter how busy I was, because I knew what it felt like when the person you admired said he was too busy. It was something, as a manager, I tried to instil in my players, and it used to shock me when I was playing for Hamburg that my teammates in Germany found it such a drag. They just didn't want to do it, whereas I would spend hours signing my name for the fans, not least because it was one way to meet new people and improve my language skills.

It was quite a culture shock, though, when fame started to engulf me in my first couple of seasons at Liverpool. Letters from all around the world began to pile up and, with help from Jean, I made an office in a back room of a junk shop on Prescot Road. Ray Clemence had introduced me to the owner, 'Lennie the Junk', and it was here that I set up the Kevin Keegan fan club, as well as using it as the headquarters for my limited company, Nageek Enterprises (Keegan spelt backwards).

It was incredible how many companies suddenly wanted to put my name and face to their products. My first boot deal was with Stylo Matchmakers, but I also had my own range of pyjamas, my Pirelli slippers, a deal with Smith's Crisps, the Kevin Keegan 'Goal' ice lolly (with a plastic stick shaped as me), my own football annual, my Mettoy football, the Grundig 'Hit Boy' radio, a sticker album, a skills book, a Grandstand electronic action game, and much, much more. My only rule was that I would not advertise beer: I was not a drinker and I thought it set a bad example to be promoting alcohol.

Until I appeared on the scene, George Best had been the go-to man for commercial deals. The problem with George was that he rarely turned up to the events he was being paid to attend. I was a lot more reliable, and even took over his *Daily Express* column – which paid me more than I was earning at Liverpool. I became the face of the Green Cross Code, filming an advert outside Anfield in a pair of flares so wide I could barely even see my shoes, and I am still reminded about showering with Henry Cooper in the television commercials for Brut – the deodorant with muscle! It's funny when I am doing talks now, and ask everyone to put up their hands if they have ever splashed on a bit of Brut aftershave. Every man over the age of forty will raise his hand.

In those early days at Liverpool, however, that side of life was all new to me, and I have since been told that the staff felt uneasy about all the attention I was suddenly getting. Nobody else at Anfield was being offered so many commercial arrangements, and at one point Shanks did wander over for one of his little chats. 'It's going great, son,' he said. 'You're doing fantastic, team's on fire, you're playing better each week . . . but just one thing, son, always remember your main contract is playing football, that's why you get everything else.' I knew what he was doing. It was a little shot across the bows, a reminder not to lose my focus. I don't think I ever would have done, but he was making sure anyway.

I went on to score ten more times in my first season for Liverpool, and my partnership with John Toshack was so effective that we were even put through a test on television to find out if there was anything in the theory that we had a telepathic understanding. Each of us had to look at a colour and a shape and then transmit the image to one another using only the force of our minds. It came back negative but, rather than spoiling everyone's fun, we kept that quiet and carried on living up to the perception that the pair of us could somehow read each other's minds.

The negative results didn't particularly surprise me, because Tosh and I never particularly socialised and were not what I would call close friends. But I did like him, and on the pitch it was uncanny how we knew what the other was going to do. We were one of the first genuine partnerships, the big guy and the little guy hunting together in tandem, and he was one of only two players in my career with whom I have had that kind of understanding. The other was Trevor Brooking, who seemed to know everything I was thinking, and vice versa, when we were playing for England. Tosh knew instinctively when I was going to run, when I wanted the ball short and when I wanted it long. He was a tremendous finisher, one of the best I ever played with, and I certainly wouldn't have scored so many goals without him providing the ammunition. Little and Large, Batman and Robin – we got called all sorts and we were happy to play up to it, having our photographs taken in the appropriate costumes.

At Liverpool, there was a pecking order and, for most of the younger players, there was an unwritten rule in place. You did as you were told, you kept quiet, and you didn't have too many opinions. I was a bit different. I felt I was playing well enough to have a voice and, if something needed to be said, I would say it. But it was a tough school, and there was no doubt which player was at the top of the tree.

Tommy Smith was a hard man. He was the leader in the dressing room, and a very good one. I liked Tommy, and always felt it was unfair that he was notorious because of the fear he instilled in his opponents. 'Tommy,' Bob Paisley once said, 'doesn't tackle players so much as break them down for scrap.' Tommy made that reputation for himself and there was no doubt some players were frightened of him, but he was not as dirty as people made out. Smidge went in hard but mostly for the ball, not the man. He looked tough, and he was tough, but a lot of it was finger-wagging rather than anything more sinister, and he spent a lot of his career being a very accomplished footballer without really getting the credit he deserved.

Early on, though, I have to admit I did think he was a bit of a bully. You couldn't go past Tommy if you were part of his group on our training runs – 'Hey, you little swine, where do you think you're going?' he'd bark – but the bigger problem, as I saw it, was his perception of me and the way that he had been at Liverpool a long time and resented the publicity I was getting.

It began to dawn on me that we might have a problem during one trip away when I came down to the hotel restaurant in the morning and, unbeknown to me, ordered the same breakfast as another player. When the waiter put a plate in front of me, I got stuck in without realising it might be somebody else's. 'That's not yours,' Tommy shouted. 'Wait your turn – you're not as big as you think you are.' He was trying to bring me down a peg or two, and it was important I stood up to him. I told him where to go, to put it bluntly, and made it clear he wasn't going to intimidate me like he might some of the other young players.

It was always likely there would be some afters and, sure enough, there was one occasion at Melwood when we raised our fists and started trading punches, until big Larry Lloyd jumped in to separate us. From that point on, however, the bad feeling disappeared and everything was OK between us.

Tommy was Liverpool through and through, and streetwise enough to use me at times. There was the time Hummel offered me a small fortune – £3,000, if I remember correctly – if I would wear a pair of their white boots. Alan Ball, then at Everton, had been signed up to do the same, as had Martin Chivers at Tottenham and Alan Hinton of Derby County. It was really good money, but I felt I should ask Tommy, as captain, what he thought about me ditching the traditional black boots that everybody wore in those days. Tommy asked how much I was going to make and looked very impressed when I reeled off the figures. But then he held up the boots I had been sent from Hummel, looked at them closely and shook his head. 'They're not for you,' he explained. 'Just picture it. Martin Chivers of Spurs – white socks, white boots: that will look OK. Alan Hinton, same again at Derby – white socks, white boots, fine. Everton, white socks, white boots – perfect for Bally. But Liverpool? Red shirts, red shorts, red socks and white boots. You're going to look a right prat if you're not careful.'

It wasn't what I wanted to hear, but I didn't want to push my luck if that was what the captain thought of it. It was a lot of money to pass up but, equally, I knew there would be other offers, and by that stage I was doing well for myself anyway. I didn't want to be seen as too flash, and Tommy made the point that if I carried on doing the business for Liverpool, I would have all the other boot manufacturers fighting over me. We turned up for the game the following weekend and, just as we were about to run out, I looked over at Tommy and did a double-take. He was wearing a red shirt, red shorts and red socks – and you can probably guess the colour of his boots. He saw me staring. Then he lifted up his foot so I could get a better look. 'Hummel,' he announced. 'Can't turn down £1,500 at this stage of my career, lad.'

I had to laugh at his sheer nerve. Tommy was coming to the end of his Liverpool career and I couldn't begrudge him his new boot deal. It did make me feel slightly better, though, that he was very self-conscious in those white boots. He even started dabbing on streaks of red boot polish to stop them dazzling quite so brightly under the floodlights. Tommy being Tommy, that just started a rumour that it was the blood of his opponents.

When he wasn't doing me up like a kipper, Tommy was one of the prime reasons why Liverpool had the best defensive statistics in the league in each of my six seasons at the club. Ray Clemence's presence was another major factor because, on his day, our goalkeeper was virtually unbeatable. We prided ourselves on being parsimonious at the back, but we generally finished near the top of the scoring charts as well. We also did it without spending an absolute fortune, if you consider that I cost £33,000, Clem was £27,000 and Steve Heighway had come straight from university, costing us nothing. Brian Hall was another university graduate, whereas Tommy and Chris Lawler were also local discoveries. Ian Callaghan was another Liverpudlian who would go on to become the club's record appearance-maker. Jimmy Case came from non-league, two years after me, for £10,000. Ray Kennedy cost £200,000, whereas Tosh and Peter Cormack were £110,000 each, and I suppose £65,000 would have been a big deal when Emlyn Hughes signed from Blackpool in 1967. But we weren't beating teams because we were blowing everyone out of the water in the transfer market. Liverpool managed to do it while being prudent with their spending. We never came close to breaking the transfer record in all my time there.

A lot of our success was built on a sense of togetherness, though it is well known Tommy and Emlyn had a huge fall-out that was never resolved. Tommy resented the way Emlyn replaced him as captain. Emlyn had also moved back from midfield to play in the centre of defence and that meant Tommy being shunted out to play at right-back. That put his nose out of joint, and it got even worse when he found out that Emlyn had gone behind his back to Bob Paisley to complain that Tommy was too slow to play in the back four.

I can still remember the moment after a game at QPR when Bob let it slip. Phil Neal had joined us from Northampton Town and was playing at right-back. That meant Tommy was out of the team. We lost 2–0 and Bob was having a go at Emlyn, blaming him for the first goal. 'You asked me to bring in some extra pace at right-back,' Bob shouted, gesturing to Phil. 'Well, I did that for you and that's the last time I listen when you come calling.'

There was an awful moment when everyone realised Bob had dropped Emlyn in it. Tommy, a substitute, rose to his feet, and his face changed colour as he turned to Emlyn. 'You bastard,' he snapped. 'I should knock the living daylights out of you.'

From that day on, Tommy held a terrible grudge. He was very bitter, convinced he had been stabbed in the back. I have lost count of the number of times that people have told me they have seen him on the after-dinner circuit and been shocked by the way he can't let it go. I liked them both, and the saddest thing is I have photographs of the two of them together in the early days when they got on fine. I did try to speak to Tommy about it after Emlyn's death, telling him it was time to put it behind him and remember all the happy occasions. He didn't want to listen, though.

That apart, it was a happy ship and – to give them their due – Tommy and Emlyn were too professional to let their personal feelings affect what happened on match-day. People assume that our only consideration was winning trophies, and the old Bill Shankly ethos that first was first and second nowhere. But there was more to us than that. Shanks, in particular, taught us a way of life, how to deal with people and understand the importance of doing things the right way.

He also understood there had to be laughter at any successful football club. Shanks was never short of a line, whether he was joshing with the fans or having a bit of fun at the expense of one of the players. He always used to mention his daughter during practice matches – 'Christ', he'd shout, 'our Jeannette could have scored that one!' – and he was blessed with such great comedy timing that there were times when I was actually laughing while running for the ball. Liverpool was a happy place, full of banter and levity.

It was on his watch that the 'THIS IS ANFIELD' sign went up above the stairs leading from the tunnel to the pitch. Shanks never missed a trick when it came to building up Liverpool's profile. That sign was put there to intimidate and worry the opposition, and it soon became tradition for us Liverpool players to reach up and touch it for good luck as we ran out.

Malcolm Macdonald, one of the more prolific strikers in the country during his Newcastle days, was a friend of mine, but he made a few mistakes when it came to Liverpool – and Bill Shankly – and one of them was to poke fun at that sign. Shanks was talking to the Newcastle manager, Joe Harvey, at the time. I was coming out of the dressing room as Malcolm looked up at the sign and, grinning, turned to Joe. 'I told you we had found the right place,' he joked.

'Aye,' Shanks shot back. 'Wait till you get out there, son, and you'll know you're at Anfield. You can run but you canna hide!'

I am struggling to think of another man who spoke with such authority and gravitas. The supporters loved it when he waved to them in his 'lucky' grey suit and deep red shirt, like a messiah acknowledging the worshipping faithful, and I always felt Shanks could have been a great socialist leader because he had such a human touch. He won people over because they knew he was genuine and he used those socialist ideals in his approach to football. Liverpool didn't want fancy-dans or big-time Charlies who were in it for themselves. Shanks demanded the players worked as a team and gave everything for one another.

He also had the knack of making you feel like any mountain could be climbed. The time, for example, we played against West

Ham, and I was up against the great Bobby Moore, captain of the England team that had won the World Cup in 1966. Shanks liked to stand in the passage outside the dressing rooms. He did it deliberately so he could inspect our opponents, checking if anyone was missing and listening into their conversations. Then he came back to our changing room to deliver his verdict. 'I've just seen that Bobby Moore,' he announced. 'Big bags under his eyes. Limping. He's been out in a nightclub again last night, I can tell.' His gaze darted round the room, and then he was staring straight at me. 'He's scared stiff of playing against you, son. You'll run him silly. It wrenches at my heart, it's tragic, because he was a great player. He's gone, but show him no mercy. Do your job, son, massacre him.'

By the time he had finished, I was convinced one of the legends of our game was actually playing on one leg and the worst defender in the entire league. We won 1–0 and I scored the goal. Afterwards, the boss sat next to me, beaming. 'Jesus Christ, what a great player that Bobby Moore is. You'll never play against a better or fitter player. He's a master, but you had the beating of him today. Grow in confidence, son. You were up against world class and you ran rings round him.' It was classic Shanks psychology. Having built me up before the match, he was making sure I would not go away thinking I had done well because of a flaw in my opponent. And it was true – Moore was magnificent that day, despite being on the losing side.

It was very simple really. When Bill Shankly talked, you listened, and reminded yourself that you were lucky to be in his presence. He didn't actually speak as much as some people assume. But his team-talks were always interesting and he had the priceless knack of being able to articulate himself in two or three perfectly clipped sentences when it might have taken another manager ten minutes to make the same point.

His greatest team-talk came the day before we played Newcastle in the 1974 FA Cup final and I doubt it lasted thirty seconds. This time, Malcolm Macdonald had been spouting off in the press about how much better than us they were. 'Super-Mac' had become 'SuperGob'. John Tudor, another of the Newcastle players, also had plenty to say, but Malcolm, in particular, had gone over the top. 'We were too slow at the back . . . Tommy Smith was past it . . . we wouldn't be able to handle Newcastle's pace.' He and his teammates made a few quid out of those interviews, but it played straight into our hands, winding us up something rotten.

We were staying at Selsdon Park Hotel in Croydon when word got round that Shanks had called a team meeting. He marched in, pinned the latest offending article to the wall and then strode out again. 'There you go, boys,' he growled. 'I don't need to say any more than that. It's all been said.' There was no need for a proper team-talk the following day. We couldn't wait to get on the pitch and make a few people eat humble pie.

Even when he didn't mean to, Shanks had a habit of saying exactly the right thing. On the night before the final, the television people had arranged for him and Joe Harvey to take part in a two-way interview from the respective team hotels. We were all watching from our rooms and I'm sure the Newcastle players were doing the same. Shanks was saying all the right things, being polite and respectful about Newcastle and talking about what a wonderful occasion it would be. But Joe looked very ill at ease, staring into the camera without the same kind of telegenic presence. Shanks removed his microphone, turned to someone in the room and said very audibly, 'Joe's a bag of nerves, isn't he?' But his microphone was still switched on and everyone could hear him. It was a killer line and, knowing how Shanks worked, I wouldn't rule out the possibility he knew exactly what he was doing. The next day it seemed to be contagious. Newcastle's players were all a bag of nerves whereas it never really entered our minds that we might lose or not play well.

That final always comes to mind when I am asked to pick out the highlights from my time as a Liverpool player. It was my first club appearance at Wembley, back in the days when it felt like the

FA Cup was the most important competition in the world, and I've never forgotten the anticipation of driving to the stadium, convinced we were going to win, with 100,000 people in the crowd and millions more tuning in. It was a supporters' final, with almost constant chanting, and I said afterwards it must have been the closest you could get in football to a psychedelic experience. After everything they had to say in the build-up, Macdonald and Tudor barely had a sniff.

We didn't rub it in, though. I actually felt sorry for the Newcastle lads, seeing how devastated they were as we waited to walk up the steps to collect the trophy. Shanks chatted among them and tried to console them, which was typical of the man, and it was only when we were three-quarters of the way through the lap of honour that I realised, in all the elation, we had somehow left the most important person at Liverpool behind. Shanks was not with us. He had walked back to the dressing room, alone, and when we finally joined him it did occur to me that he was not quite his usual self. What I didn't know was that life at Liverpool was never going to be quite the same again.

5

EUROPEAN CHAMPIONS

When I heard Bill Shankly was retiring from his role as Liverpool manager, my first reaction was that it had to be some kind of joke, though not a particularly funny one. The news plunged the whole of football into shock and on Merseyside we were hoping it was all a terrible misunderstanding. It was difficult to take in and, amid the general sense of disbelief on that summer day in 1974, I will never forget the stunned responses when Granada TV sent one of its correspondents into the centre of Liverpool to get the reaction of the team's supporters.

The footage is still on the internet. The first group of Liverpool supporters who are approached opposite St George's Hall, with their big 1970s haircuts, their flared trousers and super-sized collars, clearly think it is a prank. 'You're kidding?' one says, and he actually takes a nervous step back as the reporter tells him the news. He's smiling, but it is the smile of a man who wants to be told it is all a wind-up. 'I'm not kidding,' the reporter tells him. 'I'm deadly serious, I swear it's true.'

Still, nobody believes him. Or, at least, nobody wants to believe him. Further down the street, the next guy shakes his head. 'Nah, I don't believe that.' An elderly lady with glasses chides the interviewer – 'you'll have me crying' – and scuttles away to continue her shopping. 'This isn't in the papers,' another guy points out, full of indignation.

'Shankly?' someone asks, disbelievingly. 'Bill Shankly?'

But it is the youngest fan whose reaction is etched on my

mind. He is no older than nine or ten, with a shrill Scouse accent and hair cascading over his ears, and there is a look of sheer helplessness on his face.

'You're having me on, aren't you?' he asks.

'No,' the reporter tells him. 'I'm not having you on – I've just been to Anfield. Honest . . .'

The man with the microphone is starting to sound exasperated about the way nobody is willing to believe him. But the poor kid still isn't having it. 'Who said?' he asks, and his eyes are flitting to someone off-camera – a parent, presumably – for reassurance. That boy will be in his mid-50s now, and I wonder, all these years later, if he can still remember the sense of desolation that day. He looks as if his whole world has fallen in.

I knew how he felt. The news hit me like a sledgehammer and, in all the confusion, all sorts of thoughts flashed through my mind, not least that Shanks might be ill. The official explanation was that he wanted a rest, but it made no sense that he could just walk away from his life's work, at the age of sixty, when he was still fit and healthy. Shanks said it was because of his family, but I still ask myself whether there was more to it. Everyone was hearing different things, and the story I was told was that he would often threaten to resign when it came to negotiating a pay rise at the end of each season. The club used to think it was all hot air because they knew how much football meant to him and never expected him to see it through. Maybe they called his bluff this time. Or maybe he just wanted to go out on the high of winning the FA Cup. I would dearly love to know.

Even now, I still get emotional when I watch the old clips and hear that sharp, distinctive Scottish accent, undiminished by all those years south of the border. Shanks retired much too early. I will never change my mind on that front and, as much as I liked and respected Bob Paisley, a little bit of the club died for me when the great man left. That is no disrespect to Bob, Joe Fagan, Ronnie Moran or anybody else, but in my last three years it felt as though Liverpool were never quite the same club. It was still the place to be in English football, playing for a formidable team in front of a vibrant crowd and representing a city that was full of character and attitude, but I could never recapture the same feeling. We carried on winning trophies but something had been lost for me.

Worse, the club then allowed a rift to develop that meant, in later years, Shanks would say he felt more welcome at Everton and Manchester United than he did going back to Anfield or Melwood. Liverpool didn't often get things wrong, but they did this time, spectacularly. It was the saddest, saddest thing, and I blame the club, because someone should have had a quiet word when Shanks started turning up at Melwood. He just couldn't let go. The players would see him and instinctively greet him with 'Hello, boss', whereas Bob Paisley would get a 'Morning, Bob'. We were all pleased to see Shanks but it undermined the new manager and that, I suspect, was when the aggravation started. Shanks could have shown more tact, but the people behind the scenes should have nipped it in the bud. More should have been done to keep him involved at the highest level of the club, but the situation was allowed to fester and it was a scandal that he was made to feel like his face didn't fit.

In my view it wouldn't have been too much if Liverpool had built a throne for him in the middle of the directors' box. Indeed, I have argued in the past that Anfield should have been renamed the Bill Shankly stadium. It pained me that the bad feeling was not resolved before his death in 1981. It was wrong to let a man like that just drift away from the club, but Shanks had his pride and he would not have wanted to be anywhere he did not feel welcome.

Ultimately, though, it will never change the way he is revered on Merseyside. Shanks will remain loved and respected and it sums up his legacy that the stories of the man have lived on long after him, growing with time rather than diminishing. Everyone knows the line about football not being 'a matter of life or death – it's much more important than that', but there were a thousand more where that came from. Shanks was always quotable. He must have been a dream for the Merseyside press corps. He certainly was as a player, and I will never forget the moment, walking beside his coffin on the way to his funeral at St Mary's Church in West Derby, when the cortège turned the corner from Bill's house to pass Bellefield, Everton's training ground. All the Everton players, still in their muddy kits, had stopped training to line up by the entrance, their heads bowed in respect. It was very emotional, one of the loveliest things I have ever seen in football.

Several of his old stalwarts were invited to be pallbearers. It was an honour to be alongside Ron Yeats, Emlyn Hughes, John Toshack, Ian St John and Tommy Smith, still doing our best Shanks impressions through teary laughter in the front room of his house, and I just wish I had never lost the silver medallion my old boss gave me, in the shape of a number thirteen, after he had retired. It wasn't my number but it still meant an awful lot to me that he felt I should have it. He told me a woman in Prague had given it to him and that she had said if he wore it every day he would never die. The first time it went missing I don't think I scored for eight games. Eventually, it turned up again, and I wore it for two years before a game against Derby, when it came loose again and was trodden into the mud of the Baseball Ground pitch.

I wear another medallion now, in the shape of a number seven, but for Shanks to give me a personal gift, and me to lose it, was very upsetting. I do, however, still have the commemorative sword from when I won my second European Footballer of the Year award in 1979 and Hamburg gave me permission to fly to London for a presentation arranged by Wilkinson, the razor-blade company. Shanks had travelled down to surprise me, and when I took the sword from him I passed it straight back. 'Please,' I said, 'take it. Without you I would never have been in a position for anything like this.' It was the first time I have ever seen Shanks look emotional. His instinctive reaction was to try to hand it back again. 'It's yours, please take it,' I insisted. He paused for a few moments, looked down at the case in his hands, then replied quietly, 'When I die, I'll make sure you get it back, son.' That was all he said. A week after his funeral, his widow, Nessie, called me to say she had the sword, and that Bill had told her that when he passed away he wanted me to have it back.

Bob had been Shanks's right-hand man, and also doubled up as the club's physiotherapist, even though he wasn't actually qualified medically. It took a long time before it felt natural to call him 'Boss', and in his previous role we used to refer to him as 'The Rat', because of the way he liked to regale us with his exploits as a Desert Rat during the war. Bob was a hard taskmaster and Shanks used him as his hatchet-man if something had gone wrong or someone needed disciplining. It wasn't Shanks, for the most part, who would tell a player if he wasn't in the team, it was Bob. That made the players a bit suspicious of him, and a lot of us wondered whether he was really equipped to be Liverpool manager rather than sticking as the number two.

Bob definitely didn't have Shanks's communication skills, and his biggest problem, certainly in the early days, was that everything he did was always going to be compared to his predecessor. Shanks was a legend at Liverpool – *the* legend. Bob was a very different person, and I will never forget the day he gathered us together at Melwood for our first meeting of the new era.

Those meetings can be crucial for a new manager, with all the players waiting to see how he projects himself, and when Bob turned up he didn't even stand in the middle of the room. He had his back against the wall and his first words were, 'Eeeee, I didn't want the job anyway.' Classic Bob: he could have pretended the opposite was true, but it was never his style to play to the gallery. Bob was always to the point, and no messing. He was born in Hetton-le-Hole, where my father was raised in the north-east, and they were very similar in that respect, brought up to say exactly what was on their minds.

Bob had all sorts of strange sayings, such as warning us to keep an eye on Tony Currie of Sheffield United because 'he can flick a far-flung one', meaning he could hit a decent long ball. When we played Newcastle they had a winger called Stewart Barrowclough, and Bob would say, 'Watch that fellow Wheelbarrow, he's fast.' He used to tell us, in his County Durham accent, that something was 'a pound to a pinch of shit' – in modern parlance, that it was a no-brainer – and his first team-talk before a game against Luton was infamous among the lads because of his inability to conjure up the names of the opposition players. Tommy Smith was told to look out for 'whatcha-me-cally on the wing' and Brian Hall was under instructions to 'keep an eye on thingy-me-bob'. When the players asked Bob who he meant, he started clicking his fingers, trying to jog his memory, and eventually gave up. 'Ah, bollocks,' he exclaimed. 'Just go out and beat them.' Then he casually made his way out, humming a little song.

We finished second in the league in his first season, two points behind Derby, and the fact that was considered a failure on Merseyside showed the size of his task. After that, however, Liverpool went back to creating a dynasty. The championship trophy returned to Liverpool in his second season, and we were also reunited with the UEFA Cup, after a three-year gap, when we beat Club Brugge over two legs.

The first leg was one of those Anfield occasions I will never forget, as we came back from two goals down at half-time to score three times in six minutes. I scored the third from the penalty spot and I followed that up with the equaliser in our 1–1 draw in Belgium during the second leg. I still have a photograph of my dad from that trip to Bruges. Happy days, indeed.

The following season, 1976–7, we did even better, defending the First Division title and winning the European Cup against Borussia Mönchengladbach at the Stadio Olimpico in Rome. The only disappointment was a poor performance against Manchester United in the FA Cup final, which denied us an unprecedented treble. Yet that 2–1 defeat at Wembley fired us up even more to make sure there was no more disappointment in Rome four days later, and overall I am proud to say I worked with two of the greatest club managers there ever were, not just one. In total, I won nine trophies at Liverpool, if we include the two Charity Shields, and six were with Bob. I might not have been able to relate to him as I did with Shanks, but that was because the man who signed me from Scunthorpe was a complete one-off. Bob had a different way, but he helped the team scale even greater heights and continued winning trophies, including two more European Cups, after I had left. Bob was tremendous for me. I owed him a lot and still do.

I was cut up when Shanks left, though. I was in a dark mood and it probably wasn't a coincidence that I reacted so aggressively when we played a pre-season friendly in Kaiserslautern and one of the German players scythed down Ray Kennedy with an awful tackle. Several of us went for the perpetrator but I got there first. The referee sent me off for violent conduct, but I was let off when we came back to England because Liverpool cooked up a story that it was a case of mistaken identity. Peter Cormack, one of my closest friends at Anfield, came up with the idea. Peter was not too much taller than me. He had a similar build and the same hairstyle and, trying to spare me a ban, he suggested Liverpool pretend the referee had mixed us up. 'And, besides, I would have been proud of that punch, Kev,' he said, smiling mischievously. It would be impossible to get away with something like that now, but no further action was taken and the case was dropped.

Unfortunately, there was no escaping what happened four days later when we played in the Charity Shield and I had the ignominy, along with Billy Bremner of Leeds United, of being sent for an early bath because of our infamous punch-up on the Wembley pitch.

To describe it as embarrassing would be an understatement, and it resulted in the pair of us being charged with bringing the game into disrepute and banned for eleven games. Nobody had ever been suspended for that length of time for throwing a punch on a football pitch, but it might have been even worse given that one Harrow resident applied to the local magistrates' court for a summons to be taken out for 'behaviour in a public place likely to cause a breach of peace.' The magistrates turned down the application, but we were shown a letter which had been passed on to the Football Association by the Home Office, with one MP calling for us to be banned for life. Bob summed up my views with a line that Shanks would have been proud of. 'People who don't know how to run the country are trying to run football, which they know even less about,' he said.

As punch-ups go, it is fair to say Billy and I were trying to spark each other's lights out. The red mist had well and truly descended, and I doubt it helped my cause at the disciplinary commission that Tommy Smith, of all people, was called to give evidence on my behalf. Tommy was so notorious in those days it was like asking one of the Great Train Robbers to pass judgement on a case of petty shoplifting. Tommy set the tone by asking how one member of the commission qualified for the role when he was on holiday at the time of the match. When he was told he was not supposed to be asking questions, the iron man of Anfield burst out laughing, and that was the point at which Matt Busby, another member of the commission, stepped in to say, 'That'll be all, Tommy, thanks for coming.' I was grateful for Smidge's support, but perhaps I could have chosen a better character witness!

I deserved to be punished, and I know Billy regretted it every bit as much as I did. Billy even knocked on our dressing-room door, with the game still going on, to apologise. I was still in my shorts and had no intention of prolonging the argument when I saw this tough midfield general, the captain of Leeds and Scotland, in tears. My dad, who was coming up for seventy, had come down from the stands to console me, and I seriously thought he was going to chin Billy. 'You bugger off,' he was shouting, 'or you're going to get hit again.' I had to calm him down or the old man might have landed another right hook. Then I told Billy there were no hard feelings. 'It's no good being annoyed with the fellow, Dad,' I said. 'He's as sick as I am.'

Unfortunately, the word 'charity' was not one that automatically came to mind during Liverpool–Leeds fixtures in those days. There was no love lost between the two sides and that year, in particular, there was even more needle than usual. Leeds had pipped us to the title, which hurt us badly – and this was to be *the* confrontation. Shanks had been invited to lead us out at Wembley one last time. Don Revie had just taken the England job but was there to see Brian Clough take charge of Leeds for the first time. Clough wanted Leeds to ditch their reputation as the dirtiest team in the country. But old habits die hard, clearly, and it suited them to draw us into a scrap.

I suspect they were after me from the first minute because of what happened when the teams met at Anfield the previous season. I was flying that day, and had the nerve to knock the ball one side of Terry Cooper before running round the other side of him to whip in a cross – my old schoolboy trick again. I imagine the Leeds players thought I was taking the mick, trying it on like that with a seasoned old pro, and had decided it was time to 'sort that little bastard out.' I wasn't intending to humiliate Terry, but that was my death warrant as far as the Leeds lads were concerned.

The tone was set inside the opening minute when Allan Clarke went in, studs high, on Phil Thompson. The referee, Bob Matthewson, didn't see it, because Clarkey was sly. Leeds had plenty of hard men in that era. Jack Charlton could dish it out. Paul Reaney had a nasty side, Paul Madeley was another one who could 'do' you, and Norman Hunter was a lovely guy until you went on a football field with him. Billy was a fiery little so-and-so, Joe Jordan would battle anyone, and Bobby Collins, who was smaller even than me, was scared of nobody and had taught most of them their dirty tricks. All marvellous players, but all with an edge. Clarkey, however, was snide with it. That was the worst type. He was a fine footballer but I didn't trust or like him as a player.

I wasn't feeling too chuffed with Johnny Giles either when we went for the same ball and he lamped me with a savage right hook. Giles was another outstanding footballer with a habit of crossing the line. It was incredible he wasn't sent off, but that reprieve was partly due to me telling the referee that nobody should be dismissed in the Charity Shield. My cheek was throbbing but I asked for leniency when, on reflection, I should have kept my mouth shut. They were gunning for me, and it was not long afterwards that Giles lunged in with a diabolical tackle that, if I hadn't jumped out of the way, would have taken off both my legs. Billy suddenly appeared, standing in front of me as if throwing down the gauntlet, and I can't deny it – my temper sometimes rips. I took the law into my own hands. I clocked him and he took a swing back. We had to be sent off. The enormity of what I had done quickly set in and it was a long walk back to the dressing room.

I did not often drink, but when I got back to my parents' house in Doncaster that night I went straight out to drown my sorrows. Shanks had only one more game left for Liverpool, which was to be Billy McNeill's testimonial at Celtic two days later, and I was devastated that I had let him down so badly. I went to a nightclub and found a corner; it was one of the few times in my life I was determined to get drunk. Then, around one o'clock in the morning, I saw a face I recognised. Shanks must have been worried about me because he had rung the Doncaster Rovers manager, Maurice Setters, and asked him to find me. Maurice had been traipsing around every drinking establishment in town and he told me Shanks was insisting that I got myself to Glasgow for the game. 'Don't let him down,' he said. 'He wants to see you at Parkhead on Monday.' I sobered up, caught the train the next morning, and set up Tosh for our goal in a 1–1 draw. It was a big occasion, as Liverpool–Celtic fixtures always were, and the noise when Jock Stein and Bill Shankly, the two managerial giants, walked out together was the loudest I had heard at any football ground. I was glad I was there because it would have been a permanent regret if my last game with Shanks had been the one at Wembley.

The ban meant I did not play a league game for Bob Paisley until the first week of October and I was also fined £500. Billy had to fork out the same and we were told the punishments were increased because of the way we had both thrown our shirts to the ground as we left the pitch. I hadn't meant anything by it. It was pure rage and frustration and Billy, some yards behind me, had done exactly the same. It was the first Charity Shield to be shown on television and that image of us leaving the pitch bare-chested was front-page news.

We knew they were going to throw the book at us, but it was still a bit rich to have Vernon Stokes, the chairman of the FA's disciplinary commission, lecturing me for my behaviour when this was the man who had been suspended for financial irregu-larities during his time as chairman of Portsmouth. Matt Busby was a great man, but I had to bite my tongue again, knowing the reputation of Manchester United's supporters at that time, when he said our behaviour might encourage trouble on the terraces. I found it bizarre that Busby could be involved in the first place, passing judgement about players from two of his club's major rivals without any apparent concerns about the obvious conflict of interest. But that was the FA for you. Can you imagine a dis-ciplinary hearing involving Liverpool now and the uproar if, say, Alex Ferguson was asked to deliver the verdict?

It was certainly a different environment from the one in which I had previously encountered Busby. I often used to social-ise in Manchester when I was a Liverpool player, and on that particular evening I had come across Matt, who was out with one of his players, Paddy Crerand. They were great company and I can remember having a couple of drinks with them and trying to suppress my laughter as they played a trick on one of the people on our table. The trick was for Matt and Paddy to rub a burnt candle-wick between their fingers and, without this guy twigging, blacken his face in as many ways as possible throughout the night. The poor guy was covered in smudges by the time they were finished, and I was still laughing when I popped into the gents at the end of the night. Then I looked in the mirror and realised the swines had done me too! One–nil to Manchester United, on that occasion.

People assume there must still be bad feeling between myself and the Leeds players, but the opposite is true. I have a lot of respect for those guys, many of whom I count as friends, and I even played in Norman Hunter's testimonial for a Don Revie XI in the same season that Billy and I were banned. Even then, however, I felt like a marked man and Norman, bless him, took great pleasure in harpooning me with a trademark challenge. It was a bad one, even by his standards, and when I gingerly got back to my feet I did ask him whether it was the done thing to crock someone that way in a benefit match. Naively, I believed him when he smiled and said it wouldn't happen again. The next time he poleaxed me, he looked down at me and smiled again. 'You don't think I'm going to change for a testimonial, do you?' he asked. After the game, he gave me a clock to thank me for my contribution and I limped away from Elland Road to count my bruises, as I often did in those days.

As for Billy, he and I once had a great night out in Paris after we had played for a Europe Select XI in a friendly against the Brazilian Olympic side at Parc des Princes. We went out in a group with Ruud Krol, Wim Suurbier and Wim van Hanegem from the Holland national team. Our three Dutch companions were not only highly accomplished footballers but also determined to prove they could outdo us at drinking.

I stayed well out of it, knowing my limitations, but Billy accepted the challenge as they started on the beers, sinking pint after pint, before it was time to move on to the hard stuff.

'Whisky?' Billy suggested.

'If it ain't Dutch, it ain't much,' our Dutch trio chorused, slamming down their empty beer glasses.

'Let's make them doubles then,' Billy purred, and I swear he winked at me on the way to order the drinks.

An hour or so later, I was chatting to someone at the bar, clinging safely to my half pint, when Billy tapped me on the shoulder and gestured for me to look over at his table. Three of the great Dutch players of the 1970s – Total Football, and all that – were slumped over one another on a settee, completely out for the count. They were blotto, and Billy had that same look of cheeky innocence on his face that I had seen in the Charity Shield, gazing up at the referee with open palms and his finest 'Who, me?' expression.

If that game at Wembley counted as the lowest point of my time as a Liverpool player, it was only a fleeting period of unhappiness. I was proud to be associated with Anfield and, when I am asked to pick out the highlights, where do I even begin when the choice is so vast? My debut against Nottingham Forest will always be special, of course, and the quarter-final of the European Cup against Saint-Étienne in 1977 will take some beating. I was injured when we lost the first leg 1–0 in France, but the return game at Anfield is the one everyone still talks about, with our opponents wearing their shiny green shirts, the chants of 'Allez les Verts' from the away fans and the sheer drama after they took a 2–1 aggregate lead to leave us needing two more goals to go through. I have heard the roar of the Kop many times, but the volume was surely never turned as high as when Ray Kennedy put in our second and David Fairclough, the original 'Supersub', ran away to score the game's decisive goal. You never forget those kinds of occasions.

I opened the scoring that night, and that season I ended up with twenty goals and finished as runner-up to Allan Simonsen in the European Footballer of the Year vote. Indeed, if the scoring system had been different, I might actually have won the trophy in 1977, as well as the following two years with Hamburg. Of the twenty-five voting countries, eleven picked me in first place whereas only seven selected Simonsen. The Dane had seven runner-up votes, as opposed to my three, and gained extra points by being nominated in third position three times. No complaints here, but I must have played pretty well to finish ahead of Michel Platini and Johan Cruyff, to name but two.

I make that point because there was always a certain amount of scepticism once it came out, at the start of the 1976–7 season, that I had agreed a deal to leave Liverpool and move abroad the following summer as long as the club received a British record transfer fee of £500,000. I wanted to make it public so nobody felt deceived when the time arrived, but it was tough at times and I didn't enjoy the way my commitment was questioned. If I had a good game, the reaction in the newspapers, and with some supporters, seemed to be that I was playing to get a move, whereas if I didn't reach my usual level it was a case of, 'He doesn't care anyway, he's off at the end of the season.' I did care, immensely, but the critics really turned on me after we lost against Manchester United in the FA Cup final. I hadn't played well, but it hurt and irritated me that people were saying my heart was not in it.

There were even a few suggestions that I should be dropped from the European Cup final four days later. Yet I still maintain it was better to be open about my plans and begin my long goodbye with a year's notice. It gave Liverpool time to find a replacement and they certainly chose well when they signed Kenny Dalglish from Celtic. I had the motivation of trying to bow out as a European Cup winner, and I also think it made the club reassess how they looked after everyone in the dressing room. Liverpool's players should have been the best paid in the world. We were winning the biggest honours and establishing ourselves as the dominant team in Europe. Yet I was joining a club that had not finished higher than sixth in the Bundesliga for twenty years and my new salary of 400,000 Deutschmarks a year, the equivalent of £100,000, was more than three times what I earned at Anfield. For too long, Liverpool had offered disproportionately low salaries and abused the fact that everyone was so desperate to play for them. The club sorted it out after I left and stopped trying to do everything on the cheap. It was about time.

That complaint aside, it was still a wrench to say goodbye to such a fabulous club, and it saddened me that some Liverpool supporters obviously felt let down – betrayed even – that I could possibly imagine there were other adventures to be had elsewhere. Not many players decided in those days that they wanted to leave Anfield and, even now, I still meet fans who tell me they were moved to tears when they heard the news. As a result, I didn't hear my name being sung quite so often in my final season. The fans had always been brilliant with me, but maybe a little of the love started to ebb away. I think they respected my honesty, but many on Merseyside found it impossible to understand why someone wearing a Liverpool shirt would ever want to put on another team's colours. I still get asked the question now and I know Ian Callaghan thought I would regret my decision. 'Why do you want to go?' he asked me. 'They love you here. We're successful, you earn good money and we're going to keep winning trophies.'

The irony was that when I signed for Liverpool it was meant to be as a replacement for Cally because he had a knee injury. He ended up playing for the club for another seven years, finishing his Liverpool career with 857 appearances, and I have wondered occasionally what it would have been like to be a one-club man. But I was never going to be a lifer. I was always more of a four- or five-year man and then I would be looking for something new, and it had started to feel I was playing almost from memory at Liverpool. I knew the entire routine from corners, free kicks, where I had to stand at throw-ins, what to do when I had the ball, where exactly Steve Heighway or John Toshack would be when I wanted to release it. I felt in a rut. And I had the Kevin Keegan wanderlust. 'Cally,' I said, 'maybe the rest of your life here, as a Liverpool lad, is all you dream of. I completely respect that and always will. But there's something else out there for me and I have to go with that instinct.'

It wasn't until late on that Hamburg made their move, and at least I had the chance to bow out on the exhilarating high of a European Cup final. The UEFA Cup wins of 1973 and 1976 were incredible. That night in Rome, however, against Borussia Mönchengladbach, was something else. The Eternal City was a sea of red and white and when I close my eyes I can still hear our fans.

> *Tell me ma, me ma*
> *I'm not coming home for tea*
> *I'm going to Italy*
> *Tell me ma, me ma.*

I would have hated to leave Liverpool as a loser, and when the game kicked off that night I knew the eyes of the football world were on me. I also had to contend with the fact that one of the world's greatest defenders, Berti Vogts, was man-marking me. I once said that a team of eleven Berti Vogts would be unbeatable. He was known as 'Der Terrier' and it quickly became apparent he didn't intend to give me an inch. He was on me like a rash and I didn't get away from him until the eighty-second minute. Berti was fast. But I was faster, and as we ran together, step for step, into the penalty area, he mistimed his challenge and clipped my heel. Phil Neal's penalty put us 3–1 ahead and Liverpool, in my farewell game, were the champions of Europe.

My only minor regret is that I could not get anywhere near the European Cup during the celebrations because the other lads were hogging it so much. If you ever see a photograph of me with the trophy, you will have done better than me, because I doubt I held it for longer than the five seconds when it was passed down the line. It seemed to be welded to Emlyn Hughes's hands, in particular. I do, however, have a lovely photograph of me celebrating with Ray Clemence – the two lads who had started at Scunny – and one of the greatest memories of all my time in football came back at the team hotel, toasting our success at the winners' post-match banquet, when I felt a tap on the shoulder and turned round to find an unexpected guest.

Berti Vogts could have been excused for being sick of the sight of me. I had got away from him for the crucial penalty and three years earlier I had scored two against his team in the UEFA Cup final. Yet here he was, with a smile on his face. He had left his teammates to find our hotel and now he wanted to have a drink. 'You were fantastic tonight, Kevin,' he told me. 'I wanted to come here to congratulate you all and have a beer.'

It blew me away that someone could show that kind of character and sportsmanship and I have often wondered how many other people in that position would have shown such magnanimity in defeat. Very few, I imagine. I would love to say I belonged to the small number. Deep down, though, I know I could never have done the same. For me, there was only one thing – winning.

6

AN ENGLISHMAN ABROAD

When I arrived in Germany for my first season with Hamburg in the Bundesliga, I had no idea there would be such a distinctly unhealthy atmosphere in the dressing room and it would be so difficult convincing my new teammates I was worthy of their time.

The first six months were a nightmare, as it became painfully obvious a lot of my new teammates saw me as an unnecessary luxury. Hamburg had just won the European Cup Winners' Cup and the players resented the bold pronouncements from Dr Peter Krohn, the club's business manager, about the arrival of a 'superstar' from England who would 'transform an average team.' They shunned me and there was jealousy over money – understandably, given that I had arrived as a £500,000 signing, almost doubling the German transfer record, and was being paid more than any player in the history of the Bundesliga.

I was picking up bad vibes almost immediately. In my first training session I can remember feeling deflated that I saw so little of the ball. If I made a run, it was amazing how many times the pass did not come. If I shouted for the ball, I lost count of the number of times the player in possession went the other way. I was ostracised and marginalised from the start and, of course, I did not have the language skills to do a great deal about it. All I could do was wave my arms about and hope I would be noticed. It was not something I had ever experienced before and, though I wanted to put it down to the communication barrier, I knew enough about footballers' body language to understand this was a more serious issue. It was a hard-faced refusal to accept me.

I was baffled and upset, but over time I did come to understand why my new teammates were so cold and standoffish. Dr Krohn wanted to portray me as the club's saviour. Unfortunately, he didn't seem to appreciate that interview after interview lording me up, as well as announcing exactly how much I would be earning, might cause friction with the other players. He had been ramming it down their throats all summer and, frankly, they were sick of hearing about this rich little Englishman who was going to take the club to the next level and was so much better at football than they were. They wanted to bring me down a peg or two. They wanted to make their point – that their play was not going to be geared towards me, whatever my reputation and however much I was being paid.

It didn't help that the rules at that time restricted clubs to a maximum of two foreign players and Hamburg had also signed Ivan Buljan, the captain of Yugoslavia, meaning the Dutchman Horst Blankenburg had to be moved out. Blankenburg was a popular member of the dressing room, not just because he was a splendid footballer, but also because he was a fine socialiser who was always up for a night out. The other players resented his treatment and held me partly responsible. Blankenburg, a three-time European Cup winner with Ajax in the early 1970s, ended up moving to Neuchâtel Xamax in Switzerland, and my name was mud because of it.

Dr Krohn had brought in a new coach by the name of Rudi Gutendorf and that had also gone down badly because the players liked the previous one, Kuno Klötzer, and didn't see any reason to change. Gutendorf was a worldly German with a long, nomadic coaching career. His main team-talk was in German but then he would converse with Buljan in French and, unlike Klötzer, he could also speak fluent English. That made life easier for me, but it convinced the other players the change of manager had been for my purposes. That made the atmosphere even frostier, and it was probably for the best that I could not read what was being said about me in the German newspapers. Manny Kaltz, Hamburg's international right-back, was one of the players whose misgivings about 'the Englander' turned up in the press. He wanted to know why there was all this fuss about Kevin Keegan. 'What's so special about him?' he asked. 'When did he last score for England?'

I remember thinking at the time that if a leading European footballer had signed for Liverpool, the players would have seen it as a boost for the club and gone out of their way to help him integrate. In Hamburg, it was more a case of: leave the little sod to fend for himself – and let's see what he is really made of.

As if that wasn't bad enough, my living arrangements were hardly ideal. Hamburg had promised they would find somewhere for Jean and myself to live, and we had brought over our Old English sheepdogs, Oliver and Heidi, because the contract stipulated we would have a house with a decent-sized garden. Instead, they put us in a room on the nineteenth floor of the high-rise Hamburg Plaza Hotel in the middle of the city. There wasn't even a balcony for the dogs to get some fresh air, and the promises the club had made seemed to have been forgotten. My poor wife was stuck in the same hotel room day after day, taking the dogs down in the lift to walk them in the park. It was only when we moved out to the suburbs, buying a bungalow in a village called Itzstedt, that we started to feel as though Germany could become a proper home. Itzstedt was quiet, just as we wanted, and it suited us to have some fresh air away from the hustle and bustle of the city.

My first game for Hamburg was a friendly against Barcelona and I scored in a 6–0 win. I was determined to show the crowd I was worth the transfer fee and, despite the tricky start, I was still confident I could win over my new teammates. We then beat Liverpool 3–2 in a fixture that had been arranged as part of the transfer. I scored again, and it was nice to see some friendly faces, even if my former Anfield teammates let me know in the bluntest terms what they thought of my new haircut.

Yes, *that* haircut. It was just before leaving for Germany that I decided it was time for a new look. Little did I know, however, that my perm was about to start a new trend in football; it still amuses me that a lad from Donny, with flared trousers, sticky-out collars and platform shoes, could suddenly be thought of as a trailblazer for the fashions of the time. I wasn't even sure at first whether a perm was a good idea, and I must confess that when my hairdresser friend, Herbert Howe, convinced me it was time for a change, I timed it deliberately so I was booked into the salon after my final Liverpool appearance. There was no way I would have dared turn up at Melwood with big, dewy curls.

Jean's instinctive reaction did not fill me with great confidence, either. I had arranged to meet my wife at Bluecoat Chambers, a restaurant in Liverpool, and when I walked in, feeling like a Coldstream Guard and at least six inches taller, she collapsed in uncontrollable hysterics. My agent, Harry Swales, opted for the approach of pretending he didn't know me. Nobody else in the place even recognised me, and every time I caught Jean's eye she started cracking up again. She was still laughing twenty minutes later after sending me to the toilet to put some water on it.

It took a bit of getting used to, but I became quite attached to that hairstyle, and my advice to anyone who fancied getting the same look was that it was a lot more manageable than the 'feather cut' that was popular at the time and needed endless blow-drying. There were still times when I caught sight of my reflection and it felt as if I was staring into a fairground funhouse mirror. Yet they say imitation is the greatest form of flattery, and it wasn't long before a lot of other footballers were putting in the curlers. Phil Thompson, Terry McDermott and Phil Neal all took the plunge. Nor was it just a Liverpool thing. Charlie George tried it out. Bryan Robson was next, followed by various others. The players in Germany might not have been sure about me, but at least I could console myself with the thought that there were people going into hairdressers across Britain to ask for 'a Kevin Keegan please'.

Back in Germany, however, I had bigger issues than worrying about what people made of my hairstyle. Our first Bundesliga fixture was against MSV Duisburg and Dr Krohn had been telling anyone who would care to listen that everything would be fine now Hamburg had a new superhero. 'With God and Kevin Keegan,' he trumpeted, 'we will win.' In fact, we lost 5–2. Gutendorf, who was facing the beginnings of a player mutiny, and vying with me to be bottom of the popularity polls, even suggested the players had conspired to 'sabotage' the result.

What I didn't realise at the time was that a delegation of players – four or five of the influential ones – had already been to see Gutendorf to try to force me out of the club. The captain, Peter Nogly, was among them, and Gutendorf later recalled the message was, 'If you put this little English guy in, we don't want to work with you. We don't need him and we don't like him.'

Gutendorf lasted only until October, and was so hurt by the attitude of his players he said he wanted to get as far away as possible for his next job, keeping to his word by becoming the national coach of Australia. Dr Krohn also left and there were rumours that Hamburg would offload me too if they could get their money back. I was shocked about how quickly I was being written off and, though I had always tried not to take my worries home, I did confide in Jean that I felt unusually vulnerable.

Even without these issues, living abroad was a permanent challenge. Language was the main problem, but there were also laws to observe that were entirely new to us. The obvious one was driving on the other side of the road, but we also learned that everyone in Germany had to keep their driving licence in their car and carry an identification card at all times. Nobody had told us, and the first time a policeman stopped me to ask, 'Ausweis, bitte,' I didn't have a clue what he was talking about.

Shopping was hilarious, and we often came home with the wrong items because we were too embarrassed to explain that we had wanted something else. We went into a hardware shop to buy a fuse but didn't know the correct word, so just kept trying to show what it looked like through gestures and repeating '*sehr klein*' to emphasise it was very small. The shopkeeper brought out a plug at first. '*Nein, nein,*' we said, indicating that what we wanted was much smaller. The next time he came out it was with a set of Christmas lights.

Strangely, one of the things I missed was the good old-fashioned English pub, which didn't make a great deal of sense, bearing in mind I rarely went into one when I was in my own country. It was a twenty-mile round trip for the British newspapers, which were five times the normal price and usually the Welsh editions, and when heavy snow fell in winter we learned that anyone taking their car on the roads was liable to a £500 fine and a year's disqualification. There was no such thing as a satnav in those days, and we lost count of the number of times a twenty-minute drive turned into an hour of confused sightseeing.

It was fun, though, learning about a new culture. Jean had studied German for A-level and I was determined to absorb the language. Everything English seemed to be obtainable, apart from the television channels, and the Hamburg fans couldn't have done more to help us settle in. In one interview I mentioned I was missing my favourite cereal. Very soon, my cupboards were bursting with the packets of Shredded Wheat that had been sent in by fans, along with lists of all the local suppliers.

I liked meeting the fans because it helped me pick up the language and, thankfully, not everyone in the dressing room wanted to freeze me out. Horst Bertl, my roommate, became a loyal and trusted friend who helped keep me sane during those troubled times. Horst was married to an American girl and, apart from Jean, he did more than anyone to help me understand the language.

It wasn't an ideal start, though, and the lack of unity hurt us badly when we renewed acquaintances with Liverpool in the European Super Cup, a two-legged final bringing together the winners of the European Cup and the European Cup Winners' Cup. The first leg in Hamburg was a 1–1 draw, but the return game was a personal humiliation for me: a 6–0 defeat at Anfield. The crowd gave me a wonderful reception at the start but they were soon chanting that I should have stayed where I was. Terry McDermott scored a hat-trick and Kenny Dalglish put in the sixth goal. We were outclassed, and it was another occasion when I suspected I was purposely being denied the ball.

I was trying my best not to let it get me down, but a lot of pent-up frustration was building inside. I didn't want to let it out but that was exactly what happened on New Year's Eve, 1977, when the Bundesliga was on its winter break and we went to the marzipan town of Lübeck, forty miles north of Hamburg, to play a friendly.

Before the game, our opponents arranged for me to be presented with a bouquet of flowers on the pitch. A nice gesture, you might think, but it quickly became apparent that one of Lübeck's players had no intention of keeping things amicable. Within a few seconds of the game kicking off, he had run beside me and smashed me to the ground. His name was Erhard Preuss and there was a look on his face which told me that was just the start. He was smirking as he picked me up. *Here we go*, I thought. *I've known days like this all over the world when idiots have tried to upset me. I can cope, though. No way will this fellow make me lose my head.*

A few minutes later, I made a diagonal run, and the same player chopped my legs from beneath me. The referee did not see it because he was following the ball on the other side of the pitch and, as I picked myself up, I was telling myself again not to get wound up. But the next time I tried to go round Preuss he came in with his shoulder and smashed me in the chest, leaving me doubled up and winded. The referee awarded a free kick, and I knew enough German to point out that was the third time already. 'Don't tell me how to referee,' he snapped, and moved off.

I was wise to Preuss by now and, the next time the ball came my way, I was ready for him. He was standing in my path, making no attempt to get the ball, but he wasn't to know that, as a lad in Doncaster, I used to do a bit of boxing in the gym owned by Bruce Woodcock, the former British heavyweight champion. Preuss was smirking. I lumped him and he went out like a light. I didn't even wait for the red card. I sent myself off and walked briskly towards the tunnel, with my opponent laid out flat in cloud cuckoo land.

I regretted it very quickly, of course. I knew there would be repercussions, but my fists that afternoon were powered by frustration, by my difficulties adapting to a strange country, by the refusal of an anti-Keegan clique within my own dressing room to accept me, and by the inescapable sense that my first season in Hamburg was turning into a personal ordeal.

All my frustration was unloaded in that punch and, with barely ten minutes played, I didn't bother waiting for the game to finish. I ordered a taxi, shot off back to Itzstedt and then – the final indignity – I had to sit outside my house in the biting cold because Jean had gone out, not expecting me back until much later, and I didn't have keys or any way of contacting her. That was probably the lowest I felt in all my time in Germany. I couldn't be sure how long I was there, but I can remember darkness falling and shivering in the winter temperatures. I was frozen to the bone, knowing I was going to be suspended and that I had no defence for what I had just done. I felt sad, confused, helpless. And I couldn't remember hitting anyone that hard in my life. For a split second it had crossed my mind that I might have killed the guy.

The consequences were a big fine and an eight-week ban, plus the etiquette in Germany meant I had to drive back to Lübeck to apologise – not just to the club but to the town as a whole. That meant shaking hands with Preuss and trying to force a smile as we exchanged bunches of flowers. It was awkward, to say the least, and when I got back that night, Bill Shankly was on the phone. Shanks would often ring me in Hamburg to talk about the games and see how I was getting on. I still had tremendous respect for my old boss and feared an ear-bashing. 'Aye, it's me,' he barked. 'I want to know, did you punch him properly, son? Did he stay down and take a count of ten? Was it a left or a right?'

Can you see why I loved him so much?

The most important thing, driving back from the scene of my crime, was that I had reached the conclusion I could not feel sorry for myself any longer. My mind was made up. A lot of players would probably have sought an escape route back to England. Not me. I wasn't going to let my time in Germany fizzle out. I was going to honour my contract, work even harder to master the language and make even more of an effort to break down the barriers with the players who were cold-shouldering me. If these guys weren't going to pass it to me, I would ask them why the hell not. I needed to spend more time in their company, speak their language, show them I cared about the club and follow them to the cafe across the road after training, even if I did not fully understand what they were talking about. I had to be stronger and find my voice, like I had at Liverpool. I wasn't going to give up. I wasn't going back to England a failure, admitting I had been unable to cope and filled with embarrassment. Not in a million years.

What I did have going for me was that, despite everything, I was actually playing very well and the fans could see it. At Liverpool the players called me 'Andy McDaft' because of the way I liked a bit of fun. The fans in Hamburg had a new nickname for me – 'Machtig Maus', 'Mighty Mouse'. I was small, muscular and, despite my size, I scored headers. It was the kind of nickname that told me the fans liked me and it was strange how it worked out because those eight weeks when I was suspended, as frustrating as they were, probably turned out to be the best thing that could have happened to me.

Hamburg's results in that period quickly deteriorated. The slump included a 3–0 home defeat to Fortuna Düsseldorf, followed by a 6–1 thrashing at Cologne, and as the team started sliding down the table, the players began to re-evaluate the little Englander. Slowly but surely, attitudes began to change, as my teammates realised I was an asset not a threat. Suddenly they were telling me how much they were looking forward to me being back. Players who had barely said two words to me were now inviting me out and trying to do me favours. One even told me he could get me cheap meat for the dogs. There were still a couple who were a bit awkward, but they left at the end of my first season and, for the most part, the barriers were down. It felt like a new start. Peter Hidien, the full-back, even had a perm!

It also helped that Günter Netzer, the former West Germany international, had replaced Dr Krohn. Günter was one of the most reliable and trustworthy people I have ever known and, having been a player himself, he was fully attuned to my needs. Özcan Arkoç, the goalkeeping coach, had initially taken over from Gutendorf, but that arrangement did not last long and Branco Zebec, a Yugoslav taskmaster, was hired as the new coach.

We had heard about Zebec's reputation for working players to the bone, but for the first two or three days the training was very light. It was then he got us. I will never forget him placing a ball on the centre spot, then sitting on it, watching us through his dark glasses. A lot of people thought he wore those shades to exude hauteur, whereas the truth was he was a big drinker and if he was shielding his eyes it was invariably because he had been out the night before. He sat on that ball for an hour and a half while we ran and ran and ran. These were almost all sprints, running down one side of the pitch, across the goalmouth and back again, over and over. I had never trained so hard in my life, not even under Jack Brownsword at Scunthorpe, but Zebec had decided the team needed toughening up. In the coffee shop across the road I was picking up all sorts of new words. He was '*bekloppt*' – crazy! Our new coach was '*verruckt*'. We thought he was nuts.

But there was method to the madness. After a while, those

punishing sessions became second nature, and we started putting our extra stamina to use. Zebec introduced a twice-daily training regime, and in my second season with Hamburg, 1978–9, we were overwhelming opponents with our superior fitness. I always remember coming back to play for England in one game and the other players in the Wembley dressing room staring at my bulging physique in awe. I was absolutely ripped, fitter and more muscly than I had ever been, and playing some of the best football of my life at a time when there were some people in the game – not least Bob Paisley – who wanted me removed from the England team now I was fraternising with 'the enemy'.

To give Bob the benefit of the doubt, he came from a generation when it was just a fact of life that many people would have disliked an England international defecting to Germany. I could understand why he felt that way, because if my dad had still been alive I doubt I would have even contemplated playing in the Bundesliga. Dad was another one from an era when, to many, there was no such thing as a good German. Yet it did upset and irritate me when Bob declared that I shouldn't be allowed to play for England if I earned my wage in another country. It was a ridiculous thing to say and I would have loved to ask him if he could come up with any legitimate reasons. I would have listened to what he said and then respectfully asked whether, in his view, Kenny Dalglish should have been banished from playing for Scotland once he had moved from Celtic to Liverpool. Or was it just a German thing?

The only other person who tried to press those buttons was Brian Clough when we were television pundits for the 1978 World Cup. Cloughie made an art of rubbing up against people like sandpaper. He took pride in being that way, and I was never going to escape the snake-lick of his tongue. 'Well, young man,' he drawled, so patronisingly, live on air. 'Who have you bet your *Deutschmarks* on at this tournament?' He even mentioned the fact that my wife was having our baby in Germany. Maybe he didn't expect me to stick up for myself. 'That terrific suntan of yours, you didn't get that by being patriotic,' I pointed out. 'That didn't come from Bournemouth, did it?'

That wasn't the only time I tangled with Cloughie, and I can still remember shuddering with embarrassment during his 'tribute' speech at a charity dinner one year, when the toast was supposed to be 'Peter Lorimer, Yorkshire sports personality of the year'. Clough used the occasion to criticise the man he was meant to be honouring, while also criticising Leeds United and most of Lorimer's teammates. I was on a table with Steve Heighway and some of the other Liverpool players, and because it was a Sunday night with no midweek game, we had ordered a bottle of wine. Clough turned to us – chin in the air, wagging his finger – and announced, 'If you were my players, those glasses would be swept away.' But he wasn't our manager. Nor did we need to be lectured about how to behave.

I respected Clough's achievements, but I wasn't interested when Peter Taylor, his assistant, followed me into the toilets at London Weekend Television one day to mention they might like to sign me. Cloughie wouldn't have been right for me. Our personalities would have clashed and I would not have tolerated the eccentricities such as plying players with booze on the night before big matches. His record of taking Nottingham Forest and Derby County into the European Cup put him at the top of his business, but I didn't see the attraction. I was never fascinated by Brian Clough in the way other people were.

All that hackneyed wartime stuff – 'They bombed our chippie!' – felt very tired anyway, bearing in mind the respect I received from the German public. My teammates would rib me as *der faule Engländer* – the lazy Englishman – because I came from a country where most people didn't bother learning more than their own language. But there was never the same obsession in Germany with dredging up the past as there was in England, and the only problem Jean and I encountered, as the team started to win more games and my popularity grew, was that we couldn't go shopping together any longer because I would get mobbed.

We had to improvise after Laura, our first daughter, was born in November 1978 and we wanted to check out Hamburg's Christmas market. One of our friends, Thomas Metalmann, was going out with a girl from the local amateur dramatics society, so I put on a wig with a pair of glasses and an old beanie hat and then she set to work with her make-up skills, applying wrinkles to my face, as well as super-sized bags beneath my eyes, to age me by about twenty years. Amazingly, it worked. We had great fun at the *Weihnachtsmarkt* and nobody recognised me until the balloon we had bought for Laura came loose from her pram and floated away. I went back to buy another one and the man on the stall gave me a knowing look. 'You don't want to be recognised, huh, Kevin?' I could disguise my face but the accent gave me away.

As you may have gathered by now, I do enjoy going under-cover. We went on holiday to Disney World some years later and I had thought, maybe naively, that my fame wouldn't follow me to Florida. I was wrong. I had never turned down an autograph in my life, but I was conscious Laura and her little sister, Sarah, were missing out on all the fun. This time my disguise came as an American tourist. I bought a Green Bay Packers top from a souvenir stall. I picked out some glasses with mirrored lenses and I rounded it off with a pair of Bermuda shorts and a baseball cap that had a grey ponytail dangling out at the back. I looked a right prat, to be honest. Then I went to get some drinks from the supermarket and the next person in the queue tapped me on the shoulder. 'Any chance you could sign this, Kevin?'

My contract at Hamburg was due to expire at the end of my second season, but everything was going so well by that point that I turned down a move to Juventus to stay in the Bundesliga. By that stage I had won the 1978 European Footballer of the Year award, edging Hans Krankl of Barcelona into second place, as well as being named 'Man of the Year' by the German players themselves. My life in Hamburg had completely turned around and we were on our way to winning the league. Real Madrid were tracking me, and there was also a money-spinning offer to play for the Washington Diplomats in the North American Soccer League. I even explored whether it was possible to play in both Germany and the USA, but the rules would not allow it and I decided to stay at Hamburg to have a go at winning the European Cup. I always felt sorry for the Diplomats – they had to make do with Johan Cruyff instead!

After finishing sixth in my first season, our improvement under Zebec eventually led to Hamburg's first Bundesliga title since 1960. Horst Hrubesch, a giant striker who had signed from Rot-Weiss Essen and was known as *Das Kopfball-Ungeheuer* (The Header Beast), had been an important signing. Manny Kaltz was one of the best five footballers I ever played with, with his brilliantly whipped-in crosses from the right, and Felix Magath was a prompting force in midfield. The fitness levels demanded by Zebec had paid off. While other teams were tiring towards the end of the season, we went on a run of nine wins from ten games. We didn't look back after beating the leaders, Kaiserslautern, and when we reached the top we stayed there, until everything was confirmed with a game to spare. I was a champion of Germany, scoring seventeen league goals in the process. *Fantastisch!*

On top of everything else, this was also the period of my life – no sniggering, please – when I had the makings of my own pop career. To be fair, I have to laugh when I look back at some of the old clips of me singing 'Head over Heels', in particular when I was invited on a television chat show in Austria to perform the song. England were playing in Austria at the same time, and all the lads were watching at the team hotel. I had to mime the entire song while sitting on the knee of a middle-aged lady, staring into her eyes and even removing her spectacles at one point.

Two Yugoslavs from the music industry, friends of my team-mate Ivan Buljan, had set the ball rolling by coming to see me one day to ask if I fancied making a record. I was game for anything. Too many people are frightened to go outside their comfort zone, whereas it never worried me. I was always willing to push the boundaries and try new things. I enjoyed my dalliance with the music industry and consider it an achievement that I recorded a chart hit.

'Head over Heels' was written by Chris Norman and Pete Spencer, who were in the group Smokie. It stayed in the German hit parade for weeks, hovering around number ten, and sold 220,000 copies. It also reached number thirty-one in the UK charts, at a time when Blondie was number one with 'Sunday Girl' and the Top 40 featured David Bowie, ELO and Roxy Music. I would like to have gone higher but I did spend two weeks above ABBA and The Police, which can't be too bad. I performed on *Top of the Pops*, as well as the German equivalent, *Der Musikladen*, and there were a few occasions, I must confess, when I asked myself what the hell I was doing. But people did like that song. They used to play it on the bus to games with Hamburg and, even now, I have met people who have it as their ringtone. It was featured on an album called *Franz Beckenbauer's Football Hits*, which was a massive seller in Germany, and another LP, *One-Hit Wonders*, which also flew off the shelves.

I could have made a fortune from royalties, but I never expected it to take off the way it did and, at the time, I was delighted to be offered a flat fee of £20,000. There are some really bad singers who have had hit records and some really talented singers who have never even brought one out. My thoughts were, why not give it a try? I had a decent voice and was in the choir at school. I can still remember the elation when I heard my record being played on a radio slot called 'Smash of the Week'. My mood was quickly punctured when I realised the title of the slot was a clue, the DJ proceeding to break the record into little pieces for being his least favourite track of the week.

It was a wonderful time. In Liverpool, the open-top bus parades when we brought our trophies back to the city always made me feel as though we were back in Ancient Rome, like warriors returning from a bloody conquest to show off all the gold and loot we had plundered. For Hamburg, we stood in open-top Jeeps as we were driven to Rathausmarkt, the main square, to show off the championship shield from the town hall. It was a great day for me and, it seemed, the entire city. In all the euphoria, it never crossed my mind, at the age of twenty-eight, that it was going to be the last winner's medal of my career.

That was my biggest regret from Hamburg when I recall what happened the following season, my last year with the club, and the bitter disappointment of losing the 1980 European Cup final. As they say, you cannot win them all, and I should not feel too aggrieved when I remember the trophies I did win. Yet it was not the goodbye I had wanted, and it felt like a dreadful anticlimax after coming through so many incredible ties to reach the final.

Dinamo Tbilisi, who were being tipped as the next great club side, had dumped Liverpool out in the first round. Yet we were too strong for the Georgians, beating them 6–3 on aggregate, to go with our 5–1 two-legged win against the Icelandic side Valur in the opening round. In the quarter-finals we knocked out Hajduk Split on away goals, with a 3–3 aggregate score, and then we had to face the mighty Real Madrid. Most pundits thought we were on our way out after losing 2–0 in the Bernabéu, and maybe some of the Madrid players assumed they had done enough to reach the final, which was to be held in their own stadium. Instead, when they came to Hamburg for the second leg we swept them away with one of the most outstanding performances of club football I have ever been associated with, scoring four goals before half-time and running out as 5–1 winners. We hurt Madrid so badly that Vicente del Bosque, the future Spain national team manager, was sent off for swiping me with an exasperated punch.

In my view we were a better team than the Liverpool side that won the trophy in 1977, but we still had to get past the holders, Nottingham Forest, in the final, and we knew Brian Clough's side loved to be the underdogs. They had won the cup against poor opponents, Malmö, the previous year, but to reach that stage they had eliminated Liverpool in the first round. This time, Forest had beaten Östers, Argeş Piteşti, Dynamo Berlin and Ajax to make it to Madrid. It was not as tough a route as ours but I don't think it worked to our advantage that Trevor Francis, Forest's £1 million striker, was injured and missing from their attack. That gave Forest the excuse to play with everyone behind the ball and spend virtually the entire night trying to frustrate us, especially when they went forward on a rare breakaway in the twentieth minute and John Robertson bobbled a shot past our goalkeeper, Rudi Kargus, from a distance where he was normally unbeatable.

Robertson fascinated me because he had no pace, he always looked a bit on the heavy side and whenever you saw him off the pitch he seemed to have a cigarette dangling from the corner of his mouth. Yet squeeze the little Scot into one of those shiny red Forest shirts and he always seemed to find a way past whoever was marking him. The last time I saw him I reminded him that we had twenty-four shots that night compared to Forest's one. 'Aye,' he said, with his nicotine-laced chuckle, 'but mine was the important one.'

Apparently a couple of the Forest lads tell a story that Kenny Burns psyched me out in the tunnel before the game by taking out his dentures and grinning maniacally in my direction, with his yellow hair sticking everywhere. Larry Lloyd, his partner in Forest's central defence, is then said to have come over to me and whispered in my ear that his teammate wasn't feeling too well-disposed towards me. At which point, I am supposed to have gone ashen and spent the entire match in hiding. It's a nice story, and no doubt gets a few laughs on the after-dinner circuit in the East Midlands, but they are doing themselves a disservice.

The reason Forest won the final was Peter Shilton's goalkeeping, first and foremost. I knew Larry from my time at Liverpool and Kenny, though he was no oil painting, was never frightening. He and Larry were tremendous that night, as all the Forest defenders were, and it was a terrible feeling when the final whistle confirmed their 1–0 victory, especially as Bayern Munich had already pipped us to the Bundesliga title. I was hoping to become the first player to win European Cup medals in England and Germany, but it wasn't to be.

I wasn't a lover of Nottingham Forest, though that was more to do with Cloughie than any of their players, and there was no way I could emulate Berti Vogts by turning up at the winners' celebrations later that night. I was too bad a loser and too gutted by the defeat. I saw the Forest players at the airport the next day, shook their hands and wished them well.

And that really was it for the Keegan family in Hamburg. Aside from my early problems, it was the kind of experience you could never buy. We had a fabulous time and the best of both worlds because, as well as winning over the German public, I would like to think I earned the respect of folk back home by showing it was possible for an English footballer to integrate in a foreign country.

A lot of people expected me to flop when I left Liverpool and, crikey, it wasn't easy getting everyone's acceptance. But what the people who criticised me didn't realise was that the more I heard I was going to fail, the more determined I was to make a decent fist of it. The more I was told that I would not last as long as Jimmy Greaves, Denis Law et al., the more it motivated me. Ultimately, I bucked a trend given that Englishmen did not have a good reputation when it came to playing abroad and probably, to this day, still don't. That might not have warranted a medal of any description, but it was something that always made me proud.

7

SAINTS ALIVE

When the time arrived to say my goodbyes at Hamburg, the club presented me with a beautiful hand-crafted model ship as a leaving present, inscribed with the words, 'For Kevin Keegan, from Hamburger Sport-Verein, 1977 to 1980.' The captain, Peter Nogly, also received one, because he was leaving for Edmonton Drillers, of the North American Soccer League, at the same time. I still have mine at home. It was a lovely gift and it saddened me that the famous clock at Volksparkstadion, celebrating Hamburg's unbroken status as the only club to remain ever-present in the Bundesliga, stopped ticking as I was finishing this book. That clock had recorded all the time since the Bundesliga's inception on 24 August 1963. It stopped on fifty-four years, two hundred and sixty-one days, thirty-six minutes and six seconds, and it was a terrible shame to see my old club being relegated.

My two years in Hamburg certainly left a lasting impression on me. I learned a language, made new friends, and for a long time after moving back to England I was getting more requests to do broadcast work in Germany than my own country. I am still in touch with some of my former teammates, and when it came to my final month in Hamburg they didn't take it to heart when I had a bit of fun at their expense by writing '*knast*' – the German for 'slammer' – on the inside of my locker door and drawing a picture of myself behind prison bars to show me waiting for my release. I wrote down all the numbers of the days I had left, and every morning before training I ticked one off until, finally, I could write *'frei'* on my door – meaning I was free. My three years in the Bundesliga were over, and if you want evidence that Germans have a good sense of humour (something I can very much vouch for), they kept that locker door, complete with all my drawings, and put it in the club museum – very kindly in a section marked 'HSV Legenden'.

It is still there now, almost forty years later, and on the same door there is one of my doodles of Branko Zebec, our formidable coach, in typical pose – whistle in mouth – while his players are doing press-ups, dripping with sweat, from one of his training sessions, after which I would often get home so worn out I would have to crawl straight into bed. I had enormous respect for Zebec, but when I told him I was leaving, I did point out that his training was one of the factors and that I feared burning myself out before the age of thirty. Zebec's response was that it was the same for all the players. 'Yes,' I said, 'but they don't run like I do every Saturday.'

It was time for a new challenge and, to begin with, I had more or less decided that Italy would be my next port of call. Several Spanish clubs were chasing me but I liked the idea of testing myself in the league of *catenaccio* – the famously parsimonious defensive strategy. An Italian agent, Gigi Peronace, was talking to Juventus on my behalf, and had got as far as discussing wages, negotiating for me to join the team of Dino Zoff, Claudio Gentile and Roberto Bettega, when I came back to Jean and explained we might be packing our bags for Turin. 'You can go to Italy,' she replied, without a flicker of enthusiasm, 'but I'm going home to England.'

It was my fault. I had presumed she would follow wherever my boots took me, but the newspapers were full of stories about kidnappings and terrorism in Italy and we had a young daughter to consider. Jean was married to a famous and very recognisable footballer, and she didn't feel comfortable about leading that kind of high-profile life in another foreign country when there was so much in the news about politicians and well-known personalities being targeted.

It hadn't always been easy for her in Hamburg, with all the time I spent away, and Laura's birth had reminded us both of home comforts. The facilities in Germany were excellent, but Laura had to go back into hospital with a virus, and in those circumstances it is only natural that you want to know the language perfectly and understand exactly what is going on. Laura was very weak, and you can imagine what went through our minds when we arrived on her ward one day and couldn't hear the bleeping of the machine that was helping her to breathe. It turned out she had been taken out of her incubator and moved to a new ward, but those moments were among the worst of my life.

Fortunately, I was not short of alternative offers, and I had a release clause in my contract with Hamburg, just as I did at Liverpool, that allowed me to leave if another club offered £500,000. In those days it was virtually unheard of for footballers to insert those kinds of stipulations, but it was my career and I wanted to be in control of it. I didn't like the idea that I might want to sign for one club only to be sold somewhere else – a club I might not necessarily want to join – if a higher bid came in. I didn't like the way the clubs had all the power and whenever I signed a contract I always made sure I could leave on my terms, not the club's. I'm pretty sure I was the first footballer in England to do that. I guess it tells you about the kind of person I am. I wasn't going to let myself be exploited.

That was when Lawrie McMenemy, the popular Geordie who was manager of Southampton, telephoned out of the blue for one of the more unusual conversations I have ever had with a potential new boss. Lawrie started with a long, convoluted story about wanting to buy a special light fitting for his house in Hampshire, explaining that it was produced at a factory in Hamburg and unavailable in England unless he forked out a fortune in shipping costs. He wanted to know if I could pick up this light on his behalf and, once I had told him that shouldn't be a problem, it was inevitable that we started talking about football. Lawrie was fishing about my situation, and eventually he mentioned that if it was true, as he had been led to believe, that I was planning to leave Hamburg at the end of the season, I could always think of Southampton as an option.

Once I started thinking about it properly, I surprised myself by how much I liked the idea. I had done the big-club scene and there was something incredibly exciting about playing in front of huge crowds at Hamburg and Liverpool. But I also had a vision of leading an unfashionable, unheralded team to their first-ever league title, and I could imagine the satisfaction in those circumstances might far outweigh that of doing it at a club where it was almost second nature. Southampton had won the FA Cup in 1976 and were fourth in the league when I fixed up the meeting with Lawrie to talk about everything properly (though they had slipped back to eighth by the end of the season). It was a smallish club but they were hardly no-hopers. Mick Channon, one of my best mates in football, was there – another selling point – and they also had the experience of Dave Watson, Chris Nicholl, Charlie George and Alan Ball, plus a core of talented younger lads. Before long, I had made up my mind it was the right place for me.

It was incredible nothing got out in the press until the day – 11 February 1980 – I flew in on a private jet with Günter Netzer, Jean and little Laura playing with a jigsaw on the floor of the aircraft, while my wife and I marvelled about how much life had changed since our days in Doncaster. We were there to announce I would be joining Southampton at the start of the following season. Liverpool knew what was going on because they had a first-option clause that meant I could return to Anfield (my view being that if I wanted to play for Liverpool again, I would not have left in the first place). Hamburg knew, and we knew. Not a word leaked out otherwise, and it was only later that I found out that Lawrie had nearly blabbed the news over a couple of glasses of wine the night before. Lawrie and his wife, Anne, had been hosting a dinner party. One of his friends, the author Leslie Thomas, had managed to get it out of him that Southampton were about to announce a signing, but Lawrie wouldn't say who it was. Maybe Lawrie started to feel guilty, because at the end of the night he whispered the initials 'KK' as they were saying goodbye. Leslie looked at him knowingly. 'Don't worry,' he said, 'I won't tell a soul.' Then he drove away thinking the Norwich City goalkeeper, Kevin Keelan, must be the mystery signing!

The press still hadn't twigged even when Lawrie arranged a news conference at the Potters Heron Hotel near Romsey to introduce 'someone who was going to play a big part in South-ampton's future.' Nobody had seen me land at Southampton airport, and when I walked into the press conference there were audible gasps. It was always nice to scoop the journalists, and I wasn't going to play down my ambitions. I was there, I explained, because I wanted another stab at the First Division title and gen-uinely believed a club of Southampton's size could do it. I was coming home.

When I went back to Germany after signing the contract, I even cut my second pop single, 'To Be Home Again in England', to mark my forthcoming return, with some acoustic strumming and wonderfully corny lyrics. 'Oh how I yearn to be home again in England . . . we'll sit by the fireside and sing . . . we'll walk down a country lane on Sunday morning.'

The sentiment was genuine and it was one of the records – '"Mull of Kintyre" with fewer bagpipes,' to quote one review – that they played on the *Family Favourites* radio show, when listeners could request songs for loved ones living abroad. Gloria Hunniford must have liked it too, because she changed the chorus to make an Irish version. Incredibly, though, my paean to England failed to chart and that, sadly, was the end of my solo career in the music industry. Some people have no taste!

The only disappointment when I returned to Hamburg was that Alan Ball was offered the chance to become player-manager at Blackpool. Alan was one of the players I always looked up to because of the 1966 World Cup, and when I heard he was leaving Southampton, I have to confess the move no longer seemed quite so appealing. Yet we were soon reunited. Alan's time at Bloomfield Road did not go well and when he found himself out of work halfway through the following season the first telephone call he received was from Lawrie telling him to hurry back to the Dell, where his old first-team shirt was waiting for him. Alan was coming up for thirty-six but his legs still carried him like a champion. 'When I was young I used to work up and down the pitch,' he'd tell me. 'Now I work sideways across the pitch because it's shorter that way.'

Mick Channon was another gem, and it still makes me laugh to think of his reply when Lawrie was berating him in training one day for not running hard enough.

'Lawrie, Lawrie,' Mick shot back, with exquisite comic timing. 'Remember this is only my hobby . . .'

Mick loved football but horse racing was his real passion; he was something of a rarity for such a gifted player, as he didn't take either himself or the game too seriously. His hero was Lester Piggott, not Pelé or Cruyff, and if we were ever playing on Grand National day, you would invariably find him out on the wing because he was getting updates from the spectators in the front row. He is the leading scorer in Southampton's history, and he went on to become one of the best racehorse trainers in the business. He deserves more credit than he actually gets because there cannot be too many people who have had so much success in two completely different sports.

The other attraction for me at Southampton was Lawrie himself, with his big, charismatic personality, his talent for man-motivation and infectious enthusiasm. Lawrie hadn't been a professional footballer, but he had learned the trade and was regarded as one of the top managers in the country. Lawrie once declared the perfect balance for a football team comprised 'seven road sweepers and four violinists.' I had known him for a while because of our television work and I could tell straight away that I was going to enjoy playing for him. Southampton, on his watch, were not short of violinists.

I did get a shock, though, on my debut against Manchester City at the start of the 1980–1 season, when the referee came over after ten minutes. The game was being filmed for *Match of the Day*, which was a big deal back then, and the place was packed. Lawrie had made me captain and the referee looked stressed. 'Kevin,' he said, 'if these two carry on I am going to send them both off.' I didn't know what he was talking about until I looked across the pitch and saw two of our team, Steve Williams and Ivan Golac, being held apart. The pair of them had been swapping punches. I had to run over to make sure it didn't flare up again.

I was learning quickly about my new teammates. Steve was a talented player with a few rough edges, whereas Ivan was a skilful Yugoslav right-back who used to take risks during games and didn't take kindly to criticism. If anyone ever tried to pull him up about a mistake, Ivan's stock answer was, 'I don't care.' It didn't matter if the criticism was justified, Ivan would just shrug his shoulders. 'I don't care, I don't care.' The next day, someone might gently bring it up again, hoping that he would be willing to listen outside the match environment. 'I don't care, I don't care.'

Training at Southampton was certainly different, especially on a Friday, when the players piled into the gym and the name of the game was to kick the living daylights out of each other. There were four bare walls, a hard surface and no escape. Players were squaring up, kicks were going in and vendettas forming. I was used to everything being ultra-professional at Hamburg and couldn't believe what I was seeing. I even went to see Lawrie to complain. 'It is the sort of thing I'd expect from a pub team,' I said. 'We should be protecting our players on a Friday, not trying to put them through the wall.' Lawrie's response was that the players enjoyed the rough and tumble and, sure enough, within a few weeks I was loving every minute of it. Those vicious five-a-sides were strangely addictive. It was carnage sometimes, but it helped to build a tremendous spirit, in the same way that Wimbledon used to do some unconventional stuff in the days of the Crazy Gang. I can even remember ending up trying to persuade Lawrie we should do the same on a Tuesday, too.

The Dell was a classic English ground, full of noise and fervour, and the tight confines were always packed. The atmosphere was crackling, especially when the big boys were in town, and we fancied our chances against anyone when we were playing at home. Lawrie wanted us to attack whoever we were playing, which was just the way I liked it, but we could also let in a few. A 4–4 draw against Spurs at White Hart Lane was one example, though it was our League Cup tie against Watford, of the Second Division, that showed us at our best and worst. The first leg was a 4–0 win at the Dell, then we lost 7–1 at Vicarage Road and went out 7–5 on aggregate. And people thought it was bonkers at Newcastle!

We finished sixth in my first season, which at that time was Southampton's highest ever placing, and everyone at the club seemed pleased about how the year had gone. Everyone except me, anyway. It might have been a successful season for Southampton, but I cannot pretend it was for me. My expectations were different; I was such a positive thinker I wanted us to be going for the league rather than accepting there were five better teams than us. I had taken a risk joining Southampton and, though I never thought of it as the wrong choice, it was difficult to be satisfied with sixth place.

I had also suffered some injury issues that meant I missed more games that season than any other. My hamstring went against Birmingham when we were 3–1 up and I should have come off straight away. Instead, Lawrie asked me to move to the right wing and I was told to soldier on because we had already used the one substitute that was permitted in those days. I could understand the reluctance to go down to ten men, but I wasn't hugely impressed. Today, a player would be taken off as soon as he felt a twinge, whereas I had to shuffle around in pain for another twenty minutes and inevitably made the injury worse.

I then aggravated the injury in the most pointless fashion when I was pressed into service on a trip to Morocco to play against Raja Casablanca in a friendly organised by sponsors. I was the star player, I understood that perfectly, and knew all the obligations that went with it. But I could barely jog, let alone kick a ball, and a bigger club would have understood that I needed to stay at home to recuperate. Instead I was told that the entire trip had been sold around me and it would be seen as a terrible snub if I didn't at least show my face. Eventually, I agreed to fly out with the team because Lawrie said I could stay at the hotel while the game was being played. It was made clear I was needed purely for PR purposes and that everyone understood there was no chance I could play.

I should have seen what was coming on our first morning in Casablanca, when I ordered a taxi to the Kasbah and had to get the driver to take me straight back to the hotel because of the crowds mobbing me. It used to shock me sometimes how my fame had spread to countries so far away. It was bedlam, and when the team set off for the stadium I was glad to get some peace and quiet in my hotel room. I settled down to read a book and was contemplating going downstairs to get some food when the telephone rang. It was Lawrie, calling from the stadium, and he sounded very flustered. I could hear what sounded like fans screaming my name and he was having to shout to make himself heard.

When the bus had arrived without me on it, Lawrie explained, the fans had gone ape-shit – there was no other word for it. The game was a sell-out. The security staff were panicking and the lads had bolted themselves in the dressing room. Nick Holmes, who was captaining the side in my absence, took the phone off Lawrie and told me straight. I had to get there, injury or no injury, because there was going to be a riot if I did not show up.

A police escort, sirens blaring, got me to the ground, and they delayed the kick-off so I could limp out, leg strapped up, as a late addition to the team. I played for around seventy minutes and the crowd seemed happy enough, but the whole thing was ludicrous and it was one of those occasions when my fame counted against me. It was always the star player who was needed for the photo opportunity, the press conference, the exhibition match and so on – and if you were injured, well, that was a shame, but hurry up, all the same. It was just a fact of football life, I suppose, and I used to bend over backwards to try to keep everybody happy. But it's the same at every club where there is a big-name player – and I suspect some of the other players are quite glad sometimes they don't have the same pressures or obligations.

My second season at Southampton was the most prolific of my career. I was injury-free again and finished with thirty goals, including twenty-six in the league, to win the Golden Boot as the First Division's top-scorer. We could still be far too leaky in defence but, by the end of January, a 1–0 win at Middlesbrough had moved us to the top of the table. I scored the winner that day and, on the long bus journey home, I couldn't see any reason, with a bit of luck and some shrewd business in the transfer market, why our championship chase should not end successfully.

Lawrie lumbered down the aisle to our 'office' at the back of the bus and, over a few beers, myself and a couple of the other senior players told him that if we could boost the team with one top signing, we might just finish as champions. We all deeply cared, and Peter Shilton was in my mind because he was rumoured to be available from Nottingham Forest. Maybe Lawrie will say that signing someone of Shilton's reputation was easier said than done. Perhaps he will say we were getting ideas above our station and shouldn't have been poking our noses into his business. But who knows where it might have taken us if the club had shown more ambition?

As it was, nobody arrived and our form started to deteriorate. We were still clinging to top spot until a 3–2 defeat at Spurs towards the end of March allowed Swansea City to overtake us. We went back to the top after another typical Southampton performance to beat Stoke City 4–3 the following weekend. But that was our only win in eight games. Our momentum had gone and young Steve Moran, the top-scorer in my first season, was lost to a back injury. Swansea also dropped off, but Liverpool won twelve of their last fifteen matches and, yet again, the league championship trophy was on its way back to Anfield. Top of the table at the start of April, we came in seventh – one place further back than the previous season – and finished twenty-one points off the pace.

I was disillusioned and, in the middle of that bad run, my relationship with Lawrie took a significant turn for the worse when we crashed 3–0 at home to Aston Villa. Lawrie was entitled to be angry, but he also had the temerity to say I was not trying. Nobody had ever said that to me before, and then he went even further. He called us 'cheats'. I had never been called a cheat in my life and something broke for me that day. I'm sure Lawrie regretted it later but the damage was done. After everything I had done in my career, the rejections I had suffered and the way I had worked for everything I had ever achieved, it was probably the worst thing he could ever have said.

I was starting to feel very differently about Southampton, and when we returned for pre-season training I was increasingly critical about the direction the club were taking. The final straw was the sight of all our youngsters gathering at Heathrow to check in for our pre-season trip to Ireland. We had some talented kids, but it brought it home how little we had progressed since the end of the previous season. It was deflating. We were a long way short of being title contenders and, if my ambitions exceeded what the club could offer, it was time for me to leave.

The irony is that Southampton found the money to sign Peter Shilton within a month of my departure. Even with the England international goalkeeper on board, however, they finished four-teenth in their first season without me. Lawrie will always be a hero at Southampton. He is also someone I hold in high esteem and they had a much better season the following year to finish as runners-up. But it was the right time for me to leave. I was still hurt by that 'cheat' allegation and Lawrie knew me well enough to understand it was pointless trying to talk me out of it. I went to see him after that Ireland trip and he agreed it was probably for the best.

After that, everything happened very quickly. I was on my way to Newcastle United, but first I had to break the news to Alan Ball, my dear pal. It was a tough conversation. Mick Channon had already left and Alan was very upset, even shedding a few tears. He was always a very emotional guy, in a lovely way. I miss Alan. We had some wonderful times together.

The saddest part was leaving on poor terms with Lawrie, who was such a wonderful football man, and it wasn't the cleanest of breaks. I had signed a new contract the previous November and there was an outcry from Southampton's fans when they heard I was on my way out. A lot of people had bought their season tickets expecting me to be in the team, and they convinced themselves the news had been deliberately held back until they had parted with their money.

I considered holding a press conference to make it clear that was not the case. I even contemplated taking out a full-page advertisement in the local newspaper, but the reality was there was never going to be a nice way to go. People will always feel hurt and betrayed because football is such an emotional sport. Time is a healer, though, and I am glad Lawrie and I eventually settled our differences. We are still good friends to this day, as are our wives, Jean and Anne, and maybe I did him a disservice thinking all that stuff about the light fitting might have been a ruse. I did bring it over from Hamburg for him anyway, and it illuminated the landing of his house for many years.

8

'NOT YOU, KEEGAN'

On the night England failed to qualify for the 1974 World Cup, I was sitting on the bench behind Alf Ramsey, wondering whether he would ever turn round to give me the signal that I was coming on. Jan Tomaszewski – the Polish goalkeeper Brian Clough so mistakenly described as a 'clown' – was putting in the performance of his life. The score was 1–1 and England were staring at ignominious failure, unless someone could conjure up a dramatic late winner. Then, with five minutes to go, the moment I had been waiting for. Alf turned his head and the call finally came: 'Kevin, get changed.'

As I leapt to my feet, I had visions of scoring the goal that would alter the course of English football history. Ray Clemence, sitting beside me, also knew the urgency of the situation and, in his excitement to help me get my tracksuit off, whipped my shorts and underpants down to my knees, presenting the royal box at Wembley with a rather unexpected view. Then Alf turned his head again and gave me a strange look. 'Not you, Keegan,' he said, with that posh voice, 'Kevin Hector!' And, as I shrank into my seat, it was the Derby County player who ran on with the chance to make himself a hero. Just my luck that we had two Kevins on the bench.

I watched those agonising last few minutes with a sense of helplessness, and in the dressing room afterwards it was a scene of utter desolation. We were out of the World Cup, despite having thirty-odd attempts at goal. What I didn't realise at the time was that four years later we would experience the same kind of shame and agony, the awful déjà vu that we had presided over a national embarrassment. The same numbing feeling that another World Cup was going to pass us by and that we, the players, had let down the entire country.

When I put it in the overall context of my career, perhaps I should not be too hard on myself. I am not short of career high-lights and nobody, I suppose, can have everything. All the same, it does rankle that I cannot decorate this book with treasured memories from the major international tournaments. I captained England over thirty times, won sixty-three caps and scored twenty-one goals, but how can there not be regrets when the sum total of my involvement in the World Cup boils down to twenty-six minutes as a substitute? How can I be fully satisfied when the World Cup, for any footballer worth his salt, is the greatest stage of all? Of course it is going to sting. Of course I would have wished for more from my ten years as an international footballer.

Nor does it make me feel any better that, when I did finally make it to a World Cup, in Spain 1982, my only contribution of note was a dreadful miss against the host nation to send us home. Everyone remembers the Admiral shirt with the red and blue stripe, and I still have one of those tops, along with all the other jerseys I collected over the years. My abiding memory, sadly, when I look at it now, is Bryan Robson floating over a perfect cross in our game against the host nation and me, six yards out, fluffing the sort of header I had scored all my life. I had my chance to put us into the semi-finals in a World Cup – and I blew it.

The bottom line is that we weren't good enough and, though you could find all sorts of factors to explain England's decline, it always came back to the same point. We had some fine players, and a sprinkling of outstanding ones, but not enough. We could beat our rivals in the British Home Championship, if it was a good year, but did we have the star quality to go any further? The answer is demonstrated by the fact that I had to wait until I was twenty-nine, at the 1980 European Championship, before I got my first experience of a proper international tournament. True to form, we didn't get past the first stage and were eliminated within a week.

The failure to qualify for the 1978 World Cup was an even greater setback, because that was the part of my career when I was playing at the point of maximum expression. I was the European Footballer of the Year but deprived the biggest platform of all. It was cruel, and I spent my summer trying to keep busy rather than torturing myself by watching on television. I was not what you could call a good watcher. I didn't even tune in to see Argentina beat Holland in the final.

As for the 1976 European Championship, when Czechoslovakia held off West Germany in the final, when the Panenka penalty was patented and even 'Total Football' was not enough for the Dutch, that was another difficult summer. It was soul-destroying to think England had been world champions ten years earlier, and I will never forget Holland's visit to Wembley the following February and the crushing sense of deflation when the striker Johnny Rep wandered over, with only ten minutes played, to offer his professional opinion. Johnny could never seem to pronounce the 'n' in my name. He also had that typical Dutch trait of being very straight to the point and not thinking it necessary to sugar-coat his words. 'Kevvy,' he said, 'this is the worst England side I have ever seen. Wow, Kevvy, you have big problems.'

The score was 0–0 at that stage and, though I liked Johnny and was friendly with quite a few Dutch players, I thought it was a bit off to make such a sweeping statement so early in the game. Then Holland scored one, quickly added another, and it was exhibition stuff for the rest of the match. The only surprise was that we kept the score down to 2–0. Johnny didn't mean it offensively; he was just bemused that a country with thirteen million people could be so much better than one with over four times that number. That, unfortunately, was England all over – we had quantity not quality.

My international debut came against Wales in a 1–0 win at Cardiff's Ninian Park on 15 November 1972. I liked Alf Ramsey from the start and I felt honoured to have a connection with the manager who had led England to victory in the 1966 World Cup. We drew 1–1 in my next game, also against Wales, at Wembley. As for my third start, that was Joe Mercer's first game as caretaker manager, and the opposition was Wales again. I was living in north Wales at the time, commuting in and out of Liverpool, and the other England players had started to call me 'Taff Keegan'. We won 2–0 and I scored my first international goal. It was a tap-in, but pleasing nonetheless – and that helped soothe my nerves because I must confess I didn't find it easy at first to settle as an England player.

I wouldn't normally allow myself to be afflicted by stage fright, but perhaps I could be excused a few nerves. It was, after all, only eighteen months since I was in the Fourth Division with Scunthorpe. Alan Ball told me I looked scared stiff in my first couple of England appearances, and that wasn't far off the truth. It was different to Liverpool, where I had a three-year contract and felt the trust of Bill Shankly from day one. With England, there was no guarantee that I would be invited back if I didn't impress straight away. I was out of my comfort zone, still only twenty-one, and filled with tension. All the publicity about me being the brightest young star since George Best had left me feeling under pressure to do something out of the ordinary to live up to it. Alf tried me twice and I flopped both times.

It took a while before the penny dropped and I started to think that, hold on, if I was lighting up one of the better teams in the country, of course I deserved to wear an England shirt. For my first call-up, I could scarcely believe it was true. Then I turned up and felt like an intruder. 'Here's this lad Keegan,' seemed to be the attitude of the senior players, 'let's see what he's got then. He's had the publicity – let's see him prove it.' It needed quite a few games, maybe more than a dozen, before I truly found my feet.

I can laugh about those moments now and, despite all the

1. A postcard commemorating the 1909 West Stanley Colliery disaster, where my grandfather, Frank, helped to rescue the few men that survived. He is in the front row, third from right.

2. St Peter's High School football team of 1963–4, winners of the Doncaster district Lord Mayor's Trophy. I am in the first row, second from right.

TACTICAL SWITCH TURNING POINT OF TIGHT DUEL

by TOM TAYLOR

A GOAL by centre forward Rusling, laid on by man-of-the-match, inside left Keegan, after 108 minutes, was sufficient to take Scunthorpe United into the second round of the FA Cup at Everton's plush Goodison Park last night. They did so after a third grim defensive battle against Tranemer Rovers.

The tie had gone on for 318 minutes before Scunthorpe got in front for the first time. But once they had the lead their passage into a second round home game against Mansfield Town was assured.

Scunthorpe won because they proved vastly the superior team in extra-time and they finished the game with a confident exhibition of "keep ball" which Tranmere had not the physical strength to resist.

For me, the turning point came mid-way through the second half with a Scunthorpe tactical switch which changed the course at a time when Tranmere were threatening to dominate up front.

Closer watch

Right back Joy had been coming through as an extra forward on the flank where Scunthorpe had no recognised winger. But Davidson was switched to the left and as a result Joy was given closer attention and without the extra man in attack Tranmere were forced back from what had been a determined effort to make the break. It was fitting that Keegan should have played the vital

| TRANMERE ROV. | 0 |
| SCUNTHORPE U. | 1 |

Rusling (108 min.).
Attendance: 7,235.

87th minute when Beamish pulled back a cross from the left and with time to pick his spot, Hinch hit the foot of a post with the ball going behind for a goalkick.

As early as the 69th minute Tranmere had pulled off Moore and brought on Yardley, but the substitute made little impact when faced by Welbourne's determined tackling.

And the leggy Hinch was marked right out of the game by Deere in the man-for-man marking scheme. He worked out for the centre of the Scunthorpe defence. Scunthorpe's full backs covered well with Foxton the master of Gill, and Barker forcing Beamish into a wandering role after his early successes along the line-side.

Woolmer's impact

Barnard played his usual competent game handling the ball well and making far better use of his clearances than his opposite number.
Although giving much

to the threat of King who had moved forward in an effort to break the threatened stalemate.

At their best

Scunthorpe's extra time play saw them at their best with Keegan going close on three occasions in the first five minutes.

These shots gave Scunthorpe the inspiration they needed and against fast-tiring defenders they must have sensed that the game was fast going their way.

And so it proved, with Rusling, as he has done so often in the past, getting himself in the right spot at the right time.

For Tranmere it must have been highly disappointing. But the fact is that this compact Scunthorpe defence held all that King and his colleagues had to offer, and then produced the game's best football when it was most required.

Stamina told in the end with Scunthorpe going forward throughout extra time while Tranmere wilted when they were most in need of defensive stability.

Tranmere Rovers: Lane, Joy, Dempsey, Mathias, Moor-

3. The Scunthorpe United first team for the 1969–70 season, who played in the then Fourth Division. I'm in the second row, second from left.

4. The newspaper report on the fateful FA Cup second replay game versus Tranmere Rovers that Bill Shankly's scouts came to watch. As luck would have it, I put in a man-of-the-match performance, setting up the only goal.

5. A reunion with Sister Mary Oliver, who was my first footballing mentor and a huge influence on me growing up.

6. With 'Lennie the Junk', whose shop hosted the Kevin Keegan fan club and my limited company, Nageek Enterprises.

7. Jean and I on our wedding day.

8. Celebrating our 1974 FA Cup win over Newcastle with Liverpool captain Emlyn Hughes.

9. Myself and Leeds United's Billy Bremner being sent off by the referee in the 1974 FA Charity Shield.

10. John Toshack looks on as I celebrate scoring against Wolverhampton Wanderers, in a victory that confirmed the league championship would be returning to Anfield.

11. Celebrating winning the league championship with my father in 1976, who sadly died later that year.

12. Reunited with my old colleague 'Taf Davies in 1977, the man who kept me out of the Peglers Brass Works first team.

13. Ray Clemence and I, two lads who started out playing for Scunthorpe, celebrating Liverpool's 1977 European Cup victory.

14. The great Bill Shankly trying to present me with the commemorative Souvenir Press International Football Book Sword after winning my second European Footballer of the Year award – I insisted he kept it.

15. In action for England, scoring a close-range header against Denmark to help secure qualification for the 1980 Euros, England's first major tournament in a decade.

frustrations, I must not portray my international career as one long struggle against adversity. Far from it – it was one of the highlights of my life to play for England. It was even more wonderful, in my time as captain, to be leading out the team, knowing we were the best eleven footballers in the country. It was special. I was representing the finest team England could put out and, trust me, it was an incredible high to stand at the front of that line, knowing it used to be Bobby Moore in that position. The national anthem would start and I would sing the words. Then, a few days later, one of the traditional England caps would arrive, in rich blue velvet with silver quartering and a tassel. I'm not a showy person by any means, but I have all mine in a display cabinet.

For someone with my competitive instincts, however, it is bound to grate that so many of my caps came in the home internationals rather than the tournaments that really mattered. Seven were against Wales, six versus Northern Ireland and four from our tussles with Scotland. Add in the three against the Republic of Ireland and that is almost a third of my collection. I didn't actually play for England outside the British Isles throughout my initial eighteen months as an international footballer, and the first occasion, on a 1974 tour of Eastern Europe, was one of the worst experiences of my life.

That was the period when Joe Mercer had been placed in temporary charge. Joe knew he was keeping the seat warm for somebody else and quickly made himself popular with the players. He made a big impression on all of us and was determined to take the pressure out of playing for England. Football was a game of pleasure, he said. 'Enjoy it. You're here because you can play, so go and play. And if you want a beer, have a beer.'

Our first game was against East Germany in Leipzig and we drew 1–1, with a goal from Mick Channon, before following Joe's advice by going for a few drinks. Then it was on to Bulgaria, where Frank Worthington gave us a 1–0 win in Sofia and it was the same again in the hotel bar afterwards. There were a few bleary eyes on the flight to Yugoslavia for the final leg of the tour, and maybe our happy-go-lucky attitude counted against us when we landed at Belgrade airport. For a start, we were travelling in our own gear, so there was nothing to signify that we were actually an international football team. Usually, the FA officials would lead the players through customs and we would all wear blazers with a collar and tie. This time the players went through in dribs and drabs, all in our civvies. I was in the first group and, once my passport had been stamped, I followed the signs to the baggage-reclaim area and sat on the edge of the stationary carousel.

I was carrying a bag containing two pieces of beautiful pottery that I had bought in Sofia, one for Mum and the other for Jean. Alec Lindsay, my Liverpool colleague, had a tape-player going, and started fooling around on the carousel, walking the wrong way like the character in a silent movie. Frank Worthington, or 'Roy Rogers' as we called him because of his cowboy boots, ambled through, and I remember Bob Harris, one of the journalists who covered England, being there. It was all completely harmless until one of the airport guards grabbed Alec and threw him against a wall. It was a complete overreaction. I was doubled up laughing when suddenly I was grabbed from behind and lifted violently off the floor.

Everything happened so quickly, I wondered at first if it was one of the other lads messing around, but the sheer amount of force made me realise it was sinister. My carrier bag split open and the pottery smashed on the floor. I swung my arm back instinctively to try to fend off whoever it was. Then a guy in uniform appeared and suddenly there were two of them on me. This one was a policeman, and when I was dragged into a side room, the battering really began. Oh my God, I lost count of the number of times I was punched, clubbed and kicked. Then I was forced to my knees and, worst of all, made to bow my head like a prisoner of war.

I tried to appeal for mercy, but the more I spoke the angrier they became, and I was kept in that position – head bowed, on my knees, hands behind my back – for around twenty minutes, looking down at the blood spattered on my trousers and wondering what the hell I had done to deserve such a beating. There was no communication, just a series of angry grunts to accompany the occasional blows. It felt like an eternity and, every so often, one of these goons would start laying into me again.

I was not easily scared, but I was shivering with fright and shock. I dread to think where it might have led had Ted Croker, the FA secretary, not turned up. These police officers belatedly realised I was not an England supporter, as I presume they had thought. All of a sudden, they were trying to clean me up, mopping away the blood and doing their best to make me look respectable. They had done such a good job with their fists and boots it was almost impossible, though, and I still have the photograph of the team doctor, Neil Phillips, checking me over. Malcolm Macdonald is sitting beside me and I have a handkerchief in my hand to wipe my bloodied nose. I look shell-shocked, which is exactly what I was.

The entire incident was painful, humiliating and frightening, and the other players were so horrified when they saw the state of me they wanted to catch the next flight home and abandon the match. Joe talked them into staying and, when he offered me the chance to sit out the match, I told him that was the last thing I wanted. There was no way I was going to lose an England cap on top of everything else. I always played well when I was angry, and on that occasion I was livid that I could be treated so badly. I didn't need any more motivation. We drew 2–2 and I took a great deal of personal satisfaction from scoring one of our goals.

I vowed to myself that day that I would never return to Yugoslavia, and that wasn't just a heat-of-the-moment reaction. I was psychologically scarred by the ordeal, and when Hamburg drew Hajduk Split in the European Cup some years later, I went to see the manager, Branko Zebec, to let him know I didn't want to go. Branko was upset, as a Yugoslav, to find out what had happened, and told me I could not let one terrible experience turn me against a whole country. My teammate, Ivan Buljan, had the same message, assuring me that the people in his country liked and respected me. I'm glad they talked me round, but it was touch and go for a while, because when you have been put on your knees in the way I was, like a man waiting to be executed, it is not something that is easy to forget.

After that incident, a new rule was brought in to stipulate that the England players always had to travel in uniform, and on our next trip, with Don Revie now in the hot seat, there was a new sense of order and discipline. That was only correct, but I can't pretend I was too chuffed initially about Don's appointment. In fact, my heart sank, because for us Liverpool lads he was the enemy. Being a Liverpool player, I had to think that way. I hated everything his Leeds team had stood for, and there was so much needle between the two sides, I even wondered whether he might take a malicious sense of pleasure from being the manager to finish my international career.

I was wrong on every front. Don was not always portrayed kindly, but there was a lot more to him than the popular carica-ture of the hard-faced, gruff Yorkshireman. There was a soft-focus Don Revie. He always spoke with deep respect of Liverpool, and there was never any favouritism towards the Leeds players. His team-talks were incredible, and sometimes he, and we, would be close to tears by the time he had finished. He wanted the Wem-bley crowd to sing 'Land of Hope and Glory' and, though a lot of the lads were sceptical when he gave us our own team song, all of us sang it together, over and again, in the dressing room after we had beaten Czechoslovakia in his first match, even after he had gone out of the room. 'It's a grand old team to play for, it's a grand old team to see . . .'

That didn't mean I agreed with all his decisions, and I was as disappointed as anyone when he left us to coach the United Arab Emirates (Don would say he was going to be sacked anyway). There were times when I thought we talked so much about the opposition's strengths and weaknesses that we overlooked what our own players could do. It riled the players that the manager was so close to a couple of Fleet Street hacks that we invariably found out the team via the newspapers and, for the life of me, I could never understand why Alan Ball was cut adrift when he still had so much to offer. Don was big enough to admit he had made a mistake when he left out Emlyn Hughes and, eighteen months later, recalled him to the side. But there was no reprieve for Alan after the decision was taken that he could no longer cut it at international level. Alan had just turned thirty and continued to excel in the top division for another seven years. It was far too early to sacrifice a player of that quality.

The joke about Don was that it was difficult for him to fly with the England team because his filing cabinet did not fit on the plane. He was incredibly thorough with his tactical dossiers on our opponents, and that attracted a lot of debate because, in the 1970s, nobody else did that kind of preparatory work. Some of the team thought it was over the top and turned over the sheets of paper to use as scorecards for their card games. That, however, said more about them than him. Don was ahead of his time and what people perceived as faults then, would actually be regarded as good qualities now. In six years at Liverpool, I was never given a file on the opposition. Heck, we never even had a qualified physiotherapist. We were the best team in the country, yet we used a Subbuteo board for tactics. Different days, indeed.

Don's other obsession was team-bonding and, again, some of the players didn't get it. What they didn't understand was that Don had no interest in finding the best golfer when he arranged golf-putting competitions in the team hotel. It was purely to create some togetherness with a competitive element. We used to draw lots to have various rounds of two players against one another, FA Cup-style, and each person had three goes to sink the ball. Stan Bowles hated it. He had his first go – knocked it miles past the hole. Second go – whacked it even further, barely even looking. Third one, bang again. 'Cheers, boys, see you in the morning,' he said, and was already walking off. Stan wasn't one for team-bonding.

I grew very fond of Don. I could see why the Leeds players were so devoted to him and, years later, we spent a lot of quality time together when we were living in Marbella and trying to disprove the theory that golf was the perfect way to ruin a good walk. Those times confirmed my view that he was a good man, and it was tragic to see him fall to motor neurone disease. For such a proud and independent man, it must have been terribly upsetting that he needed assistance even to go to the toilet. I bought him a golf buggy so he could still come round the course with us and he would sometimes have a bet on 'the little fella', as he called me, to make things more interesting. Eventually, he wasn't even able to drive the buggy. He was just wasting away.

Our only disagreement came early on, in May 1975, after a game against Northern Ireland, when a letter, purportedly from the IRA, was sent to the FA offices saying that if I showed my face in Belfast I was a dead man. Another letter went directly to a member of the FA Council, naming me again, and Don took me aside to suggest it might be safer for me to have a few days at home. When I rang Jean she made it clear she wouldn't be able to rest until I was back. Anyone would be worried in that position, but my point was that I couldn't live my life in hiding because of some crank writing letters. What if it was a hoax, as I suspected, and another player scored a hat-trick in my place? Did I really want to lose out on another England cap? And what if someone, possibly an opposition fan, realised what could be done and delivered the same threat to Liverpool before a big match? 'Well, look,' Jean said, 'I know what I think, but I also know the way you think and it won't do me any good telling you what I think.'

Once the decision had been made that I should go with the team, it wasn't easy clearing my mind and, perhaps unsurprisingly, I didn't play brilliantly in a goalless draw at Windsor Park. But you can imagine my reaction when Don put up the team-sheet for our next game against Wales and I wasn't on it. I was stunned, not just by the decision, but because there was no explanation whatsoever. After going to Ireland with a death threat hanging over me, an explanation was the least I deserved. I even started wondering whether Don had tried to use the IRA scare as an excuse to get me out of the team. I should have had it out with him face to face, but I waited all day for an explanation and, by early evening, he still hadn't said a word. I was young, stubborn and impulsive and prone sometimes to making rash decisions. I packed my bags, checked out of my hotel room and went home.

It was childish of me, and if I thought the public would take my side, I was mistaken. The press were camped outside my house and the general reaction was that I was behaving like a baby, throwing my toys out of the pram because I couldn't get my own way. Luckily, Don took a more understanding view, and thank heavens for that, because he would have been within his rights to tell me to take a running jump. Instead, he rang me to say it was a misunderstanding, explaining that he had wanted to keep me back for our game against Scotland the following Saturday, and said we would both regret it if I didn't come back. I don't think I would have been quite so forgiving if the roles were reversed, but Don chose not to make an example of me. 'What happened is forgotten,' he assured me. And within ten months he had made me captain – which, for me, was the greatest honour of all.

My first game as skipper came on a wet, muddy Wednesday night against – you've guessed it – Wales, and we won 2–1 at the Racecourse Ground in Wrexham. Those clashes with Wales could be quite tasty. I was kicked to the ground in one pitch invasion at Cardiff, and in another game Joey Jones clattered into me so forcefully that nobody could possibly have thought we were Liverpool teammates. When we returned to Anfield, Joey walked straight into an admonishment from Bob Paisley. 'Just remember you have to play with Kevin on Saturday,' Bob reminded him.

That was nothing, however, compared to the treatment I had to suffer against Italy at Wembley in November 1977, when I found out the hard way why our opponents had a reputation as the dirtiest international team in Europe. I was a marked man that night. Marco Tardelli, who will always be known for his goal celebration in the 1982 World Cup final, gave me the first warning, dropping me to the floor with a vicious elbow to the jaw. I don't know how I got up from that one, or how my assailant wasn't sent off, and my jaw was still aching when Romeo Benetti, whose style of play could be generously described as 'tenacious', introduced himself by digging his elbow into the top of my head.

Even with my perm offering an extra layer of protection, it was a painful way to make acquaintances, and I retaliated with an elbow of my own, catching him flush in the mouth. One of his front teeth popped out and then I knew I was in serious trouble. Benetti was frightening. He gave me a murderous look – imagine the Jaws character from the James Bond movies – and growled in broken English, 'I get you, Keegan. Before finish.' He spat straight in my eye. But as the game wore on I was starting to think I might have got away with it. I had managed to keep out of his way, using all the evasion tactics I had fine-tuned on the pitches of the South Yorkshire amateur leagues. The clock was showing ten minutes to go and I was confidently thinking, *You won't get me, chum*. He did, though.

His moment arrived when I played the ball through for Trevor Brooking to score our second goal. I had given us a first-half lead and that was Trevor's first goal for England – at last, in his nineteenth appearance. He would have to forgive me for not joining in the celebrations because, as he was tucking the ball past Dino Zoff, I was lying on the turf in a crumpled heap. Benetti had seen his chance, waited for me to play the pass and cleaned me out. In fact, he came in so high I wonder whether he thought it was possible to detach my leg from the rest of my body. My knee ballooned and I had to go off. It was a fair price, I suppose, for a broken tooth.

By that stage Ron Greenwood had taken over, and I have to admit it was a blow when he decided to take the captaincy off me. I did understand, to a degree. I had just moved to Hamburg and

the Germans wanted me to sit out one or two of the less important England friendlies. Ron's view was that it would be better to
have a captain who was always available. He wanted the captain
to represent an English club and, ideally, to be a defender or midfielder. 'Don't take it personally,' he told me, 'but I'm giving the
job to Emlyn Hughes.' I couldn't pretend to be happy, having had
the role for the previous nine games, but I never made a big issue
of it. Then Emlyn started to drift out of the team and, within two
years, the role was mine again.

Ron had been chosen for the role of England manager, despite
Brian Clough being built up in the newspapers as the 'people's
choice'. I was quite relieved Cloughie didn't get it because there
would have been fireworks between us. Trevor Brooking, who
had been one of Ron's players at West Ham, had told me good
things about the new manager, and it was a step in the right
direction when the team qualified for the 1980 European Championship.

It was the first major tournament England had reached in a
decade. I've had a bit of stick over the years for that photograph
where Emlyn Hughes and myself are pretending to give Margaret
Thatcher a peck on each cheek during a reception in Downing
Street before we flew out. Yet that is not exactly fair. It was 1980
when the FA received the invitation to meet the prime minister
and, whatever your political allegiance, that kind of event is par
for the course if you are the England captain going to a major
tournament. I have never voted Conservative in my life and, if
you remember my family's background, you can probably guess
what I think about the way Thatcher's government treated the
miners, leading to the strike action and the devastation of so
many pit communities. That, however, was some time later. Every
England team makes those kind of public appearances prior to a
tournament and that, in 1980, was all it was – no more, no less.

Some years later, I was invited to take part in a photo shoot
with Tony Blair during the Labour Party conference in Brighton.
We took a football to see how long we could keep it in the air

with a game of head-tennis. Longer than I had presumed, is the honest answer. Tony was always interesting company, as was his wife, Cherie. We had them round for dinner when we were living in the north-east and he was leader of the country. Jean cooked everyone a lovely meal and, halfway through the main course, a message came that Tony had an urgent telephone call. He needed somewhere private and the only place we could think of was our bedroom. What we didn't realise when we left him sitting on the end of our bed, with Jean scurrying round to make sure there were none of my socks on the floor, was that he was working on the Good Friday agreement for the Northern Ireland peace process. After the death threat of 1975, it was nice to think the Keegan family could help in our own small way!

Ron Greenwood did at least get England back into the habit of qualifying for tournaments and, realistically, 1982 was always going to be my final chance to make a lasting impression at a World Cup. I was thirty-one. I had just had my best scoring return for a season, with twenty-six league goals for Southampton, and when we set out to Spain I was determined to make the most of it.

Instead, an old back injury flared up and that tournament turned into a nightmare. The timing was terrible, five days before our opening game against France in Bilbao, and the pain was so excruciating I was more or less confined to bed. My roommate, Trevor Brooking, had suffered his own misfortune, with a groin injury, and at times like that all you really have is gallows humour. We even painted a red cross on our door to make sure everyone knew it was a hospital ward.

Even when I had an epidural, it still brought no relief, and I was so depressed that Ron came over at breakfast one day to ask if I could start smiling more in case I brought down the other players. How could I be all sunshine and light when I was going through the biggest disappointment of my career? I couldn't just flick a switch to make myself happy again. So I closed the bedroom door and lay on my bed, alone with my thoughts, staring out of the window. I spent so long in that position that the view – two chimneys on a nearby power station – is still etched on my mind. Like I say, it was a nightmare.

By the time England had qualified for the second group stage, where we were drawn against West Germany and Spain with a place in the semi-finals up for grabs, I was still racked with pain and had already missed three matches. The choice was clear. I could either accept defeat, put it down as a cruel twist of fate and get a flight home, or I could fly to Germany to see the specialist, Jürgen Rehwinkel, who had looked after me when my back started playing up in Hamburg.

On that occasion Dr Rehwinkel had worked out that three or four vertebrae were slightly out of place and clicked them back so I was better within twenty-four hours. It had worked before and I was convinced it could work again. Indeed, I had already said to Ron earlier in the tournament that it was the best chance I had. Ron didn't like the idea of one of his players flying to Germany for treatment, and the team doctor, Vernon Edwards, seemed offended by the suggestion I wanted a second opinion. All I wanted was to get my back sorted. I should have stood my ground but I left it for three games before going back to Ron to say I had tried it his way and it hadn't worked. Now, I asked, could we try it my way?

Ron still had doubts, especially now we were about to play West Germany, and seemed to think it was a national embarrassment that an English footballer might need treatment from a German doctor. He was worried about it getting into the press and said the only way I could go was if I agreed to accomplish the entire operation in secret. That was absurd. I asked how he imagined someone with a face and hairstyle as well known as mine could be expected to get to Germany and back in the middle of a World Cup without anyone noticing. But I had to give it a go. I left in the dead of night and the hotel receptionist kindly lent me her car, a tiny Seat 500, for the long, uncomfortable drive from Bilbao to Madrid airport. From Madrid, I caught a 7 a.m.

flight to Hamburg, wearing sunglasses and a hat to conceal my curls, and by lunchtime I was in Dr Rehwinkel's surgery, trying to explain why the FA had not let me fly in as soon as the problem flared up. He was horrified about what I had been through, the politics that had delayed me and the fact that the FA had let someone with a bad back spend nearly five hours in a cramped car. And, just as I had thought, he quickly came up with a way of massaging everything back into place.

The incredible thing was that I kept to my side of the bargain, and nobody outside a select few knew anything about my secret expedition. As you have probably gathered by now, I was a master of disguise when I needed to be. I knew I could trust Trevor to keep it quiet. I stayed overnight with a friend in Hamburg, rather than checking into a hotel, and after some more treatment in the morning, I flew back into Madrid before setting off in the Seat 500 on the 250-mile drive to Bilbao. The whole trip was done and dusted within forty-eight hours. Nobody was any the wiser and I just wish I had never been talked out of it in the first place because, frankly, the England medical staff had misdiagnosed the problem. The whole thing was a fiasco and when I look back on it now I could be forgiven if I felt bitter. Instead, I just feel sadness.

After all that, the game against West Germany came and went without me playing a single minute. That was tough, and I felt like an actor putting on a smile, as Ron had asked, in front of the other lads. I thought I was going to start the match and I'm pretty sure everyone in the team reckoned the same. I felt like a new man. Ron even had me in the team for a practice match the day before. Trevor was also left out, despite recovering from his own injury. We were England's best two players, hugely influential in the way the team played and desperate to make up for lost time. Equally, I can understand why Ron was torn. England had beaten France, Czechoslovakia and Kuwait and I had always gone by the old maxim that you shouldn't break up a winning team. I had profited from it and now, sadly, I was the victim of it.

What I will never understand, though, is the logic of keeping us on the bench for the game against Spain. Your best players are your best players, and our 0–0 draw against the Germans meant we needed to beat the Spaniards to go through. The circumstances had changed. We both should have started and – hypothetical, I know – maybe if we had been on from the first minute, it would have been England going through to the semi-finals. Maybe the World Cup would never have had that semi-final between West Germany and France, and Harald Schumacher's infamous assault on Patrick Battiston. Don't forget, either, that we had already shown we could beat France. I am not saying it would have definitely happened, but nobody will ever talk me out of the view that it was Ron's biggest mistake.

It was the sixty-fourth minute when Trevor and I came on and straight away we showed we could trouble the Spanish defence. That, however, means nothing now, and the only detail of significance is that when my big chance came, with virtually my first touch, my header flew wide. Bryan Robson had put it on a plate for me and that miss is probably the only moment of my England career that people remember now. The game ended goalless and that was my one and only taste of the World Cup. We were out, even though we hadn't actually lost a game in the entire tournament. Ron handed in his resignation and I had no idea, walking off the pitch at the Bernabéu, that it would be the last time I would ever be picked for my country.

9

WE'RE IN HEAVEN

St James' Park dominates the Newcastle skyline like a medieval castle. Beneath it, it can feel like every other person is wearing a black and white shirt. Even when the stadium was a lot more dilapidated than the shiny, modern ground we see now, there was something about the place that held my fascination. It felt like home and, right from the start, there was an incredible sense of belonging, the feeling that I was coming back to my roots, arriving at the very place that had always filled me with wonder and awe. It was the right club, right place, right time, and I knew it was my destiny.

The excitement infected me from the day I arrived in August 1982, when hundreds of fans converged on the Gosforth Park Hotel for my first press conference. They gathered on the grassy verges, peering through the windows, peeking from behind curtains and running down the corridors. The *Newcastle Evening Chronicle* confirmed the story on the front page – 'HERE HE IS!' – and it was a special moment for me when I felt one of those Newcastle shirts against my skin for the first time.

All the memories of hearing my father singing 'Blaydon Races' and listening to his stories about Jackie Milburn and Hughie Gallacher came flooding back. I remembered the times when relatives from the north-east came to visit and the way Dad's Geordie accent suddenly became so much stronger. Dad's favourite word was 'champion'. Even when the cancer took hold. I'd go, 'How are you today, Dad?' He'd reply, 'Champion, son.'

He would have loved to see me wearing those black and white stripes. I felt proud and humble, flushed with gratitude.

Not everyone could understand why the England captain would contemplate dropping into the Second Division, and there were plenty of people who wanted to know if I had lost the plot. But they also thought I was crackers when I left Hamburg, the European Cup finalists, for unfashionable Southampton. What those people didn't understand was the tremendous pull that Newcastle had for me. They didn't appreciate the urge I had to be among the Geordies and the feeling in my bones that, at some stage, it was inevitable I was going to end up in this football-daft city.

Strictly speaking, Doncaster was my home, but Newcastle had been a part of my life for as long as I could remember. I was born into a black and white world. It was a Geordie, my uncle Frank, who gave me my first ball. I had been told from a very early age about the passion of the Newcastle fans, and there were times with Liverpool, especially in the 1974 FA Cup final, when I had been given a glimpse of it for myself. Now it was time to experience it properly, and it didn't take long to realise it was all true: the entire week in Newcastle was shaped around three o'clock on a Saturday afternoon. The fans got behind the team, they queued for two hours before kick-off and when the players left the ground, two hours later, they were still there waiting for the chance to see their heroes. St James' was a place of worship, the focal point of the city and community. The other six days of the week could feel bland in comparison.

I felt a bond with these people straight away. The club was something very special to them but they hadn't had a hero since Malcolm Macdonald was sold in the mid-1970s. All the years of drift had made them even hungrier for success. I was there to help them start believing in the future rather than always looking back and, without wishing to sound conceited, they weren't used to signing players of my ability. Newcastle had rarely shown that kind of ambition before and that meant an incredible outpouring of emotion directed towards me.

Everywhere I had been, the fans had embraced me. At Newcastle, however, it was something out of the ordinary. I had never experienced that kind of deification before. No man could have been made more welcome, and when I scored on my debut I did something I had never done before and threw myself into the Gallowgate End to show I was one of them. It was pure instinct, completely off the cuff, and it took a while before I managed to prise myself free. 'I didn't want to come out,' I told the press later. 'I just wanted to stay there for ever. I've seen it all . . . but playing before thousands of passionate Geordies will equal everything in my life.' As my life had already featured a European Cup, England caps and league titles, that was some compliment. But it was how I felt.

There were 36,185 inside St James' for our game against QPR that day and, even before the game had started, two fans had broken through the police cordon to hoist me aloft. Newcastle had attracted a crowd of 10,670 against the same opponents four months earlier – and lost 4–0. Fleet Street writers who had not travelled that far north in a decade had filled the press box. The game was a sell-out, with thousands more trying to get tickets outside. People had tried to warn me what it would be like. 'Whatever you think it is going to be,' they said, 'you're not going to believe it.' I liked what I heard but I was thinking, *I've played at Anfield, I've been in a European Cup final in Rome, I've played at Wembley and Hamburg and the Maracanã.* But they were right. The atmosphere felt more like a cup final than a league match. At Liverpool all the noise used to come from the Kop. With Newcastle, it was from all four sides, like speakers on a surround-sound system. All I could think as I ran out that day was, *You can't let them down.* My goal was the winner. It felt amazing how I kept finding fairy tales.

My two years as a Newcastle player culminated in promotion to the top division, and that was the perfect way for me to say my goodbyes and retire from professional football. It was some way to go, and everyone remembers that final dramatic scene when a white helicopter landed on the centre-circle to whizz me away. Newcastle were on the way back into the big time. I had achieved what I wanted, and there was never a single moment when I regretted choosing Newcastle ahead of some of the other clubs – Manchester United, for one – who were trying to lure me away from Southampton.

It did, however, come at a significant cost to my England career, if I was correct to presume my new status as a Second Division player was the overriding reason why I was never selected for the national team again. Unfortunately I can never say with absolute certainty, because Bobby Robson, the manager who discarded me, did not think it necessary to offer any form of explanation. All I can do is try to second-guess him, and it is sad, knowing the way Bobby came to be revered on Tyneside, that my experiences of him are so tarnished as a result.

What upset me, more than anything, was the way I heard about it. Bobby had taken over as England manager from Ron Greenwood after the 1982 World Cup, and I wasn't naive. When I moved to Newcastle, I was fully aware that it might not count in my favour to be playing for a team outside the top division. I knew it was a gamble, and that a new England manager was bound to make some changes. Bobby was fully entitled to look at different options and, even though I was England captain, I would never have been so arrogant as to assume my position was watertight.

With that in mind, I did briefly fear the worst after the match against QPR, when I was told Bobby had been in the crowd and wanted to meet me for a chat in the manager Arthur Cox's office. Yet the man I encountered that day could hardly have been more effusive. Bobby was a Geordie, devoted to his hometown team, and he was bubbling with enthusiasm about how we had played, telling me how happy he was that I had joined the club and that it was not just marvellous for me but for everybody in the city.

He was delighted with my goal, commenting that I had lost none of my sharpness. We talked and talked and talked, and when it was time to leave he clasped my hand, told me again what a fabulous day it had been and left me with the words, 'I'll see you in a few weeks.' His first England game was coming up against Denmark and, straight away, I felt a connection. England-wise, it felt like a marriage made in heaven.

What happened next will always be shrouded in mystery for me, and it was the way he handled it that shocked me. I had to learn from the press that I had been dumped, and it seemed incredible, after everything Bobby had said to me, that he never thought it would be the decent thing to pick up the telephone to explain.

Time is a healer, of course, and it goes without saying that I wish it had never been that way. Bobby was so cherished in his time as Newcastle manager, from 1999 to 2004, that he is now immortalised with a statue outside the ground. Yet I felt immensely let down when, let's face it, I wasn't a player on the fringes of the squad who had picked up a handful of caps. I had finished the previous season with Southampton as the leading scorer in the country. I had sixty-three caps for England and I was a two-time European Footballer of the Year. Was it asking too much to think a player in that position should be shown a little courtesy? Was it so unreasonable to think I deserved better?

I know I would never have treated a senior England player so badly. It was the worst way possible for any footballer to find out, and when I went into management years later, I made a point of trying to explain my reasons to every single player I was leaving out. It became too much in the end to get round everyone, and I realised over time that I did not always need to explain myself. Yet I always tried to let down people gently, and I certainly would have handled it the correct way, face to face, if it was someone who had captained his country thirty-odd times.

If Bobby had explained to me that he didn't want to select someone who was playing in the Second Division, or that he felt it was time to experiment with younger players, I would have looked him in the eye, shaken his hand and thanked him for having the decency to break the news himself. If he had asked me to keep the news to myself, rather than creating a media hurricane before his first England squad had been announced, I would have respected his wishes, no problem. If he had afforded me a bit of respect, there would never have been a huge issue. Instead, he had the opportunity to tell me to my face and didn't have the guts to go through with it. That stung. I felt betrayed, hurt and humiliated, and I didn't hold back when the press asked what I thought of it. I told them I was finished with England and had never been treated so shabbily in my entire career. 'Often in life it's the little things which let you down,' I said. 'Surely Bobby Robson could have phoned me. After being involved in the international set-up for ten years, surely I'm worth a ten-pence phone call.'

When Bobby took the job he was widely quoted as saying, 'Kevin Keegan is very much part of my plans.' I found it very difficult to forgive him and, after the deed was done, it could be awkward whenever we bumped into one another. Little was said. There was never any explanation because the time had gone. All I was left with were assumptions and hearsay. Maybe he thought I was slowing down and that too many of the players he had inherited were on the wrong side of thirty. Maybe he felt I was too strong a personality. I read somewhere that he might have suspected I had too much influence over the other players. But if that was genuinely his belief, I would like to know where he was getting his information. My influence was no more or less than any other international captain.

Ultimately, it was all guesswork on my part. I never talked to him about it, and I will never know why, almost overnight, I went from being England's team captain to being jettisoned from the entire squad. Our only conversations tended to be a brief hello, and that was it. I never knew Bobby properly and it always felt very unsatisfactory that there was such a distance between two football men who cared passionately for Newcastle and probably had a lot in common. Bobby was knighted in 2002 and football royalty, not just in the north-east but throughout the entire sport. Equally, I have to be honest and say the friendliest I have ever known him was in the meeting when he told me he was looking forward to working with me – then dropped me like a hot stone. I would like to give him the benefit of the doubt, but I do think sometimes that actions speak louder than words.

All I could do was show he had made a mistake and, with the disappointment still raw in my mind, I was absolutely deter-mined to demonstrate I was still the best player in my position in the country. I set out to use the snub as a form of motivation and, when we played Rotherham shortly afterwards, in a game shown on *Match of the Day*, it was the perfect opportunity.

I was marked that day by Emlyn Hughes – my former Liver-pool teammate had become Rotherham's player-manager – and at one point I even suggested to my old pal that he substituted himself to spare any more embarrassment. I scored four in a 5–1 trouncing. I am not sure I have ever played better and I could hear the crowd singing, 'Are you watching, Bobby Robson?' fol-lowed by 'Keegan for England'. I appreciated their support, but I was far less impressed when I found out Bobby had been spat at and verbally abused on his next visit to St James'. It shows how strongly people felt about it, but he did not deserve that treat-ment.

Newcastle had been relegated in 1978 and finished ninth, eleventh, ninth and eighth in the four seasons before I arrived. People talked about the club being a sleeping giant though, at times, I wondered whether it was actually in a coma. Yet I liked Arthur Cox immensely. Arthur had been in charge for the previ-ous two years. He was solid, trustworthy, reliable – all the old-fashioned virtues – and I could see bits of Bill Shankly in him.

Arthur was a taskmaster who would have us running up the steepest hills he could find or throwing ourselves into the sea at

Whitley Bay or Tynemouth in all kinds of wintry weather, pointing to the elderly ladies on the beach if anyone had the temerity to complain about the freezing temperatures. Arthur claimed the salt water had therapeutic qualities, and had a good sense of humour behind that dour sergeant-major image. I respected his honesty and the way, in particular, in our first-ever meeting he admitted the team were pretty ordinary. St James' had been filled with optimism when I arrived, but it quickly became obvious that there was not enough for promotion in my first season. We dipped to fifteenth at one point and, even when we went on a decent run after the turn of the year, we still managed to lose to Derby and Burnley when they were both in the bottom two.

We finished fifth. It was a flattering position but Arthur was tremendously committed to getting it right, and I liked the way the senior players had the kind of relationship with him where we could knock on his door to have our say. He wanted our input and he chose well on that front when he brought in Terry McDermott, my old mate from Liverpool, as well as Dave McCreery, formerly of Manchester United, and Jeff Clarke from Sunderland. I finished the season with twenty-one goals from thirty-seven appearances, as well as the North-East Player of the Year award. But it was Jeff, not me, who should have been collecting that award.

There was plenty of laughter at Newcastle in those days. Arthur used to have us running up these great big hills in Gateshead. It wasn't quite as brutal as 'Ackie's Warren', when Jack Brownsword was cracking the whip at Scunthorpe, but the players would still complain that it was like being in the army. Arthur would have none of it. 'Get up there', he'd shout. One time we were due to go on a run, Terry and I went to a fancy-dress shop in Newcastle and came back dressed as commandoes, complete with camouflage and face paint. Arthur loved it – but we still had to tackle those hills, carrying all our war equipment.

Another time, a story appeared in the newspapers about a Middle Eastern club wanting to sign me. The speculation was huge and Terry still had all the Arab regalia – the dishdasha, the headdress and so on – from a trip Liverpool had made to that part of the world. First, though, he rang the chairman, Stan Seymour, and put on an accent to pretend he was a billionaire sheikh, announcing that he was due to arrive in Newcastle that afternoon to make the club 'an offer that cannot be refused.' Stan told him that he wouldn't sell me for all the money in the world. But Terry – His Royal Highness Prince Al Terrymac, as he introduced himself – told him it would be disrespectful to his country if he was not allowed the courtesy of a meeting. We borrowed a friend's Mercedes for Terry, all robed up, to drive into St James', with Stan, Arthur and all the directors peering out of the boardroom window, wondering what to make of their guest. I went in first and told everyone they had to take off their shoes in the presence of royalty from the Gulf States. Then Terry knocked on the door and I swear all the directors, with their shoes lined up, jumped to their feet and bowed instinctively. I can still hear Stan's yelp of outrage when he realised it was Terry's moustache behind the red shemagh.

My strike partner in my first season at Newcastle was Imre Varadi, who could be a touch erratic but matched my total of twenty-one goals. We also had a young Chris Waddle coming through and, though we could all see he was immensely talented, he was still learning the game. Chris didn't have the posture of your typical star footballer; he was all drooping shoulders and bowed head, and he could be painfully shy. He had been working in a sausage-seasoning factory and Arthur threatened to send him back a couple of times. Arthur knew Chris had special qualities and devoted an awful lot of time to making sure all that rich potential could flower fully.

It was obvious, though, that we needed something else to spark us off. We were a good way short of being a top team, and there was a brief period in the summer of 1983 when it crossed my mind that perhaps I would be better with a club in the top division. Those thoughts did not last long, but I wanted more for

Newcastle and I was learning how, geographically, the club were at a disadvantage. 'Star players should never be afraid to come here,' I'd say. 'Tyneside is a paradise.' Yet it was seldom easy, as I discovered when I was managing the club, to convince the best players to relocate to the north-east.

Imre Varadi was sold to Sheffield Wednesday, and I didn't have a clue who we were lining up as his replacement until one night, lying in bed, the phone rang. It was Arthur on the line and his first words were, 'We've got one.'

Arthur liked to keep me informed about transfer business. Yet I had taken one of these late-night calls before. On that occasion he got me up at 1 a.m., not even bothering to say hello, to announce down the line, 'We've got him, we've got him.' I thought we must be signing some world-class player, but it turned out we had persuaded a boy of fourteen to join our youth system. 'A young lad called Nesbitt,' Arthur announced. 'Best player in the area. Sunderland wanted him but we've got him. See you tomorrow.' Then the phone went dead and I was left listening to the dialling tone, wide awake.

I wasn't going to get too carried away, therefore, when he rang the next time. 'Beardsley's his name,' he said.

'Beardsley?' I asked, completely nonplussed. 'Who's that then?'

'You'll like him,' Arthur said. 'I've got him from Vancouver Whitecaps. See you in the morning.' And then the phone went down again.

I wasn't exactly filled with the joys of spring. The newspapers had been talking about us signing Kenny Dalglish, who was now in his early thirties at Liverpool. I trusted Arthur to know his stuff, but I had never heard of this lad Beardsley. None of my teammates had either, and we were dubious, to say the least, when we found out some more about our new signing. Beardsley was another Geordie, but Newcastle had released him as a teenager and he had gone to Carlisle United instead. He was twenty-three now and playing in Canada because Manchester

United had taken a chance on him and decided he wasn't up to it.

It wasn't a glittering CV, and when he wandered in a couple of days later, with that pudding-bowl barnet, he looked like a bloke off the street who had won a competition to train with us for the day. Dressing rooms can be harsh places, and when he shuffled back out there weren't many of the lads who were willing to give him the benefit of the doubt. None of us thought this innocuous-looking kid from a Micky Mouse league thousands of miles away was going to be the answer.

'He doesn't even look like a footballer.'

'Look at the size of him, there's nothing on him.'

'Vancouver Whitecaps?'

Well, what could you say about Peter? It took five minutes of his first training session to realise that Arthur had indeed 'got one'. It was his touch, his movement, his quick feet and intelligence on the ball. He could do everything. He came, he showed, he turned, he shimmied, he played passes nobody else could have seen.

At Scunthorpe I always thought Terry Heath had the wow factor, because of his skill on the ball, and when I moved to Liverpool I had never seen anyone with Peter Thompson's ability. By the time I started playing for Newcastle, however, I had played against Cruyff, Maradona and Pelé, and yet I have never had my mind blown as I did on the first day I saw Peter Beardsley.

I went to see Arthur afterwards and the two of us sat in a daze. 'Where the hell did you get this lad?' I asked. 'He's not rapid but he gets there. He's not big but he holds it up. He shoots, he passes, he twists, he turns . . . he's all over the place. Wow!' And, Peter being Peter, at the end of the session he was running around to tidy up after everyone, collecting all the balls without any fuss whatsoever. He always wanted to help. Arthur, a great football man, didn't say a great deal. He never did. He was chuckling to himself, though.

Peter's arrival was a significant reason we got our act together in the 1983–4 season to win promotion. I loved his approach to football. He would be there at seven in the morning sometimes, to help the groundsman get everything ready, and I've heard all sorts of stories over the years about him lugging his own kit around when he started playing for England. They will all be true. Nobody questioned it either, because it was just the sort of person Peter was. He would do anything, from carting off the skip to laying out the training-ground cones and, if we were ever short of a goalkeeper, volunteering to go in the net. His enthusiasm was incredible. I called him 'Pedro' and the nickname stuck. Arthur had started to get the best out of Chris Waddle and, between us, Newcastle's front three contributed sixty-five goals over the season. We went up in third place behind Sheffield Wednesday and Chelsea, and I could see we had players who should thrive in the top division.

By the time we clinched promotion, however, I had already made up my mind that I would not be going with them. My decision had been made at the start of the year – on 6 January, to be precise – and I can still vividly remember the exact moment. We had drawn Liverpool in the third round of the FA Cup and a return to Anfield was always going to mean a lot to me. Yet I feared the worst. Liverpool were at the top of the First Division, as they always seemed to be in that era, and I knew it would need something almost freakish for us to get anything. I said all the right things in the build-up and told everyone I was looking forward to being back at my old ground. But I had never forgotten what it was like to go to Anfield with Hamburg, in the European Super Cup, and take a 6–0 hammering. Hamburg were a decent side, whereas I knew, in my heart of hearts, that Newcastle were not ready for a test of that magnitude.

We lost 4–0. They were better than us in every department, from A to Z. But it wasn't the score that shocked me. It was the moment one of my teammates knocked the ball behind Liverpool's defence to send me clear, bearing down on the goal at the

Anfield Road end with only Bruce Grobbelaar to beat and 12,000 Geordies packed in the stand.

I had been in that position, one-on-one against the opposition goalkeeper, more times than I could remember, and in that split second I was already thinking about Grobbelaar, sizing him up, working out my angles. Was he going to come out to me? Would he go down early and give me the chance to lift the ball over him? Should I try to take the ball around him? Or would there be a gap if I took the shot early and kept it low? All those thoughts hurtle through your mind at a million miles an hour. The important thing is the defender is out of the equation. There is only a second or two to get it right.

In my first game for England, I had a similar chance against Wales at Ninian Park, with only the goalkeeper, Gary Sprake, standing in the way of a dream debut. Sprake refused to move. I jinked right, I jinked left, but he held his ground. He stayed still, crouching down, watching my approach – waiting for me to go first. The only gap was between his legs, so I went for the nutmeg and tried to drill it through the hole. The ball struck his knee, bounced out and the chance was lost. Sprake had been too clever for me and I didn't get a kind press the next day.

That, however, was a long time ago. I was coming up for thirty-three now – older, wiser, and I knew exactly what to do. Stay calm, pick your spot. In my head the net was already bulging. I was shaping to shoot and, in that moment, the goal-scorer's instinct takes over. I was back at the ground where I had so many golden memories. It felt written in the stars.

Suddenly there was a flash of red at my shoulder and, in an instant, Mark Lawrenson had appeared beside me. Everything happened so quickly. And then, in a split second, the Liverpool defender had taken the ball off my foot. It was all a blur. One moment I was racing through – the next, the ball was gone and, with it, the chance. And that was my epiphany.

People have said to me since that I should not have been so hard on myself, bearing in mind Liverpool were on their way to a third league title in a row. They point out I was playing against the best defence in the country, and that the man who caught and overtook me was grease lightning. But I had always thought I was, too. Nothing like that had happened to me before, and that was the precise moment, with the game still going on, that the truth hit me like a mallet. I had lost my place in the England team, I was a Second Division player, and I was on the slippery slope, no matter how many times the people in Newcastle hailed me as their king.

Nobody else would have realised quite how jarring that moment was for me. At the final whistle I shook hands with the Liverpool players, thanked the Kop for their applause and waved apologetically to the Newcastle fans. Inwardly, however, the stuffing had been knocked out of me. It wasn't the 4–0 defeat. It was the knowledge that I had been a yard too slow. I felt that I had fallen short of my own high standards. My mind was made up: it was my last season as a professional footballer.

It was an easy decision, and when I told Arthur straight after the game, he knew me well enough not to try to talk me out of it. It must have been a shock for him, but he told me there was nothing he could say that would change my mind. He was spot on. When I made a decision, whether others thought it right or wrong, I generally stuck by it.

I announced my impending retirement on Valentine's Day, my thirty-third birthday, and a lot of people might think it was absurd to end my playing career based on one bad moment. Not me, though. If Newcastle were going up, I didn't want to be going back to the First Division as a one-time superstar who had been at the top and was now on his way down. I didn't want to be going to all those famous grounds with people saying, 'You know what, he can't do it at this level any more.' I didn't want to take the easy option by moving back into midfield and spinning out my career for another three years, possibly longer. I wanted to go out as a top player.

Plus I wasn't frightened about coming to the end. I had made good money out of the game. I didn't have a clue what I was going to do, or where I was going to end up, but I wasn't going to be short of options and, if anything, it excited me knowing there was so much more in life for me to discover. Jean and I had a villa in Marbella where I could work on my golf swing and comfort myself with sunshine and chilled wine. I was always going to keep busy, and there was the whole world to explore. Football had controlled my life ever since I turned up at Scunthorpe, aged sixteen, in a furniture van – and look where I had been since then. I didn't mind the uncertainty and it didn't worry me that I would be waking up for the first time in my adult life without having to shape everything I did around professional football. There was nothing to fear.

The important thing was to go out on a high – and I did that, literally, with my exit. Newcastle's final league game of the promotion season was against Brighton, with St James' bathed in sunshine and a party mood inside the ground. But we also had an end-of-season benefit match against Liverpool, and that was another carnival atmosphere, with fireworks exploding in the sky and a Royal Marines marching band on the pitch. There was a message on the scoreboard reading '*Auf Wiedersehen*, Kev' – this being the time when *Auf Wiedersehen, Pet* was popular on television – and if you speak to anyone who was there they always remember the pure theatre after the final whistle when my transport for the evening zoomed into view.

It had never been done before, and the police weren't very happy, to say the least, that a helicopter had been arranged without anyone checking with the authorities. Ironically, the idea was that it would be safer to fly me away because of the crush that was anticipated outside the players' exit. The helicopter was to take me to a party at Gosforth Park Hotel and the emotion was incredible as I walked round the pitch, waving goodbye to everyone and trying to catch some of the scarves that were thrown from the crowd.

The ballboys joined me on the lap of honour, and I never

realised until many years later that a thirteen-year-old Alan Shearer was among the lads jogging with me in their tight-fitting Co-op tracksuits. I paused in front of the old West Stand to pick out my family in the directors' box. Then I went down on bended knees to bow and genuflect in front of the Gallowgate End and made a dash for the helicopter door, turning to wave one last goodbye.

As I climbed aboard and the rotor blades started whirring, I peeled off my Newcastle shirt, dropped it to the ground and shouted to the nearest steward that I wanted it to go to Peter Beardsley. I had already said in the press that Peter was the man to fill the number seven, and that was my way of anointing him publicly. In my mind it was a grand gesture and fitting for the occasion. Yet when I asked Peter if he ever received that shirt, he stared at me blankly. That steward, I imagine, got a nice souvenir!

And then, whoosh – I was off, still in my muddy kit, peering down at all those people, with their necks craned and their arms raised, until the ground was a tiny speck in the distance. After 831 club appearances in England and Germany, 285 goals, four league titles, one FA Cup, four European finals and now promotion with my beloved Newcastle, it was all over for Kevin Keegan, the footballer. It was one of many cathartic experiences I have had at St James' and apt, perhaps, that I left that way when I had always wanted Newcastle to reach for the skies. What I never realised was that I would be back one day to take the club even higher.

10

TO BE HOME AGAIN

I was in the fast lane of the M25 motorway when the blaring horn told me I had started to drift across the traffic and was in danger of causing a crash. I had been driving virtually all day, taking in three different countries and several tanks of petrol. I was exhausted and I had been dozing off at the wheel when the driver behind me started hooting madly to bring me to my senses.

If you have ever been in that position, you will know what a horrible feeling it is to hear that noise at seventy miles per hour. I was used to nightmarishly long journeys, as many of us are in football, but this one had taken its toll and it was frightening to realise how close I had come to putting myself, and others, in danger. My heart was pounding and, in my zombie-like fatigue, I knew I had to get off the motorway before something terrible happened.

The date was 8 April 1991, and what I didn't realise at the time was that it was going to turn into one of the worst days of my life. I was coming back to live in England. It was a new start, for myself and my family, after seven years in Marbella, living the good life in the Spanish sunshine. Jean and the girls had already flown back and were staying with friends in Southampton, waiting for me to arrive. I was driving the family's Range Rover, filled with our possessions, on the final leg of the journey.

But I was desperately tired. It was almost 700 miles from Marbella all the way through Spain to the border with France, and nearly the same again to Calais. I did manage a little bit of sleep at one of those roadside rest areas in France, but not very much, and my intention was to get my head down on the ferry. Instead I sat next to a guy who recognised me, introduced himself as a Spurs fan, and soon we were involved in one of those football conversations that can go on longer than you anticipate.

The next thing I knew we were docking at Dover and I hadn't managed to close my eyes once. I went through customs and then set off on the last 150 miles of a long, hard slog. I was happy to be back on English soil and relieved I had broken the back of the journey, but when I got on the M25, everything started to catch up with me. It was getting dark. My eyes were beginning to close and I was drifting over the white lines when that blaring horn jolted me awake. Jean had given me a pillow in case I needed a break and, though I was only an hour and a half away from my destination, I knew it would be foolish to drive any further.

At the next junction, for Reigate, I pulled off the motorway to find somewhere for a doze. All I wanted was an hour to rest my eyes, freshen up, then get going again. But the first layby off the junction was barely 200 yards from the motorway, with all the cars and heavy goods traffic rattling by, and not exactly an ideal place to get some rest. I drove a little further and turned off Reigate Hill to a country lane. I could see the lights of a pub not too far down the road. It was a quiet spot, half a mile from the motorway, and there was a car park with nobody else around. It felt safe enough. I pushed down the locks, propped my pillow against the window, and before long I was out for the count.

The only way I can describe what happened next is that it felt like a dream – or a nightmare – until the taste of blood in my mouth told me I was very much awake and in serious trouble. Initially, it was a rock that was hurled through the driver's window, against the exact spot where my head was resting. It was big enough to have killed me, and I was lucky that my pillow was there to cushion the blow, saving me from serious injury. I could hear someone shouting, 'Give us your wallet,' but everything occurred so quickly it was all a blur and, in my confused state, I was still thinking this couldn't really be happening.

The first vicious blow from a baseball bat made it clear that no nightmare could be this realistic. There was glass everywhere and my assailant was swinging wildly as he laid into me through the shattered window. After three or four blows I must have been close to unconsciousness, but in those awful moments I still had enough sense to shift across to the middle of the car, making it harder to strike me with so much force. I remember screaming at whoever it was, asking him what he wanted. But I could tell even in the dark that there was more than one person and I feared the worst when I heard another voice saying, 'Get on with it.' It was chilling. At that point I really thought I was going to be left for dead.

As I tried to scramble clear, the baseball bat came through the window again. This time my assailant had stopped taking wild swings and rammed the end of it straight into my mouth. He kept shouting that he wanted money and I knew my only chance was to do as he said. I started scrabbling through my pockets to give him whatever I had. I flung my wallet at him and a fistful of notes and then lay back, desperately hoping that would be enough. And suddenly it was all over. As quickly as they arrived, they were gone.

For a few moments I lay still, dazed and confused, trying to take in what had happened. I was in a terrible state, blood pouring from my head, and something foolishly told me I should go after them. I wasn't thinking straight and my natural instinct, despite the obvious dangers, was that I could not let them get away with it. I put the key in the ignition and stuck the car into reverse, only for it to go into a skid. While the guy with the baseball bat had been laying into me, his mates had slashed my tyres. I wasn't going anywhere fast.

They had smashed the back window to pull out my suitcase and whatever else they could get their hands on. But at least I was alive, and when I staggered back to the roadside, trying to wave down the traffic, a passing motorist stopped to help. I was delirious with shock, babbling away in Spanish – forgetting, in my confused state, that I was back in England. I must have looked a dreadful state and when I got to the hospital they told me I was fortunate – in the extreme – that I was escaping with only eight stitches in my scalp. I had lost count of the number of times I had been hit, and when I felt around my mouth it was a pleasant surprise to find my teeth all seemed to be where they belonged. Given the ferocity of the attack, I knew I was lucky to be walking away.

When the people who inflicted this unprovoked and vicious beating were arrested and taken to court, it turned out they owed money to a drug dealer and thought I was an easy target. What they could never have imagined was that my wallet would be filled with pesetas. I doubt that currency was much use to them and, unless they were totally stupid, I am not sure they would have got too far using a credit card in the name of Kevin Keegan. The gang was from the Newhaven area and the youngest member, the one with the baseball bat, was only eighteen years old. They were caught bragging about it in a pub and the judge described it in his sentencing remarks as a 'disgraceful use of criminal violence against a defenceless individual.' Three of them were given prison sentences, while a fourth member of the gang was spared because he turned Queen's evidence and told the police what had happened in return for his freedom.

It wasn't easy coming to terms with what had happened – and a horrific experience for Jean too – and I was so traumatised at first I wasn't even certain I wanted to move back from Spain after all. For the next few weeks I kept getting calls from the police saying they had found some of my items and asking me to drive back to Reigate to identify these possessions – my belt, my shorts and some other bits and pieces – as possible evidence.

It dominated my life, and for a while it made me question whether England was still the place I wanted my family to be. I always liked to have a positive outlook but it was difficult in those times. *Is this what England has become?* I wondered. *What exactly am I coming back to here?* Plus it didn't help that the worst elements of the press were desperate to find some salacious spin. Tabloid hacks were despatched to find out if there was another reason why I was down some lovers' lane. They never found anything, much to their disappointment, because there was nothing to find, but it wasn't for a lack of trying. It was typical of our red-top press, and not the only time in my life, as I will explain later in this book, that I discovered just how low they would stoop.

What a contrast, as well, from my easy way of life in Marbella, waking up virtually every day to glorious sunshine, and worrying about very little other than how to swing a golf club. Spain was good for Jean and me. It was a completely different lifestyle, a slower and more relaxed pace of life, and I would recommend it to anyone who wants to switch off and unwind for a few years. When the children were at school, we would pop out for lunch, and in the evenings we often ate out again, watching the sun go down above the waves. Our house overlooked the seventh fairway of the Rio Real golf club and, with such a beautiful location and climate, we wanted a name that felt apt for where we were living. We called it 'Seventh Heaven'.

I brought my golf handicap down to four during those years in Marbella, and spent a long time trying to reach a point where I was playing off scratch. I played tennis, I did a lot of running and I had a morning swim most days. The beach was nearby and, after ten hard years of football, sometimes playing fifty-two weeks a year, it was good to be out of that grind, catching my breath and enjoying some family time.

That was not to say I had lost my enthusiasm for new adventures. It was just channelled in other directions. I had time in Marbella to start making the kind of plans that were impossible when I was playing. I started looking forward to all the things I could do, all the places I could visit, knowing I now had the freedom to do as I liked. There were invitations to go to Australia,

New Zealand, Canada and Japan. I spent a month training the Tigers under-21 team in Malaysia. Other offers followed – to Sweden, Finland, and all sorts of far-flung places. I was always on the go: autograph sessions, awards presentations, hospital visits, charity games, television appearances. It was my own world tour before I settled down into a much less hectic schedule, making the most of the Spanish weather, and cutting myself free from football.

Málaga was the nearest club, but I wasn't tempted to drive the twenty-five miles to Estadio La Rosaleda. There were times when I saw the odd Spanish game on television, but I never set my clock around it, and those were the days before English games were beamed around the world on satellite channels. I knew the basic facts, the results of the big games, who had won the league and so on, and I came back occasionally to cover a game for ITV. On the whole, however, I had lost touch with English football. I was quite happy for it to be that way.

It was golf that was my passion, honing my swing on the circuit that saw me become close friends with Don Revie, playing in pro-celebrity tournaments with the likes of Sean Connery and Jimmy Tarbuck and – showing us how to do it properly – Gary Player and Lee Trevino. Golf dominated my life for a couple of years and, for myself and Jean, the drawbacks of bringing up Laura and Sarah in such beautiful surroundings were very few.

Yet it was never our intention to stay in Marbella for ever, and I can vividly remember the light-bulb moment one day at Las Brisas, the golf course where I hit one of my two career holes-in-one, when I was standing over my ball on the twelfth hole, worrying about what club to take, and it struck me that maybe I had blurred my life's priorities. I was forty years of age and my golf partners tended to be retirees in their sixties or seventies. I had made some good friends and it was an enjoyable lifestyle, but it didn't seem right that my biggest problem in life was whether I should take a pitching wedge or a nine-iron to the green. I had needed a break and I had been in the fortunate position of being able to take one but, at my age, was this what I wanted for the rest of my life? Did I really want to retire in middle age? No, the answer was clear in my mind. It was time to get going again.

Jean was on the same wavelength. We also wanted to bring the girls back to England for their schooling and, once we started readjusting to life in Hampshire, there was plenty to keep me busy. I joined the after-dinner speaking circuit, attended golf days, played for Pelé in Tokyo, went horse racing and much more. We had a farmhouse near Broadlands, where Lord Mountbatten used to live, and 180 acres of land. If you go there now, it has been turned into a housing estate, but it was sprawling countryside back then. Every morning at six I was up to muck out the horses, and by the time that was done I was full of energy and ready to go. I set up and patented my Soccer Circus business, my intention being to open the country's only football-based theme park. I saw myself as an entrepreneurial person who could devise my own ideas and put them into practice. BSkyB had asked me to join their punditry team covering the Bundesliga, and I was enjoying being my own boss. The phone was always ringing with new offers.

Still, though, I didn't have any overwhelming urge to be at the sharp end of football, nor to remind myself what it was like to watch a game under floodlights. Although I was back in England, living close to Southampton, there was no burning desire to visit the Dell – or any other football ground, for that matter. Even when Liverpool played at Southampton, pitting together two of my old clubs, I had no urge to ring up for a ticket. That wasn't a slight on either club. I just didn't make a habit of hanging around my old clubs.

In early 1992, I got a phone call out of the blue from Alistair Wilson. Alistair was high up at Scottish and Newcastle Breweries, the sponsors of Newcastle United, and we had got on well when I was playing for the club. We had remained in touch, but when the telephone rang that day I could never have guessed what he was going to say: that the Newcastle board wanted to know if I would be the club's next manager. It was a lot to take in. Alistair did not even sound sure himself, and followed it up by saying he knew he was probably wasting my time even floating the idea. But I didn't turn it down. I didn't say I wanted it either, but when we had finished talking and I went through to tell Jean, I will never forget her first words. It must have been the look in my eyes. 'You'll take it,' she said.

If it had been any other club, I wouldn't have been tempted. But there was still something about Newcastle that fascinated me – all that energy, all that untapped potential, and my vision of what could happen if someone lit up the place. I knew the club. I knew the area, I knew what the fans wanted and, just as importantly, I knew what they did *not* want.

The temptation was irresistible, but it wasn't straightforward because the Newcastle directors had just given the existing manager, Ossie Ardiles, a public vote of confidence. Ossie hadn't even been in charge for a year. He was struggling for results, but the club had explicitly stated that he didn't have to worry about losing his job and, at that time, managers tended to get a lot more slack than they do nowadays. I felt uneasy that I was being approached about a position that had not been vacated, but the directors assured me that, regardless of my decision, they were intending to break the news to Ossie the following day. Publicly, they had described him as 'safe as houses'. In reality, the decision to sack him had already been taken.

The offer was a three-year deal, and that suited me fine, until I had my first meeting with Sir John Hall in London and he explained that the club were in a genuine crisis. Sir John was a successful businessman who had overseen the development of Gateshead's Metro Centre development, and taken a position of influence on the Newcastle board. He was in London because he and his wife, Lady Mae, were buying some trees from Kew Gardens to take back to Wynyard Hall, their country house in the Tees Valley. Sir John had broken away to meet me and he brought his son, Douglas, plus the two other directors, Freddie Fletcher and Freddy Shepherd, who would become such a massive part in the club's story.

Sir John told me there would be money to spend, but he also made it clear the club were fighting for survival in more ways than one. Newcastle were second from bottom of the old Second Division and, incredibly, had played up to four more games than some of the other teams in relegation danger. They had managed only one win from their previous thirteen matches and I had to be realistic. I wanted to know what would happen if Newcastle were relegated. 'That will be the end of this football club,' Sir John said, matter-of-factly. 'We will fold.'

My gut instinct was to believe Newcastle's fanbase was far too vast for that to be a genuine possibility. Yet he sounded like he meant it, and this was a man who knew about business. I was shocked to hear what had happened to the club since I left in 1984, and I told him it would make better sense in those circumstances for me to take the job until the end of the season and then see where we were. We had four months – sixteen games – to save ourselves, and I made it clear that was all we should really think about. They offered me £60,000, with a bonus of the same again if we stayed up. The deal was signed and a press conference was arranged at the Newcastle Breweries Visitors' Centre, where I waited in an adjacent room while Sir John picked up the microphone to address the assembled media. 'Ladies and gentleman, I would like to introduce you to the next manager of Newcastle United' – and that was the moment I walked through the door. Much like when I came back from Hamburg to join Southampton, we had managed to keep it quiet. There was no helicopter this time, but it was still dramatic.

Once again, I experienced the warmth and passion of the Geordie public, and I was reminded how absurd it was that a club with Newcastle's following was not at the forefront of English football. The truth, however, was that the once-mighty Newcastle – three-time champions before the Great War and six-time FA Cup winners, though never since 1955 – had not won the league championship since 1927. Indeed, Newcastle had not won anything of note since 1969. That was the Inter-Cities Fairs Cup, the precursor to the UEFA Cup, and I am not even sure that should be regarded as a great triumph, bearing in mind the entry rules. For a long time, it was open only to clubs with trade fairs in their cities. After that, there was the 'one-club-per-city' rule and that meant Newcastle – tenth in the First Division in 1968 – squeezed in because Everton, Tottenham and Arsenal were excluded by the presence of Liverpool and Chelsea. I was a fresh-faced teen on the books of Scunthorpe United when Newcastle beat the Hungarian team Újpesti Dózsa in the final.

As well as all the problems on the pitch, it was also very clear there were all sorts of politics behind the scenes, as there often were with Newcastle. Stan Seymour's time as chairman had ended in 1988. George Forbes now had the role, with Peter Mallinger his deputy, but it seemed to be the other directors pulling all the strings. Neither Forbes nor Mallinger were present when I was offered the job, and I later found out they were told about my appointment only an hour before the news was made public. Sir John was the man with the money and, it seemed, the power, trying to win control of the club.

I wanted to be fresh, positive and honest. But I went in with my eyes wide open. Newcastle had significant debts and the club had gone through five different managers since my last time on Tyneside. Arthur Cox had walked out after a fall-out with the board. Jack Charlton was the next manager in line and had given a local lad named Paul Gascoigne his debut. Jack lasted a year before Iam McFaul, the goalkeeper I had scored against in the 1974 FA Cup final, took over, staying three seasons. Jim Smith was in charge when Newcastle dropped back into the Second Division and now Ossie had gone, too.

Newcastle had a famous history, an iconic shirt and a tradition of passionate support. What they didn't have was a decent football team. I didn't have a second to lose and, after the first day of training, I went back to my hotel room to plot my next move. I wanted someone trustworthy on board with me and the first person I thought of was Terry McDermott. Terry and I had drifted out of contact since our days as Liverpool, Newcastle and England teammates, but he ticked all the boxes. He loved the club, just like I did, and we had the kind of relationship where we could bounce ideas off one another. Terry couldn't get there quickly enough, and I even agreed to pay his salary out of my own pocket, offering him £12,000 to the end of the season. I could have gone to the board for the money but I knew they wanted me to work with Ossie's staff, and I could imagine their reaction when they found out where Terry had been working. He and a mate were flogging hamburgers from a van at racecourse meetings.

A lot of critics thought it made no sense to expect me to walk straight back in after all those years out of the sport. To a degree, I could understand their scepticism. I had watched two live matches in seven years. One was the 1991 European Cup final between Red Star Belgrade and Marseille. It was probably the worst European final in history – and was not going to help me a lot, I figured, grubbing around for points towards the bottom of the Second Division. The other was on 23 November 1991, when I was invited to St James' Park for the launch of Newcastle's centenary book. Newcastle drew 0–0 with Blackburn and that was the first time I met Douglas Hall, son of Sir John. It was a poor game, and when Douglas asked me what I thought of the team, I was too polite to tell him the truth.

Three months on, it turned out it was worse than I thought. Newcastle were in serious danger of dropping into the third tier of English football for the first time in their 100-year history. I was being hailed as the 'Messiah' but, the more I think about it now, the more I realise it was an incredible gamble to put myself in that position. It was an experiment, a leap of faith, a long shot – call it what you like. I didn't know what it was like to fail, and I sure as hell didn't intend to start with Newcastle, but it wasn't an orthodox appointment and it was undeniably true that I had almost zero knowledge of the players I would be relying on to stop us from dropping into a black hole.

That was my big concern. When I looked down Newcastle's squad, a lot of the names meant very little to me. I had to look up who Bjørn Kristensen was. I had no idea whether Kevin Scott was a defender, midfielder or striker. I had met Micky Quinn at the races, so that was a start. I had seen Ray Ranson play for Manchester City and I had good reports about David Kelly, Gavin Peacock and one or two others. But there was no internet in those days to find out everything at the click of a button. Andy Hunt, Lee Makel, David Robinson, Mark Stimson, Liam O'Brien, Matty Appleby, Darren Bradshaw and on and on – all these names were completely new to me.

Then I started to look at our future opponents. We were playing Bristol City in my first game and there were only two things I knew about our visitors from Ashton Gate. One, they wore red shirts and, two, they had a robin redbreast on their badge. I was hoping my staff might be able to fill me in – but I didn't know the names of all my staff, either. I could barely name a player in the Second Division and, in my first press conference, I could tell some of the journalists thought I might have bitten off more than I could chew. How did I expect to pull it off, seemed to be the attitude, when my only qualifications were a thousand rounds of golf in Spain? 'You hope and pretend you know what you are doing,' I told them.

I still had my football knowledge and all my experience of playing at the highest level and, in my view, that gave me a hell of a start. But there were a lot of people waiting for me to fall flat on my face, and I have to admit there were times early on when a few doubts crept in. I didn't want to be remembered as the man who took this historic club into the third tier of English football. I had inherited a mess and it was difficult to forget what Sir John had said to me. He had made it absolutely clear that, if the worst came to the worst, it could be curtains.

11

THE GREAT ESCAPE

If there were some moments of insecurity early on, they quickly passed. It wasn't my way to be filled with self-doubt, and I was always confident I had the force of personality to bring some positivity back to St James' Park. I had seen the way Bill Shankly brought light to even the darkest corners at Liverpool. I had learned from Bob Paisley, Don Revie, Alf Ramsey and Joe Mercer, and spent valuable years with distinguished football men such as Arthur Cox, and of course Ron Ashman of Scunthorpe United. I would have been a fool not to have learned from these people, even before implementing my own ideas, and the motivational powers that I hoped would inspire a struggling team.

Yet I was in for a shock when I turned up for my first day and saw, close-up, the scale of neglect since the last time I had been at Newcastle's training ground. It was terrible. I had left in 1984 and, almost eight years on, I was sure I recognised some of the stains on the old communal bath. In fact, when I looked at the scum floating on the surface, it did cross my mind that it might even be the same bathwater.

The training pitches were in a horrendous state, and the gym was covered in a layer of grime. The bins were overflowing with several days' worth of rubbish, the paint was peeling, and the toilets were a no-go zone for everyone apart from the bravest individual. It was shocking to see how unloved the place had become. There were discarded plates on the side, with stale bread crusts and bits of old food that had been left for goodness knows how long. It demonstrated a complete lack of pride. The place had gone to ruin and I can still remember Terry McDermott's verdict. Terry always had a nice way of summing up his thoughts. 'What a shithole', he said.

Newcastle didn't even have a washing machine, and the players were being told to take their kit home to wash between games. It was the sort of thing you would have expected from a pub team rather than a professional football club and, though it might not have been visible from the stands, it made me wince with embarrassment when I saw what the players were wearing. Some of the more diligent members of my newly inherited squad still managed to turn out in crisp black and white shirts. Others had put their washing machines to the wrong temperature and were representing Newcastle in dishwater-grey. Some would forget to wash them at all, and run out with last week's grass stains still visible. I knew money was tight, but there was no excuse for being in that state, and I told the board that if they wanted me to do the job properly, they had to start treating the players with more respect. It was time, I said, to create an environment where the players felt valued and, first things first, that meant giving the place a good scrub. 'How can I tell my players this is the best club in the world when the bath is not clean and the toilets are dirty?' I wanted to know.

The workmen moved in on my first weekend, cleared out all the rubbish and set about renovating the place, so when the players turned up the following Monday I could surprise them, like one of those makeovers you get on television these days. The clean-up operation cost us £6,000 and the players couldn't believe it when they saw the difference. The baths had been jetted down, the walls had been painted, and the pervading smell was now of disinfectant rather than stale urine. The place was gleaming and, of all the things we did at Newcastle, the importance of that makeover cannot be underestimated. It let everyone know, right from the start, that it was going to be different on my watch, that standards and expectations were going to be raised and that, from now on, the little things mattered. Toilets cleaned, sinks scrubbed: that was just the start.

But it wasn't easy. On 1 January 1992, Newcastle were at the lowest point in the club's history, bottom of the Second Division after a 4–0 defeat to Southend United. When I arrived thirty-six days later, I inherited a side that had won six of their previous thirty league fixtures and had the worse defence in the league, conceding almost two goals a game. Ossie Ardiles's last game was a 5–2 defeat at Oxford, and the previous league match, against Charlton Athletic, was a tragicomedy played inside a half-empty St James' Park. Newcastle led 3–0 after thirty-four minutes and finally seemed to have turned a corner. Charlton then proceeded to score four times, including an eighty-ninth minute winner from Alan Pardew, a future Newcastle manager.

The malaise ran deep. The best players had been shipped out, which was a scandal as far as I was concerned, and I had been left with a young, inadequate team whose confidence seemed broken. Terry and I were in our early forties, but I am not exaggerating when I say we were the standout players in the five-a-sides. We had played international football, worked under some of the greatest managers in the business and won almost every trophy going. We had played at a level our lads were never likely to experience – and it showed. Even with our advancing years and inferior fitness, we were head and shoulders above the rest and, trust me, that was not something either of us wanted. In the bath after one training session, I asked Terry what the team should be for our first game against Bristol City, and his response made me submerge my head under the water. 'Truthfully?' he replied. 'The first two names on the team-sheet should be yours and mine.'

We had to resort to humour because that was often the only way to get through difficult moments in football. Things were so bad we didn't even get a single call when it came to my first transfer-deadline day, in March 1992, as a manager. That afternoon, Terry and I sat in my office working out which players we could move out to trim the squad of the dead wood. Yet, by three o'clock, it was starting to dawn on us that nobody wanted our cast-offs. 'Still two hours left,' Terry pointed out cheerfully, as the clock ticked towards the 5 p.m. deadline. But we were kidding ourselves and the telephone didn't shrill into life until a few minutes after the deadline had passed.

Even then, I picked up the receiver with a surge of anticipation, desperately hoping the clock might be fast and that it was still possible to arrange something. Instead, I heard someone with a Scouse accent on the other end of the line, pretending to be a buyer. Terry had popped out on the pretence of going to the lavatory and was ringing me from a phone down the corridor. He started trying to haggle for one of my players. I told him the player wouldn't come cheap and recommended he came back with a serious offer. We went through the whole routine, bartering like a pair of lunatics – him trying to knock off a few grand, me stubbornly holding out for the best fee possible. It lightened the mood, but the absence of serious calls that day didn't say a great deal about the Newcastle players.

One encouraging aspect was that the club's youth system had brought through an impressive crop of young players including Lee Clark, Steve Watson, Steve Howey, Alan Thompson and Robbie Elliott. They were north-east lads, which I liked, and desperate to play, hanging on to every word during team meetings. I likened them to a nest of baby birds – beaks open, leaning forward, trying to get every last morsel.

Clark was a tough lad with a fierce competitive edge. He had already been introduced to the first team by Ossie Ardiles, but didn't do himself any favours when he swung a punch at Alan Neilson in my first training session. The match against Bristol City was going to be a highly charged atmosphere and, though I wanted my midfield to have a bit of aggression, I couldn't risk us going down to ten men and losing because of it. He was out of the team.

Instead, on the day before the game, I arranged a training match for the reserves and included myself to make up the numbers. Then, five minutes in, the ball came my way and, wallop, I was reminded of that England–Italy game when it was Romeo Benetti on my case. Clarkey had clattered me, knee-high, from behind. I wasn't even expecting a tackle, let alone being dumped to the floor by a boy of nineteen years. But I had to admire his nerve. He didn't even pick me up, turning to get on with the game and shouting something not very friendly about getting him back in the team.

As I staggered to my feet, all I could hear was a lot of shouting and commotion – and someone with an East European accent sounding particularly angry. It was Pavel Srníček, one of our goalkeepers. Pavel was so incensed by what he had seen he had sprinted out of his goal and karate-kicked Clarkey to the side of the head. Lee was on his back and his assailant was standing over him, pointing an accusatory finger. 'You . . . do . . . not . . . do . . . that . . . to . . . the . . . manager!'

At least it showed they cared, and when I hobbled back to the dressing rooms I didn't think it was necessary to punish Lee. I liked his spirit, to be honest. He said sorry, and my bruised leg didn't bother me too badly when we won 3–0 the next day. David Kelly scored twice, Liam O'Brien got the other and the attendance of 29,263 was almost twice that for Newcastle's previous home game. It was the perfect start, and I told the players that it was up to all of us, not just me, to make sure we kept it that way.

We lost the following week at Blackburn, the leaders, which brought us back down to earth, but there was only one more defeat in the next six matches. A buzz had returned to the city, and when we beat Sunderland 1–0 in my first Tyne–Wear derby as a manager, courtesy of another Kelly goal, we had climbed out of the relegation places to nineteenth position. Newcastle, once again, felt like a happy place – or, at least, a happier place – and whatever we were doing seemed to be working.

All of which made it very frustrating that, behind the scenes, I had joined a club where it felt like half the board were at each other's throats. Sir John had been playing politics since day one and, two weeks before that Sunderland match, I had come very close to walking out when it dawned on me that he had reneged on his agreement to back me with signings.

My beef was with Sir John, and nobody else, because he had explicitly told me when I took the job that he would find £1 million for me to spend on the team and, if necessary, could stump up the same again should the right players be available. So you can imagine how I felt when the first time I asked for funds to buy a player I was refused. The player I wanted, Darron McDonough, was available from Luton for £90,000. If Sir John was going to bring down the shutters for a player costing only £90,000, what would it be like when I asked the club to dig deeper for someone else?

I felt misled. I wasn't making unreasonable demands and it was always very difficult for me to work with people who I felt were deceiving me. I saw it as personal betrayal, and when I explained the background to Terry McDermott, I told him I would have to leave if it turned out that Sir John had lured me to the club on a false promise. That must have been shattering news for Terry – for heaven's sake, we had barely been there five weeks. I wasn't exactly thrilled either, but I couldn't accept being treated that way. Trust and loyalty should be everything. I didn't want to leave the job half done, but it was a point of principle: Sir John had to keep his promises, or he could explain to the media why I had quit.

We planned to leave on 13 March, the day before we played Swindon at St James' Park, and we were on the road when Terry announced that it didn't feel right. We had checked out of our hotel, paid all our extras and, as far as I was concerned, that was it. The plan was to drop Terry off in Liverpool and then I was going to turn south and get back to my family in Hampshire. But Terry persuaded me to pull over, and we sat and discussed it in a layby at Haydon Bridge. Terry's view was that it wasn't fair on the players for them to turn up before an important game and find the manager had gone. 'Turn back, gaffer,' he suggested. 'Let's play the game, get it over with and then we'll go.'

Those are the moments when you need a good man by your side, someone who will give you the right advice and isn't afraid to tell you something you might not necessarily want to hear. The players had worked their socks off for us, and Terry was right: they deserved better. I just needed someone to point that out to me because I was so wrapped up in my own grievances. Did I want to walk out on Newcastle after only thirty-seven days in the job? Of course I didn't. Did I like the thought of leaving Newcastle in the lurch? Not for a moment. Yet I wasn't going to be anybody's fool, and I was still feeling aggrieved when I took my place in the dugout for a 3–1 win against Swindon the following day. Nothing had changed in my mind and, when I drove away that night, it was in the belief that my time at the club was over. Terry and I shook hands. He told me that it had been a great few weeks and that, if I ever fancied doing it again, to give him a call. I jumped in my car and headed for the A1, feeling sick to the stomach.

By the time I got home, the press had found out something was wrong and there were reporters camped outside my house. I stayed inside, waiting for Sir John to ring, and I was determined to show him what kind of person he was dealing with. People might think it was me being difficult but they would be wrong. It was about establishing a line of trust, standing up for myself, and being treated in the way I would treat others. And, besides, I wasn't asking for anything that hadn't already been promised. All I wanted was for people to be straight with me and I made that absolutely clear when Sir John rang the next morning. Respect had to work both ways – and I told him that, too.

Sir John asked me to take a deep breath, accepted I had legitimate grievances and promised it wouldn't happen again. He also made it clear that I would get the transfer funds he had promised and that he was not in the business of telling key employees one thing, then doing something completely different. He didn't want me to go, and he made it absolutely clear that we had to sort it out for the good of the club. 'There are only two people who can save Newcastle United,' he said, 'and we are talking on the telephone.'

He sounded sincere and, from that day on, Sir John knew that as long as he kept to his word he wouldn't have any problem with me. The ground rules were in place now. The air was clear and I knew, above all, that what he had said was fundamentally true. It was for the two of us to save Newcastle.

There was still an awful lot that needed to be put right behind the scenes. To begin with, Newcastle wouldn't even let the team have overnight stops for our away trips if the alternative was to save a few quid by travelling on the day of games. I found it staggering, bearing in mind the club's position geographically, but the directors didn't want to fork out for hotel bills and didn't seem to care, or realise, what effect a gruelling bus journey of four or five hours might have on the players. I told the club it was unacceptable and, over time, the policy changed. Yet I can also remember a night game in Cambridge when we were tipped out of our hotel rooms at 11 a.m. because the club hadn't asked for a late checkout. For the rest of the day, we just hung around the hotel until it was time to set off for the stadium.

As for my crash course in management, it wasn't easy being parachuted back into football when I had been out of the game for so long. We won 2–0 in that game at Cambridge, and afterwards I passed their manager on the way to the press conference. I had heard about John Beck, his tricks for unsettling opponents and all the infamous stories about how he used to chuck buckets of icy water over his players. It was the first time I had met him, and I stopped to introduce myself properly. We had a quick chat, shook hands, and then I went to speak to the journalists, thinking nothing more of it.

A couple of weeks later, Terry and I were watching a game at Bradford City, sitting in the stand with Ian Ross, my old Liverpool teammate, when John Beck started walking down our row of seats.

'Do you know John Beck?' I said to Ian, thinking it was polite to introduce everyone.

'I do,' he replied, 'and that's not him, Kevin . . .'

The mystery man turned out to be Gary Peters, Cambridge's assistant manager, who had been fulfilling media duties on Beck's behalf after our game at their place – and had evidently decided to humour me when I started calling him John.

There was another surprise waiting for me when I wandered on to our training pitches one morning and found a little ginger-haired fellow jogging round the track in his Newcastle kit. I had made it my business to get to know all the players – but I had never seen this lad before. I didn't have a clue who he was but he seemed to know me, judging by his cheery wave as he ran past.

'All right, boss?' he called out.

I didn't want to be rude but it was a mystery to me who he was. He did another lap and this time I beckoned for him to stop running.

'Who are you then?' I asked, offering my hand.

'Billy Askew,' he said. 'Nice to meet you.'

'You too, Billy. But if you don't mind me asking, what are you doing on our training pitches?'

It turned out he was one of our players. In fact, he had been on Newcastle's books for two years. The problem was he had been on loan at Shrewsbury Town for the previous month, and nobody had bothered to let me know. Billy had been around a bit. He was thirty-two and his career included eight years at Hull City in the lower divisions. Except for most of that time, of course, I had been in Marbella. That was an even more awkward conversation than the one with Gary Peters.

Another shock arrived when I had my first view of Steve Watson's throw-in technique and the crazy action where he would run towards the line, somersault through the air and then catapult the ball forwards as he was coming down to land. The crowd loved it and, having been out of the game for so many years, it did briefly cross my mind that maybe it was just the way people took throw-ins now.

Instead it was explained to me that this was Steve's party piece. It still makes me laugh, to this day, to think of him flying through the air like an Olympic gymnast, but I found it difficult to be too enthusiastic at the time. I saw it as a gimmick, and the fact it was so popular with the fans, getting a loud cheer every time, seemed to me just another sign of how far Newcastle had fallen. I wanted people to come through the turnstiles in the anticipation of seeing goals and thrilling football. I didn't want the highlight to be Steve Watson's throw-ins, for heaven's sake.

Steve was a talented kid who loved playing for his hometown team, but there were other players who found it difficult dealing with the pressures of playing for a club of Newcastle's size. Some of those players, I found out, used to park their cars on the far side of St James' Park and sneak in through one of the turnstiles at the back rather than face the supporters at the front entrance. There were always big crowds outside the ground, and the players had found a way to avoid everyone. One of the turnstile operators was letting them in and I didn't like the response when I tackled the players about it. 'It's better this way,' one said, 'I don't need all that hassle.' Those players, I quickly decided, needed to be shipped out. The club was too big for them.

We had some good lads such as Gavin Peacock and David Kelly, both of whom did brilliantly for me, but we needed a leader inside the dressing room. Kevin Scott, our captain, was a good guy but too quiet for my liking. We had Ray Ranson, an experienced old pro, but he was at a stage of his career when injuries had taken hold, and we could not totally rely on Kevin Brock either. Kevin was a clever footballer, but he suffered from migraines that could completely wipe him out. He was one of our better players, but there were even a couple of times, on the day of matches, when his wife rang in to say he was unavailable.

We needed someone of the calibre of Brian Kilcline, with his moustache, his yellow mane, and the slightly wild look in his eye that told everyone he meant business. We signed him, initially on loan, from Oldham Athletic, where he wasn't even getting a game, and his strength of personality was ideal for the position in which we found ourselves. What the Newcastle fans wanted was to see eleven players in black and white who would give everything for that iconic shirt. Kilcline understood that perfectly. Even on the bad days, his head never dropped. He was tough as teak, absolutely fearless, and determined to repay us for taking a chance on him. He was a ready-made captain – one of my more important signings as Newcastle's manager – and how we needed him when the team slipped back into relegation danger.

The players had made the classic mistake of thinking they were no longer in peril and, after the initial surge of improvement when I took over, we had started to look like a relegation team again. A run of five successive defeats started with a 6–2 thrashing at Wolves. We lost 3–2 at home to Tranmere, went down by the same score at Ipswich, and a 1–0 home defeat to Millwall dropped us back into the bottom three. With three games of the season to go, we went to Derby and lost, ignominiously. Kevin Scott and Kevin Brock were sent off in the first half, and Liam O'Brien followed with a red card of his own after the break. Our eight men finished with a 4–1 defeat and the pressure was cranked up to critical levels.

In our penultimate game, we desperately needed to win at home to Portsmouth and, with five minutes remaining, the game was goalless. David Kelly's late winner must count as one of the more important goals in Newcastle's history, lifting us out of the bottom three, but we still had to go to Filbert Street to face a Leicester City side that was aiming to win automatic promotion. Leicester needed only a point to go up, whereas we were still in grave danger of the drop. A defeat, or even a draw, would have sent us down, if Oxford or Plymouth, the two sides directly beneath us, had both won.

That game at Filbert Street was a nerve-shredding affair and had one of the more dramatic conclusions to a football match I can ever remember. We went ahead with a scrambled goal from Gavin Peacock but, as the clock showed ninety minutes, the ball arrived at the head of Steve Walsh, the Leicester captain, and he carefully directed it past our goalkeeper, Tommy Wright, for the equaliser. We were dazed. Was that us relegated? I was fearing the worst, until the game restarted and, amazingly, Walsh then turned the ball into his own net in stoppage time. We had done it. Or had we? It was pandemonium, with fans streaming on to the pitch, and when the referee took the players off we didn't even know if the game was over or not.

As it turned out, we would have been spared relegation anyway, because Plymouth were losing at home to Blackburn Rovers and on their way down. But we didn't know that at the time and, in all the chaos, the referee must have decided it was safer to end the match without anyone hearing a full-time whistle. That was fine by me. I have always said I break out in a cold sweat when I am reminded how close we came to being relegated and, possibly, going out of business. But we *had* done it. The battered ship *Magpie* was safely back in port and, for Newcastle United, a new era was about to begin.

12

WATCH OUT, ALEX

We had survived by the skin of our teeth and it didn't get much more dramatic than our final-day escape at Leicester City. That, however, quickly passed into history as far as I was concerned, and once I committed myself to taking the manager's job full-time, I wasn't going to fall into the trap of thinking the best we could do the following season was to consolidate and finish in mid-table. With me at the helm, Newcastle could forget that kind of dreary conservatism. The pressure was on to get results and hit new targets. I had been doing it all my career and I didn't intend to stop now. And, frankly, I loved it that way.

That was why I had a message for everyone associated with the club at the start of the 1992–3 season, when I told the press our aim was to become another Liverpool, dominate English football and capture the imagination of the whole country. Some managers might have thought twice about making such a bold statement when the Premier League had just been born and Newcastle had been absent from the birth. But I didn't care if people thought I was overdosing on optimism. I had spent hours reading books on positive mental attitude, management skills and the advanced thinking of experts such as Vince Lombardi of the Green Bay Packers. I wanted everybody at the club to think the same way, and when we began the season at home to Southend United, I used my programme notes to spread the message.

Newcastle United are a Premier League side in all but name and it is my job to make sure that becomes a reality as soon as possible. So how soon? This season. OK, I know that promises have been made in the past, targets have been set and the end result has been that our fans have been left feeling disappointed and dejected. But I have set my own personal goal of getting this club into the Premier League in just one season. That's my job. That's what I'm paid to do. I honestly believe that when we hit our targets this club will be bigger and more exciting than Liverpool. I said in a recent newspaper article that if we clinch a Premier League place next spring, it will make St James' Park a more exciting place than Anfield. And I meant it.

There were people who thought it was an outrageous statement. One of our own directors asked me whether it was wise and suggested I was putting an awful lot of pressure on everyone. 'Good, rightly so,' I told him. 'That's the problem with Newcastle. Your expectations have always been, "This is Newcastle, we don't do well." Well, if you start saying what it is you want, and you start believing it, it might actually happen.' I knew my ambitions were realistic, but there was still the familiar air of pessimism that 'we're Newcastle, we're not quite there, we always fall back.' I wanted to change that mentality. I was on a mission to make Newcastle the club I always thought it should be. I wanted a team that could challenge the elite and I wanted it to happen as quickly as possible. Some people might have scoffed. But those people underestimated me.

We had an incredible start, beating Southend 3–2 and following that up with a 2–1 win at Derby, then back-to-back victories at home to West Ham and Luton. We went to Bristol Rovers and won again. Five wins out of five. Then Portsmouth, Bristol City, Peterborough, Brentford and Tranmere. Ten from ten. We went to Sunderland, and Liam O'Brien's free kick got us our first win at Roker Park for thirty-five years. Eleven games, eleven wins, twenty-five goals scored, seven conceded. And not forgetting a 3–1 victory at Middlesbrough, then a Premier League side, in the League Cup.

I can still remember the sudden, damp silence in the final minute of our twelfth league fixture when Jim Dobbin of Grimsby Town scored an absolute rocket to end our immaculate start. That, however, was another occasion that convinced me Newcastle were in the wrong division. There were 8,000 fans locked out that day, and the police were worried it was getting out of hand and, potentially, dangerous. After that, all our home games for the rest of the season had to be all-ticket events.

The turnaround was incredible, bearing in mind we finished the previous season with the second-worst defensive statistics in the entire football league. We had opened up a ten-point lead over second-placed West Ham, and that meant I could go to the board, even with three-quarters of the season still to go, to start putting in place my plans for the following year. 'We're going to get promoted,' I told them. 'Let's start buying our players for the top division now, and get them integrated now, because they will cost us a lot more when we go up.'

By that stage Sir John Hall had taken over from George Forbes as chairman and had appointed Freddy Shepherd as vice-chairman. Sir John had his son, Douglas, and the chief executive, Freddie Fletcher, in his camp. A new, adventurous board had emerged, full of ideas and not frightened to try anything it felt would benefit the club. I was given a three-year contract, one of my stipulations being that Terry McDermott was awarded a deal of his own, and I moved out of my hotel to rent a house from Sir John on the Wynyard Hall estate. It was time to move the family up to the north-east.

That made life a lot easier because, until then, Jean and the girls were still in Hampshire and I had been trekking up and down England's road network to be with them after games. If we were playing at St James' Park at 3 p.m. on a Saturday, I wouldn't get back until after midnight sometimes, and then I would set off back the next day because I wanted to avoid the Monday traffic. It was a hell of a slog, close to a 700-mile round trip, and I would be exhausted by the time I arrived back in the north-east. Wynyard, thirty-five miles south of Newcastle, was the perfect place to make home.

It hadn't been a straightforward summer, however, and I didn't sign the contract until I was given various assurances about the club's ambitions matching mine. I had caught the management bug, but I wasn't impressed when the directors put a document in front of me that, as well as setting out my proposed salary and other contractual details, specified I had to raise £1.5 million from the sale of players and only half would go back into a transfer pot. I made it clear that I couldn't stay under those terms and the newspapers reported that I had resigned. That wasn't true for the simple reason that you cannot resign from a contract you have never signed. Yet it was in the balance until Douglas and the two Freddies flew out to see me at my villa in Marbella and made it clear that Newcastle would be a very different club under the new regime.

My relationship with the board was much better from that point onwards, and our flying start to the 1992–3 season had left me in no doubt that in the space of a year we could go from staring at relegation to walking away with the league. Suddenly the directors were coming to me, rather than the other way round, asking if I wanted to sign anyone. For the first time, we had everyone rowing the boat the same way. It was so new to everyone, so very exciting, and now we were in a position where we could go to our transfer targets and tell them we were going to be in the Premier League.

We had already signed John Beresford from Portsmouth, and that gave us a left-back who loved to get forward. Paul Bracewell had arrived from Sunderland, and Barry Venison's signing spoke volumes about the direction we were heading. Venison had won two league championship medals and an FA Cup at Liverpool, but he chose to drop down a division, leaving the most successful club in the country, because he was a north-east lad from Stanley and wanted to be part of what we were building.

Rob Lee was my next target. Gavin Peacock had mentioned that there was a midfielder at Charlton Athletic who could play at a higher level and, as soon as I saw Rob play, I wanted him in my team. Rob had the quality all the top players possess – football intelligence – but it wasn't easy convincing him because Middlesbrough, the division above us, also wanted him, and he had already been to see their manager, Lennie Lawrence, about moving to Ayresome Park.

Lennie had previously been Rob's manager at Charlton, and was desperate to clinch a deal for his former player. The odds were stacked against us, but I managed to speak to Rob and I knew I had a decent chance of winning him over when he mentioned I had been one of his boyhood heroes. 'If you go to Middlesbrough you will be on a medium-sized boat,' I told him. 'One day, soon, a massive boat the size of the *Queen Mary* will sail past you with "Newcastle United" written on the side. And you will look at it and say: "I could have been on that boat."'

That wasn't just a sales pitch. I genuinely believed it was true, and I also told him, with a perfectly straight face, that if he had any reservations about leaving London, he should take into account that it was closer for him to get to Newcastle than it was Middlesbrough.

Rob wasn't exactly thrilled when I joked about that in a press conference some time later and he was accused of some wonky geography. 'Gaffer, you've made me look foolish,' he'd say. But it was true, kind of. There were only two flights a day from Heathrow to Teesside airport, and if a Middlesbrough player was travelling by rail from London he would have to get off at Darlington, where not all the trains stopped, and find a way across. Newcastle, on the other hand, had eight London-bound flights a day, to Gatwick as well as Heathrow, and a much better rail service, with the train station just a short walk from the stadium.

OK, Newcastle was a fair bit further in terms of mileage – but I didn't labour that point.

Scott Sellars, who signed from Leeds for £700,000, was another terrific piece of business, but our biggest buy that season was undoubtedly Andy Cole. He was another one we signed to make sure we would be ready when we went into the Premier League. Not *if* we were in the Premier League, but *when*. I didn't have any doubts whatsoever, and I had seen enough of Andy to realise he would strike fear in opposition defences at the highest level.

One afternoon, Terry and I were looking through the fixtures, wondering whether there was a game we could go to see and wishing we had been a bit more organised. Bristol City were playing West Ham that evening, but it was already approaching five o'clock and we were kicking ourselves that we hadn't planned it earlier.

That was the point at which Douglas Hall popped his head round the door to let us know he was getting off for the night. 'All OK?' he asked. 'Anything I can do?'

It was Terry who decided to chance his arm. 'I don't suppose your plane is available, is it?'

Douglas kept a private plane at Teesside airport and his eyes lit up when we explained our predicament. His pilot was shopping in Yarm when Douglas rang him, and not exactly thrilled about being called out at such short notice. Yet Douglas was determined to help. He sorted it all out and, by six o'clock, we were in the air.

When we landed in Bristol, there was a car waiting to rush us to Ashton Gate. We hurried into our seats as the teams were coming out, and the first thing I noticed was that Andy was wearing a pair of elasticised cycling shorts beneath his kit. His thigh was strapped and it was obvious he was playing with an injury. Andy's game was all about sprinting power. Yet he was running at three-quarters pace. He had to be taken off early and, as we watched him leave the pitch, Terry turned to me, shaking his head. 'Well, what a waste of bloody time.'

Except I didn't think it was. The fact Cole had gone to play with an injured leg told me something about his character. Another player might have cried off rather than risk making the injury worse. I didn't want players who would look for excuses as soon as they had a little niggle. I wanted players who were willing to put their bodies on the line, and Andy had just shown me there was more to him than being a prolific goal-scorer. I might not have seen the performance I expected, but I was keener than ever to sign him.

He cost us £1.75 million and, to put that into context, it was more than twice the amount Newcastle had ever spent on a player. A year earlier, Terry and I had been going through that player-selling charade in our offices, worrying that relegation to the old Third Division might put the club out of business. Now we were preparing to smash the club's transfer record to boost what, in my view, was already a top-four Premier League side in the making. Cole's signing was a demonstration of our new thinking and another positive sign that Sir John, like me, didn't just want to make up the numbers when we reached the top division.

All that was left from my end was to touch base with the player and, as soon as I had the go-ahead, I dialled the number I had been given for his digs. I couldn't get hold of him all afternoon but kept pressing the redial button until, finally, he picked up the receiver.

'Hello,' I said, 'is that Anthony Cole?'

'No,' came a sullen reply, 'this is Andy Cole.'

Oh, Kevin – you absolute plonker . . . I had got myself in a muddle because we had a young player called Anthony Cole on the books at Newcastle. But it was an embarrassing faux pas. The conversation had started badly and, once I had apologised for getting his name wrong, it didn't get a whole lot easier.

I began by explaining why we were prepared to spend so

much money on him. I had worked out there was a flight he could catch from Heathrow that night and I was sure he would want to come up as quickly as he could to meet me. I knew that if it was me, I would have been on that plane.

'Andy, we've just broken the club record and agreed a fee for you; what I'd really like you to do now is get on that flight up here,' I said.

'I can't,' he said. 'I've got something on tonight.'

Now it was my turn to feel put out. Terry Mac was listening in and I put my hand over the receiver to mouth my frustration. 'He says he's got something on . . . what the hell?' If I hadn't dropped such a rick with his name, my instinct might have been to tell him if there was something more important than signing for Newcastle then, fine, we might as well forget it. I bit my tongue and decided to give him the benefit of the doubt. But I was pulling my hair out. It wasn't the response I had wanted and, in hindsight, it was probably for the good that he didn't give me any more details about what he was doing that night. I later found it was because he had no clean clothes. Andy always did his laundry on a certain night of the week and, plainly, wanted to keep to that routine.

We rearranged for the next day, and in fact I liked Andy from the moment I met him. He had an obsession with scoring goals. He set the tone on his home debut, a 4–0 defeat of Notts County, and his first hat-trick arrived a couple of weeks later in a 6–0 win against Barnsley. On and on he went. Andy had joined us for the last twelve games of the season. He scored twelve times and the fans adored him. He was a sensation.

We went up in style, winning our last five matches, and the thrills of that season will never leave me. It was the most exciting period of all at Newcastle – even more exciting, genuinely, than when we were going for the Premier League title. Players who had once been jeered off the pitch were now being hailed as heroes. Newcastle, the city, felt alive. Has there ever been another city where the entire mood is dictated by the fortunes of its football team?

Our final game was at home to Leicester – yes, the same team we had met in very different circumstances twelve months earlier – and my only concern was that we had a live television audience and I didn't want our standards to drop now we had been promoted. There was something about the atmosphere that day that made me feel uneasy. Lindisfarne put on a concert on the pitch. There were acrobats and dancers. I hadn't been consulted about any of it, and I was even less impressed when I came into the dressing room to find a television guy attaching a camera to the wall.

I don't think so, chum. Too much was going on for my liking, and I ordered it to be taken down. Leicester were sixth in the league – no mugs – and when we walked out of the tunnel, with the entire ground singing 'championees', I turned to Terry and told him I didn't like the way my players had been knocked out of their usual routine. 'You know what's going to happen now,' I said. 'This is going to be a damp squib. We'll lose one–nil today, just you see.'

Well, my old pal took great pleasure reminding me of that prediction just before half-time, when David Kelly headed in his hat-trick goal. That made it 6–0 in our favour after forty-four minutes against a team that had qualified for the play-offs. The crowd were having the time of their lives and Terry, gesturing towards the electronic scoreboard at the Gallowgate End, gave me that little cheeky look he does. 'Some damp squib,' he shouted above the din. 'One–nil to Leicester, you reckon?'

It finished 7–1, our biggest win of the season, and when Andy Cole completed his own hat-trick in the second half, it was the first time two Newcastle players had scored three in the same match since 1946. We had scored more goals, ninety-two, than any other side in the four divisions and, for a team that supposedly could never defend, we hadn't done too badly at the back either. From eighty-four goals conceded in the 1991–2 season, the number had come down to thirty-eight. In twelve months, we had gone from the worst defensive record in the division to the best. Only at Newcastle, eh?

The key was whether we could carry that on at Anfield, Old Trafford, Highbury and all those other Premier League grounds and, in my mind, we were going to all those places to win. Manchester United had just won their first title for almost a quarter of a century. It was no longer Liverpool in my sights, and in my programme notes I had a challenge for Alex Ferguson and the newly crowned Premier League champions. Newcastle United were on their way. 'Watch out, Alex,' I wrote, 'we will be after your title.'

13

RIDING THE MONSTER

It probably summed up our ambitions during the following years in the Premier League that at one stage Douglas Hall took it upon himself to fly to Italy and turn up, unannounced, at the home of Juventus, with the intention of bringing one of the game's authentic superstars back to Tyneside.

It's a great story. Douglas took Freddy Shepherd, Freddie Fletcher and Terry McDermott with him on a private jet to Turin. Then he walked through the entrance of the club's offices, introduced himself as a director of Newcastle United and asked for a meeting with the Juventus president, Vittorio Chiusano, to arrange a deal for Roberto Baggio or, failing that, Dennis Bergkamp.

I told Douglas he must have been round the bend to turn up off the cuff and think one of the giants of European football would let any player of that calibre go. It was never going to happen, and I did gently point out that it wasn't really the way the top clubs conducted transfer business. But I had to admire his nerve, even if it wasn't necessarily the way I would have gone about it myself. The message from Juve, unsurprisingly, was that no one at the club was available to meet them and that, in any case, their star players were not for sale – and *arrivederci*. Which, in this case, could probably be translated as 'sling your hook'. Douglas came back with a souvenir from the trip – a Juventus shirt with 'Baggio' and the number ten emblazoned across the back – laid out on the back seat of his car. Sadly, he never got anywhere near the man himself.

I can laugh about it now, and I cannot fault the man for having a go. There are all sorts of different ways to get a transfer done, and I used a few tricks of my own when it came to signing Peter Beardsley from Everton and putting together the strike partnership with Andy Cole that helped us finish third in our first season in the Premier League.

I knew Peter's qualities from our days as teammates, and I was convinced it would give him a new lease of life if we could bring him back to St James' Park. The only problem was that Peter was thirty-two. Everton wanted £1.35 million and the directors didn't like the idea of spending that amount on some-one that age. We were also interested in Benfica's Russian striker, Sergei Yuran, and on the way to meet Peter at a hotel in Weth-erby, I took a call from Freddy Shepherd to tell me the only way it could be ticked off was if I signed both players at once. I didn't understand the logic at first and I wasn't quite sure what he was telling me – until, that is, he told me to do the maths. Yuran was twenty-six and the board had decided it wouldn't be a bad invest-ment to sign a thirty-something Beardsley if it averaged out that the two players were twenty-nine.

It sounded crazy but I didn't really have a great deal of time to weigh it all up. Peter was waiting inside the hotel, completely oblivious to the fact I was on the phone to Freddy in a layby down the road. There was no guarantee Yuran would join us, and I didn't think Peter would have been impressed if I had sprung the news that the deal hinged on another striker signing later in the day. I had to improvise. 'Freddy,' I said, 'tell the chairman that Sunderland are waiting in the wings and if we don't sign Beards-ley today they will sign him tomorrow.'

'Sunderland?' he said, suddenly sounding very nervous. 'Bloody hell. In that case, you had better get it done.'

It was almost true. It was actually Derby who were after him, not our arch-rivals Sunderland, but it was only a white lie. I was convinced Peter would have gone to Derby if I had explained the board's thinking, and I figured my conscience would be clear if the Beardsley–Cole partnership terrorised opposition defences in the way I imagined. Peter, a class act, even agreed to take a pay cut to join us. Meanwhile the deal for Yuran fell through, partly because of the number of agents who wanted a piece of the cake, but also because of the negative vibes we were getting from the player. Yuran wanted his wages paid after tax and all sorts of ridiculous financial requirements. He seemed more interested in what kind of car he would be getting as part of the package and didn't make any attempt to conceal his displeasure when I told him we had a deal in place with Rover. He thought I meant Range Rover, but even that wasn't good enough and he requested a top-of-the-range BMW. When a deal rests on what kind of car the player gets, there have to be questions about whether his priorities are in the right order.

I didn't lose any sleep over that one, and my transfer-market strategy for Newcastle in the Premier League was simple: we were creating a monster which we had to keep feeding. We had good players, but if we could replace them with better ones we would always go with the upgrade. Beardsley was the classic example, taking over from the popular David Kelly, and immediately showing he had lost none of his zest. Peter had played for both Merseyside clubs since leaving St James' Park, and it saddened me that Newcastle had let him spend the best years of his career elsewhere.

Cole, in particular, loved playing with him, and those two were way above any other strike partnership that had been seen at Newcastle for a long time. Peter had a rare ability to read his teammate's mind and plot the next move. He would flog himself to death for the sake of the team and dovetailed beautifully with Andy. They scored goals for fun and, with two players of that quality leading our forward line, I wasn't surprised that we qualified for Europe, finishing above Liverpool and Arsenal, in our first season in the top division.

Everyone talked about how special the Premier League was, but we were never in awe of anybody. By the end of September we were eleventh. We were in the top six by mid-November and fourth going into Christmas. It was our honeymoon season, and when we went on a six-match winning sequence in March, it moved us into third position behind Manchester United, the runaway leaders, and Blackburn Rovers. If anything, we were disappointed not to finish the season even higher. We did, however, outscore the champions – our eighty-two goals being two more than Alex Ferguson's team, fifteen points clear of us, had managed.

Cole alone scored thirty-four league goals and his overall total of forty-one broke the club record jointly held by Hughie Gallagher and George Robledo, with thirty-nine each. It was Newcastle's highest finish since winning the league in 1927 and we did it with a side made up of virtually all English players: Cole and Beardsley up front, with Scott Sellars, Rob Lee, Paul Bracewell, John Beresford, Lee Clark, Barry Venison and Steve Watson the others to make at least thirty appearances. Brian Kilcline still had a huge influence behind the scenes, and Robbie Elliott was emerging as a talented left-back. Plus we had Steve Howey, Kevin Scott and Mark Robinson and, towards the end of the season, Ruel Fox and Darren Peacock.

The entire team could have been made up of Englishmen if Mike Hooper, the goalkeeper we signed from Liverpool for £550,000, had done enough to keep Pavel Srníček out of the side. Unfortunately for Mike, he struggled for confidence at Newcastle and never recovered after being blamed for letting in a free kick from Matt Le Tissier in a home defeat to Southampton. Le Tissier was one of the great dead-ball specialists, but Mike watched the shot go in without moving an inch and didn't understand how badly that would go down with the Geordie public. Arthur Cox did. I had invited my old manager back to Newcastle to work with me and Terry and he told our goalkeeper in the dressing room that he had just made a critical mistake. 'I know you couldn't have got to it. You knew, Le Tissier knew and everyone on the pitch knew, but if you want to be a goalkeeper for Newcastle you have to dive. The crowd will forgive you for diving and missing it. But they won't forgive you for standing still.' It might sound pointless but it was true: the fans at Newcastle won't tolerate a goalkeeper lamely watching the ball go in the net.

Srníček, who later established himself as a Czech Republic international, had originally won his place from Tommy Wright and eventually did enough to show me he was the safest pair of hands at the club. But he wasn't flawless, and when he wrote in his autobiography that he never felt I fully trusted him, he was probably correct. He was a favourite of the crowd, with their 'Pavel is a Geordie' T-shirts, and I was reminded of his popularity when I left him out for one game and an elderly lady started berating me in the corridors of St James' Park. That was Peggy, Freddy Shepherd's mother, who was a fully fledged member of the Pavel fan club and wanted me to know I was making a terrible mistake. Peggy used to give me hell, in a lovely way, telling me Mike Hooper was overweight and that Pavel was far too nice to be left out.

Unfortunately for Pavel, he wasn't entirely reliable when it came to dealing with opposition crosses. Pavel put in some fine performances, and occasionally some brilliant ones, but he was just short of that elite level, and if Mike had applied himself more rigorously he could have made the position his own. Instead, Peggy might have been right: Mike turned up for pre-season training so heavy one summer I had to send him away again. Later, I brought in Shaka Hislop and, again, Pavel showed his competitive courage to win his place back. We were always trying to find a truly great goalkeeper for Newcastle and I am not sure we ever managed it. Ours were excellent – but you couldn't call them genuine greats of their profession.

Despite my misgivings, I knew I had to take firm action when our goalkeeping coach, John Burridge, called Pavel a coward after one game. I liked Budgie. He was a larger-than-life character and, even in his forties, convinced he was still the best goalkeeper within the club. He used to have a saying, 'I'll give you my eyes, boss, I'll give you my eyes' – meaning he would give everything he had for the club. But he went too far with his criticisms that day and I had to do something about it.

John's frustration was that our goalkeeper should have been braver when he was coming out to deal with crosses in a packed penalty area and, if that meant taking a bang to the head or getting his teeth knocked out, so be it. That was fair enough, but there were ways of saying these things. It was in the press and that was the last thing Pavel needed for his confidence. Pavel was very upset when he came to see me about it and, as far as I was concerned, that meant I had to start looking for a new goalkeeper coach. I didn't want to lose John but I couldn't tolerate my goalkeeper being humiliated that way.

By that stage we had agreed a deal to rent the sports facilities at Durham University as an upgrade on our own training ground. Sir John Hall, who was such a devoted Geordie, didn't like the idea at first of taking the players outside the city's boundaries. It was a battle even to get him to talk about it – 'You do not take Newcastle United across the Tyne,' he would say – and when I finally managed to talk him round, he had kittens when he found out there was a public footpath running beside the training pitches. Sir John and the other directors were horrified by the idea that our supporters would have open access to training. My attitude, on the other hand, was the more the merrier. As Bill Shankly once said, wasn't a football club supposed to belong to its supporters?

We were soon getting huge crowds for those training sessions. The fans would turn up with sandwiches and flasks of tea and sit in their camping chairs to watch us go through our drills. There was only one security guard. We would get up to 3,000 people in the school holidays and the club even talked about putting up a mobile shop to sell a few shirts. A burger van appeared and I would often wander over to have my lunch with the fans. People would travel from Cornwall and Dorset and all sorts of remote places to see us. 'I set off at 3 a.m. to see you,' one guy told me. Their devotion never ceased to amaze me, and I made sure the autograph hunters never went home disappointed. The players would complain sometimes that it could take an hour and a half to get to their cars. But they would get short shrift from me. 'Me too,' I'd say. 'Would you prefer to go home and nobody is interested in you?'

In particular, we always made a tremendous fuss of the fans with disabilities who arrived in their busloads and often found themselves added, unofficially, to my backroom staff. The deal was that they were allowed to stand directly on the touchline as long as they let me know if they heard any of my players swearing. It was never long before they were waving frantically to alert me they had heard a rude word. Then I would stop the game so they could point out the culprit. The player would deny it sometimes and there would be uproar. 'Yes, you did,' they'd shout. 'We heard you! We heard you saying "fuck!" We heard you!' They loved the way we made them feel part of it. We'd spoil them rotten.

We shared the facilities with the university and it always makes me smile to think of David Ginola's arrival in Newcastle and the first friend he made in the city. He didn't know how the set-up worked and, assuming one of the lads running round the athletic track must be one of his new teammates, introduced himself as our latest signing, just off the plane from France. Before long they were happily chatting away. David wanted to know what Newcastle was like and if there were any nice restaurants and, in the end, they arranged to meet for a meal that evening. I'm not sure when the penny dropped and David realised this wasn't another Newcastle player, or when the student cottoned on to the misunderstanding, but I would love to have been a fly on the wall in that restaurant.

The only problem came when Robbie Elliott turned up swaying one day, reeking of beer, and it became apparent he had been on an almighty bender the night before. Terry and Arthur had clocked he was in a bad way before I came out. They could tell he was still worse for wear but, rather than create a scene, they decided it would be better to shield him from the crowds. When I turned up, I couldn't understand why thirty players were jogging so closely to one another. The ones in the middle could hardly move their arms and it wasn't until I saw the state of Robbie that I realised they were literally propping him up. 'Robbie, go down injured,' I told him. 'The medical staff will take you in. Then come to see me tomorrow when you have sobered up.'

In the modern era, now everyone is snapping away with camera phones, we would never have got away with it. I don't like the way football has changed in that regard; nowadays someone would have sold the pictures to the newspapers or put it on Twitter within minutes. Robbie was full of contrition when he came in the next day and I told him he was being fined. Well, a Kevin Keegan fine. 'That will be £200,' I told him. 'You don't have to pay me anything but, if anyone asks, you were fined £200, get it? And if you let it out that you haven't been fined, I will take that £200 out of your wages.' It was important for me to have discipline and there was no way I could tolerate a player turning up half-cut. But I didn't see the point in docking players' wages.

For less serious infringements, Arthur and I used to set up a courtroom and put towels over our heads to look like barristers' wigs. Arthur would play the part of the defence barrister, I would be the prosecution and sometimes we would invite other members of the coaching staff to be the jury. We would listen to what the player had to say, cross-examine him with our evidence and then decide whether he was guilty or not and, if necessary, what the punishment should be. Press-ups, quite often.

Training was dedicated, thorough and serious, but the players were allowed to have fun and humour was always a big part of it. Equally, we knew when to be serious. I was always on to the players about their behaviour and John Beresford overstepped the mark twenty-five minutes into one game against Aston Villa at St James' Park when I shouted some instructions his way because

I wasn't happy with how we were defending. John didn't take kindly to being singled out and, in the heat of the moment, told me where to go, in no uncertain terms. Nobody could have been in any doubt what he said to me and my first reaction was to tell the substitute Robbie Elliott to start warming up. I couldn't have players talking to me that way and showing that kind of disrespect. John knew he had made a mistake and tried to apologise. But it cut no ice. 'You are off, pal,' I said.

John was one of my first signings, a player I admired greatly, but nobody was immune if they stepped out of line and it was the same when the police let us know that Barry Venison and Paul Bracewell had found themselves in a bit of bother outside a wine bar. Barry came in with a black eye and I had to remind them about the risks of going out on the town, especially as ex-Sunderland players, when there was always a chance they might come across some idiot who had drunk too much. To be fair, though, that was very unusual. Our players were worshipped in Newcastle, and it was never really an issue that Brace and Venners, two great pros, had links to our arch-rivals. Our fans were just grateful that we had re-established ourselves as the northeast's top dogs.

My sights were fixed even higher. I wanted to go after Manchester United rather than concentrating on local rivalries, and I genuinely thought we could go all the way when we got off to a flier in the 1994–5 season. We were blitzing everyone: Leicester, 3–1; Coventry, 4–0; Southampton, 5–1; West Ham, 3–1; Chelsea, 4–2; Arsenal, 3–2. Liverpool came to our place in the seventh fixture and left with a 1–1 draw. No shame there, and likewise when Blackburn, funded by Jack Walker's millions, did the same a fortnight later. But we also beat Aston Villa, Crystal Palace and Sheffield Wednesday in our opening run, as well as dumping Manchester United out of the League Cup and putting ten past Royal Antwerp over two legs in our first UEFA Cup tie.

When we went to Manchester United on 29 October, we were four points clear at the top of the table. We lost 2–0 and, after that, it was shocking to see our deterioration. In the follow-ing three months we won only two league games and went out of the UEFA Cup to Athletic Bilbao. The blip became a slump and we had slipped to fifth, twelve points off the top, when I started thinking seriously about the ramifications of a deal which, I knew, would shake the football world to its foundations and stun the Newcastle public.

So, why did I sell Andy Cole? What was it that persuaded me that Newcastle would be better off in the long run without the player who had been the focal point of our attack? And why *them*? Why, of all the clubs, Manchester United?

Well, I've never said it before, but I suspect Andy might have been 'tapped up' anyway. I would never expect him to admit as much; it's not something anybody from Old Trafford would ever confess and I don't expect I will ever know for certain. But my firm suspicion is that someone had turned his head. Andy's body language had changed. His attitude had become questionable, to say the least, and it seemed to me that he had made up his mind he did not particularly want to be with us any more.

He might say that is not true. He is even on record saying he did not want to leave Newcastle. I would like to believe him and I have no hard evidence other than a gut feeling from all my years in the industry. But if I am mistaken it leaves several unanswered questions about why he had stopped training properly and become so detached and unresponsive.

Andy was barely lifting a leg in training. The team was built for Andy to inflict maximum damage. We had brought in players specifically with him in mind, so as soon as he stopped being fully committed, which was how I saw it, we had to move him on. He had run his race with Newcastle, as simple as that. He had lost a bit of respect from the other players, who could see he was not applying himself properly, and it wasn't a coincidence that his form had started to deteriorate. If you skive in training it is very difficult to put that right in matches. You can't just turn it on and off like a tap.

As I have said already, I warmed to Andy from the day he arrived in Newcastle. I tried to help him in his personal life and I introduced him to a new agent, Paul Stretford, when he had problems with his previous adviser. Andy was a deep character. I wouldn't call him a loner, but he was different to your average footballer and we were guilty at times, all of us, of forgetting what it must be like for a young man to be living so far from home and catapulted into the big flash world of elite football.

These days, clubs employ player-liaison officers and a small army of back-up staff to make sure there is a support network in place. Back then, however, it was very different. Andy had moved into Crook, a mining village in County Durham, where he was living his life in a goldfish bowl, nowhere near any of his new teammates, and feeling lost and isolated. We, as a club, should have helped him more with the settling-in process, but he was holed up in Crook without knowing anybody and under siege, day and night, from locals knocking on his door or hanging round his gates. We had left him to it. When we found out he was living like a prisoner in his own home, it was a wake-up call for all of us that the club needed a better support system. Andy moved into an apartment in Newcastle and he was much happier there.

I confided in Andy when I was trying to sign Peter Beardsley. I even drove Andy to Anfield one night to watch Liverpool play Queens Park Rangers, because I was thinking about making a bid for Darren Peacock. I reckoned Darren could do for Newcastle what Steve Bruce did for Manchester United but I wanted Andy's take, as a centre-forward, before making a bid. I liked Andy. I thought he was a tremendous footballer and a good guy.

Equally, I had been given a glimpse of his less attractive traits when we were preparing to face Wimbledon in a League Cup tie during his first full season with us. Andy was so uninterested in training the day before the game, I had to stop the session. He was barely moving and the other players were getting irritated with him. There was no immediate explanation for it and that was not the first time he had lacked commitment in training. I had given him the benefit of the doubt before, but his attitude was so poor I halted training and told him he needed to buck up his ideas. I said he wasn't being fair on anyone and I asked if he had any intentions of working up a sweat in the next half an hour.

'If that's the best you can offer, you might as well eff off,' I told him. Except I probably didn't put it as politely as that. And he did. He turned on his heels, effed off, and that was the last we saw of him for three days.

As Andy tells it in his autobiography, he was brooding from a defeat at Southampton the previous weekend when I had carpeted the team for a poor all-round performance. Lee Clark, such a fiery and passionate little character, bore the brunt of it from me that day because when I substituted him he tried to storm off to the changing rooms. Not on your life, sunshine. You couldn't just duck up the tunnel to escape at the Dell. The changing rooms were in a corner of the ground and, as Lee stomped away, I seized his collar and marched him back to the bench like a naughty schoolboy. Lee kicked the physio Derek Wright's bag and, as punishment, I had banished him from the cup tie against Wimbledon. Andy, who was his big mate, claims in his autobiography that he was sulking with me because of the way his friend had been treated. It's a lame excuse, and ignores the fact that if one person is not training properly it is an insult to the coaching staff who have put on the session and to all the other players.

To be fair to Andy, he did apologise when he finally showed his face again. I put him back in the team and, typically, he marked his return with a goal. It was a record-breaking season for him and nobody could ever quibble with his figures for Newcastle. Andy played eighty-four games for Newcastle and scored sixty-eight times – a strike rate of 81 per cent. Hughie Gallacher, with 143 goals in 174 matches, had a marginally better one, at 82 per cent. But it was a close-run thing, and no other centre-forward in the club's history beats Andy for goals per game. Andy was an ideal wearer of that famous number nine shirt, passed down through the ages by Gallacher, Jackie Milburn and Malcolm Macdonald, and such a prolific scorer I knew it would be a sensation, and a huge controversy, that I was willing to let him go.

There was not a flicker of uncertainty in my voice, however, when I went to the board to let them know what I was proposing. The gasps were audible. They were shocked and, to begin with, I don't think they could quite believe what I was suggesting. Yet they also knew me well enough to realise it was not a decision I would have taken lightly. I told them it would take guts and character to back me, and the fact that Andy had scored only one league goal from late October to January made it a touch easier for them to understand my logic.

That didn't mean Andy was burnt-out, or anywhere near that point. He was twenty-three, the Professional Footballers' Association Young Player of the Year, and I fully expected him to carry on scoring for fun for Manchester United. But my rationale was that we had seen the best of him in a Newcastle shirt, and that if we wanted to mount a serious tilt for the championship the following season we should take the money, use it wisely and go for a slightly different approach.

By that stage, I had received an offer from Manchester United and the deal was already being hatched. Paul Stretford was also Stan Collymore's agent, and it was the Nottingham Forest striker who had originally been in Alex Ferguson's thoughts. Yet Alex set the ball rolling by mentioning to Paul that the other English striker he would fancy was Cole. That, in turn, was passed on to me, just at the time when I was starting to question whether Andy had lost a bit of his spark. Paul thought there was no chance of me sanctioning the deal, but he dropped it into conversation anyway and for a couple of days I wrestled with the idea in my mind.

I wasn't daft. I knew that by selling Andy I would potentially be helping the best team in the country accumulate even more trophies. It would have been pretty vindictive on my part, however, to put him up for sale then stipulate we would not do business with Manchester United. I mean, what other club in England could have taken him? The fee was fixed at £7 million, a British transfer record, with Keith Gillespie joining us as the makeweight, valued at £1 million. Everything was shrouded in secrecy, just as I liked it, and when it was all signed off Alex rang to ask how I wanted to play it with the media. He had got what he wanted. But I had, too. It was a phenomenal amount of money in those days, and in that situation there was a certain etiquette between managers. 'You're the one who has broken the transfer record,' I told him. 'It should be your right to make the announcement.'

It was the right thing to do, and I knew that if I was in his position I would have wanted to put out the news. Yet the way it came out via Old Trafford, without any warning whatsoever, just made it even worse for all the Geordies. It was never going to be easy for the supporters to understand. I just hoped they would eventually forgive me and understand I was doing it for valid reasons. It would be stretching the truth to say I was not apprehensive about the reaction, however. We didn't have anyone lined up as a replacement and, though Gillespie was a talented winger, he was only on the fringes in Manchester and hardly a household name. We knew the fans were going to go ballistic, and the atmosphere in the boardroom was almost funereal as we steeled ourselves for the inevitable backlash.

Looking out from the window, it wasn't long before we could see the first fans heading to the ground. Before long they were arriving in droves and you could tell, just from the way they were stomping up the hill, they were not coming to congratulate us. Douglas Hall joined me at the window and the blood drained from his face.

'There's loads of them,' he gasped.

'And there will be more,' I said.

The crowd was 200–300 strong and getting bigger all the time when I realised I had to do something. Television crews were arriving and the anger on the faces outside was unmistakable. Douglas must have thought it was a lynch mob, because he rang security to ask for two cars 'quick as possible' to pick us up from the other side of the ground.

I wasn't prepared to go into hiding. 'All they want is an explanation,' I said. 'They want to know why, and I'm going down there to tell them.'

It felt like the right thing to do but, halfway down the stairs, I must confess I was wondering what the hell I was letting myself in for. It wasn't going to be pretty, and when I turned round I could see that, apart from Terry, I was on my own. The directors had started to follow me but held back when they heard so many irate voices outside. I was walking into a bear pit, and when I appeared on the steps at the back of the Milburn Stand it was the only time in my life at Newcastle that I had been welcomed with jeers.

Their faces were contorted with anger and hurt. It took a while just to be heard and, for those first few moments, I just had to accept the buffeting of 'Judas' and 'traitor'. It was a completely new experience for me and it took a few seconds to take it in. There were hisses and shouts, and one of the first comments I heard was from a guy saying it was typical of Newcastle to be selling their best players to finance a new stand. That wasn't true, but I could understand why he had reached that conclusion. Newcastle had been a selling club for a long time – Chris Waddle, Peter Beardsley, Paul Gascoigne – and that policy had built up years of mistrust. I had promised it would be different on my watch, but now their favourite player, with twenty-seven goals already that season, was on his way to Manchester United. The fans were entitled to think the worst when, even as this scene played out, there were two cranes working on the ground re-development behind us.

Another voice could be heard above the din. 'Hey, give him a chance, let's hear him out then.' I turned to the first guy and told him that I knew why he was so cynical. I said I understood everyone was raw and it was true that kind of accusation could have been levelled at the club in the past, but I also pointed out it was hardly fair when Ruel Fox had cost us £2.25 million from Norwich and Darren Peacock was £2.7 million from QPR. Philippe Albert had cost almost the same from Anderlecht and we had spent good money on Beardsley, Marc Hottiger, Paul Kitson and Steve Guppy. Not all those deals worked out, but it wasn't right to say that Newcastle were still a selling club.

I wanted the fans to know it was my decision, nobody else's, and that it would be me who copped the blame if it turned out to be a dreadful error. But I also made it clear the money would go back into the team, rather than cosmetics for the ground, and I promised there was a method to my apparent madness.

The next man to speak out asked how I could possibly justify doing business with Manchester United and I was ready for that one. 'Hold on a minute,' I said. 'When I came here three years ago this club's biggest rivals were Southend United and Cambridge United, not Manchester United.'

That struck a chord, and the next voice was not quite as hostile. One of the supporters thanked me for coming out and said it had taken guts to face everyone. That settled down some of the more persistent hecklers and the next guy also seemed to be on my side. 'You don't think Kevin would be daft enough to sell Andy Cole if he didn't have someone lined up, would he? But he's certainly not going to tell us who it is until the deal is done.'

Inwardly, I felt a pang of embarrassment. That wasn't the situation at all. Nor did it help that I could hear Terry, just behind me, muttering under his breath, 'Oh yes he would, mate.'

The directors now felt bold enough to make an appearance behind me. Suddenly we had all sorts of different suggestions about who we should get with the money. There were shouts for Alan Shearer. Others wanted Matt Le Tissier or Roberto Baggio. The jeering had stopped and it became a civil discussion, during which I reiterated that I wanted a team that could outdo Manchester United. I promised the supporters I would make sure the ·

money was spent wisely and I asked them to keep in mind that my only intention was to drive the club forward. 'If I've got it wrong, there's a bullet with my name on it,' I pointed out.

The entire scene was captured by television cameras and I cannot think of another club in England where the same would have happened. But that was Newcastle: there was no other club quite like us. It wasn't PR that had led me down those steps, it was just something I had to do – a natural response to a situation I had never known before. They were not a mob and there was even some clapping when I turned to go back inside. They had converged on the ground because they cared deeply, but so did I – and though I still didn't have a completely clear picture of what to do with the Andy Cole money, I was willing, as always, to follow my instincts.

14

SO NEAR YET SO FAR

By the time we began our championship chase in the 1995–6 season, nobody could have accused us of reneging on our promise to spend the Andy Cole money on top-whack signings. Les Ferdinand joined from Queens Park Rangers and quickly established his own place in the list of great Newcastle United centre-forwards. David Ginola added his elegant touches and, later in the season, we went back into the transfer market for David Batty and Faustino Asprilla. We had finished sixth in 1994–5 and that felt like regression after coming third the year before. We knew we had to do better.

It turned out to be one of the more memorable seasons in the history of English football and, as everyone knows, there was a long time when it looked as though we had it sewn up. Manchester United had other ideas, unfortunately. I still have nightmares about the way we threw it away and, with a twelve-point lead in late January, we were never going to get a better chance. No one, however, can take away what we had achieved since I found the club in the relegation quagmire of the old Second Division. I still firmly believe history will remember that team with great affection and, until our collapse, I doubt there were any neutrals who would have begrudged us the biggest domestic prize of all. We had led from the opening weekend in August all the way to 23 March and, throughout all that time, I was convinced we were going to do it.

In the end, it came down to the fact that Alex Ferguson's team had all their championship-winning know-how, whereas this situation was very new to us. We were naive in many ways. It was part of our charm, and one of the reasons why so many people liked watching Newcastle, but ultimately it counted against us. It had taken us four years to make Newcastle title contenders, whereas Alex needed longer with Manchester United from a much stronger starting position, so we must have been doing something right. But he and his players were formidable opponents and too many of our team lost their form at the worst possible time. We gave it our best shot but we were caught and overhauled by a tremendous side led by one of the greatest managers there has ever been.

It is strange, though, how people's memories warp over the years, and the modern narrative now appears to be that my television outburst is the principal reason why the championship trophy ended up at Old Trafford. The popular view seems to be that 'mind games' were the decisive factor. Apparently, my interview on Sky Sports transmitted anxiety to my players who, in turn, were reduced to nervous wrecks and raised a white flag of surrender.

In reality, the truth is much more mundane, bearing in mind Manchester United were already down to their final match when I had my 'love it' moment. They were very much in the box seat, having leapfrogged us at the top of the table five weeks earlier, and nobody really expected them to slip up at Middlesbrough on the final weekend of the season. The title race was virtually over. Never let the facts get in the way of a good story, I suppose, but the real damage was done when we went on a run of eight games from 21 February to 8 April and won a meagre seven points. We did succumb to mental tension, but that was well before my outburst, on 29 April, and it is a distortion of history to think the championship was settled by 'psychological warfare', or whatever you wish to call it.

While I am debunking a few myths, it isn't true either that our title mission fell apart because of a painfully porous defence. Or, indeed, that every single game at Newcastle was a goals bonanza. Again, it is amazing how these things gather legs, and I guess we should take it as a compliment that we are remembered for being so much fun. Yet people seem taken aback when I point out Manchester United were the Premier League's leading scorers that season with seventy-three goals and Liverpool, with seventy, also outscored us. Yes, we wanted to win the league with beauty and set a new benchmark in the English game. And, yes, we came damn close to it – but our total of sixty-six goals is not always what people imagine.

As for this perception that we were absolutely hopeless in defence, it seems to be lost in history that we conceded only two more goals that season than the eventual champions and that, until the final week, our goals-against columns were dead level. People remember the famous 4–3 defeat at Liverpool and seem to think that kind of drama was a weekly occurrence for Newcastle. In fact, it was one of only two 4–3 games in my entire time with the club. Yet I wish I had a pound for every time someone has approached me to reminisce about the déjà vu of the seven-goal thriller at Anfield the following season. I am used to it by now – but I do gently point out that I had left Newcastle by that stage and Kenny Dalglish was in the hot seat.

One 4–3 game was enough for me, and hopefully I can be forgiven for not remembering that wild night under Anfield's floodlights with the same affection as the television viewers who voted it, after twenty years of the Premier League, as the best game in all that time. No team in my memory had ever gone to Liverpool and played as well as we did, only to come away with nothing. We led twice, at 2–1 and 3–2, and is there any more gut-wrenching feeling in football than to lose with the last kick of a match? It was shattering, to say the least, and if you were watching on television you would have seen Terry McDermott and myself slump behind the advertising boards when Stan Collymore slammed in the stoppage-time winner.

When I watch that goal now the same thought comes back as

on the night, that Pavel Srníček should not have been beaten at his near post, and perhaps that demonstrates my point about our goalkeepers – as highly accomplished as they were – not being greats of their profession. Apparently, I had annoyed Pavel in the build-up to the game by asking if he could be more like Peter Schmeichel and win us a match. I don't remember that, but I can recall being asked afterwards whether I could take solace from the fact we had played so thrillingly. My reply was, 'I'd like us to play crap and win a game.'

I also remember Sammy Lee was lucky to get out of the stadium in one piece that night. Sammy was a kid making his way through the ranks at Liverpool when Terry and myself were established players at Anfield in the 1970s. Twenty years on, he was part of Liverpool's coaching staff, sitting with their manager, Roy Evans, and chose to celebrate Collymore's winner by prancing about in front of our dugout. All that anguish, all that hard work going up in smoke, all the crushing disappointment, then Terry and I had it rubbed in our faces by an old colleague. Sammy, to be fair, did apologise afterwards.

Our defeat that night was part of the eight-game sequence when we won only seven points, losing five times, and at the business end of the season, no team with title aspirations can hit that kind of form and expect to get away with it. We had already been knocked off top spot when we lost 2–0 at Arsenal in our previous match, and our position was further weakened when we went to Blackburn, again under the television spotlight, and suffered another grievous setback.

That trip to Ewood Park was another game everyone remembers. We were on top for most of it, and when David Batty put us ahead, after seventy-six minutes, we seemed on course to reinstate our title credentials. Could we show our mettle, close the game down and see out the last quarter of an hour? The answer was delivered four minutes from the end when Graham Fenton equalised for Blackburn with virtually his first touch as a substitute. A draw was no good to us. We went looking for the winner and, as we piled forward, the same player broke away in the eighty-ninth minute to score again. Fenton was a Newcastle supporter who, in different circumstances, might have been singing his heart out among the thousands of men, women and children wearing black and white stripes in the away end. It was another Geordie, Alan Shearer, who set him up for both his goals. Can you believe it? As kids, he and Fenton enrolled on the Blue Star Soccer Days I ran when I was playing for Newcastle. It was soap-opera stuff for Sky but shattering for us, again. How come these last-minute goals never went our way?

Too many players were struggling with the tension, and when we did play well we were still coming away empty-handed from key fixtures. Indeed, the only two players who could escape criticism from February onwards were Batty and Steve Watson. Batty was blamed in some quarters for the team's deterioration, simply because his arrival coincided with the slump in results. Yet it was unfair to pin that on him. He reminded me in style of Billy Bremner while Steve was young, full of enthusiasm and seemed immune to the pressures that were weighing down more experienced teammates.

Ultimately, though, how could I be too critical of my players after everything they had done? Our total of seventy-eight points would have won the title the following season and matched Arsenal's number when they finished as champions another year on. It remains Newcastle's best-ever total in the Premier League era. There was nobody to touch us in the first six months and, throughout the entire season, we lost only one game at St James' Park. That, sadly, was against Manchester United, and I am still struggling, all these years later, to understand how we were unable to turn our superiority in that match into the hard currency of goals.

We played out of our skins, but you could have chucked a handful of rice at Peter Schmeichel and the big Dane would have kept out every grain. It was the greatest goalkeeping performance I had ever witnessed, and when we came in at half-time, it was already in the back of my mind that it might not be our night. Sure enough, Eric Cantona bobbled in a volley against the run of play, and that was the moment everything started to unravel for Newcastle. Our lead had already been slashed from twelve points to four. A win would have moved us seven clear, with a game in hand, and within sight of our first league title since George V was on the throne. Now we had Manchester United one point behind us. They were in the ascendancy and, unlike us, had the experience of being in that position before. They were the last side we wanted in our wing-mirrors.

Within three weeks they had replaced us at the top. For the first time it was us playing catch-up, and it didn't help when Leeds, in thirteenth place, went to Old Trafford in mid-April and their goalkeeper, Mark Beeney, was sent off after only seventeen minutes. Leeds did not have a substitute goalkeeper, and it was unrealistic to think the ten men could possibly hold on with a centre-half, Lucas Radebe, taking over between the posts. Even when Leeds made it to half-time without conceding, the odds were heavily stacked in favour of the home side. One of the strengths of Ferguson's teams was that they never panicked, they kept going, they always trusted themselves. They knew how to grind out a 1–0 win and, true to form, Roy Keane popped up with a decisive goal.

This was the season Alan Hansen came out with his infamous line on *Match of the Day* about 'you can't win anything with kids.' What Alan didn't take into account was that Manchester United had experienced campaigners such as Steve Bruce, Gary Pallister, Denis Irwin and Peter Schmeichel to go with Ryan Giggs, Andy Cole and Roy Keane and the emerging talents of David Beckham, Paul Scholes, Nicky Butt and the Neville brothers. Crucially, they also had Eric Cantona returning from his eight-month suspension for a kung-fu attack on a Crystal Palace supporter. Newcastle, on the other hand, did not have a single player with title-winning experience, apart from Peter Beardsley, until Batty joined us from Blackburn six months into the season. Manchester

United won thirteen of their last fifteen games whereas we had started to wilt long before Fergie decided it was time to turn a fair contest into a bare-knuckle fight.

Alex was not only one of football's greatest managers, he was also one of the profession's finest stirrers, and when he came into his press conference after that Leeds match he had clearly thought of a way to manipulate the headlines for his own agenda. Leeds, he said, had tried harder than in any other game that season, and he followed that up by questioning whether they would be so ferociously competitive in their remaining fixtures. 'They raised their game because they were playing Manchester United. It was pathetic. I think we can accept any club coming here and trying their hardest as long as they do it every week. But no wonder managers get the sack. On that performance they should be a top-six team. They're not – they're struggling, so they've been cheating their manager.'

It was as subtle as a sledgehammer. Alex knew perfectly well we had a game coming up against Leeds at Elland Road. He would have known the headlines his comments would generate, the questions it would raise about the commitment of their players, and he was throwing down a challenge. It was a cheap trick. Alex will no doubt be congratulated for striking some kind of psychological blow but, if that was the intention, I am happy to state I would never stoop to the same level.

As if that were not bad enough, he also appeared to suspect the worst from Nottingham Forest, another of the teams we still had to face, and had the gall to bring up the fact we had a long-standing agreement to revisit the City Ground for an end-of-season testimonial for Stuart Pearce, their captain. Alex always seemed to take the view that everyone was out to get Manchester United. His suspicion this time appeared to be that Forest might go easy on us because of the arrangement between the two clubs, and a misplaced belief that Newcastle finishing the season as champions, rather than runners-up, might ensure a bumper crowd for Pearce.

It was a ridiculous and outrageous suggestion but, once it appeared in the newspapers, various reporters began to add their own spin, pointing out that Forest's manager, Frank Clark, had played for Newcastle for most of his career. Frank, a Geordie, was president of the London branch of the Newcastle supporters' club. The whole crazy story started to snowball. Fergie had set the hare running and it seemed blatantly designed to ensure Forest tried extra-hard against us, so nobody could turn round afterwards and say his suspicions were right.

As it was, we won 1–0 at Elland Road with a header from Keith Gillespie, and the Leeds supporters applauded us off the pitch at the final whistle. It was a scrap, but we got through. That put us three points behind with two games to go, compared to Manchester United's one, and once I had addressed the players, it was time to do my duties with the Sky cameras. I still had all the adrenalin flooding through my veins, and nobody could ever convince me I had misinterpreted Alex's comments. I was live on air with the presenters Richard Keys and Andy Gray and I surprised everyone, including myself.

Richard Keys: Why do you think all that was happening, Kevin, tension on the night?

KK: I don't think you can discount it. We just want to keep our hopes alive and a lot of things have been said over the last few days, some of it slanderous. We've never commented. We've just got on working, trying to pass the ball like we do in training. I think you've got to send Alex Ferguson a tape of this game, haven't you? Isn't that what he asked for?

Andy Gray: Well, I'm sure if he was watching it tonight, Kevin, he would have no arguments about the way Leeds went about their job and really tested your team.

KK: And . . . and . . . we . . . we're playing Notts Forest on Thursday – and he objected to that? Now that was fixed up months ago. We're supposed to play Notts Forest. I mean, that sort of stuff, we . . . it's been . . . we're better . . . we're bigger than that.

Keys: But that's part and parcel of the psychology of the game, Kevin, isn't it?

KK: No! When you do that, with footballers, like he said about Leeds, and when you do things like that about a man like Stuart Pearce . . . I've kept really quiet but I'll tell you something, he went down in my estimation when he said that. We have not resorted to that. But I'll tell you – you can tell him now if you're watching it – we're still fighting for this title and he's got to go to Middlesbrough and get something, and I tell you honestly, I will love it if we beat them. Love it!

Keys: Well, quite plainly the message is, it's a long way from over and you're still in there scrapping and battling and you'll take any of those as long as you continue to get the results.

KK: I think football in this country is honest and so, honestly, when you look abroad you've got your doubts. But it really has got to me and I . . . I . . . I've not voiced it live, not in front of the press or anywhere – I'm not even going to the press conference – but the battle's still on and Man United have not won this yet.

It was quite a show. I never actually realised how angry I was until I watched it back. It was pure emotion pouring out, heart-on-the-sleeve stuff, but that was the way I felt and I wasn't going to bottle it up just because the general rule in football seemed to be that Alex Ferguson was untouchable.

Initially, I felt sorry for Howard Wilkinson and the Leeds players because, as far as I was concerned, Fergie was using them for his own means. I was less sympathetic, however, when I read in one of Alex's books a few years later that he had asked Howard if he could have a 'pop', and that, incredibly, the Leeds manager had no objection. That was out of order. If any manager had asked the same of me, I would have pointed out that if anyone was going to have a go at my players, it should be me. But he and Howard were close, whereas Howard was no friend of mine, and it turned out they had cooked it up in advance.

My emotions were running high and it didn't help that I was wearing headphones to hear what was being said in the studio. Those 'cans' force you to raise your voice and, in the heat of the moment, jabbing my finger for extra emphasis, it must have been television gold for the watching millions. Was I ranting? Yes, I suppose I was. It was all part of that season, the drama of being so close, the roller-coaster ride of Newcastle – I let it all out, in a typical Kevin Keegan way.

I certainly hadn't planned to lose my temper but maybe, even subconsciously, there were other reasons why I reacted so spectacularly. I will probably be accused of sour grapes, but when you are taking on Manchester United it can feel like you are fighting more than just a football team. There was a fear factor in English football when it came to the side from Old Trafford – and their manager in particular. The journalists danced to his tune, the other managers wanted to cosy up to him and the authorities let him get away with some questionable behaviour, in particular when it came to referees.

On top of everything else, when we were sitting pretty at the top of the league it got back to us that the *News of the World* had arranged an editorial meeting because 'everything was going too well for Newcastle' – and it was time to put a stick of dynamite beneath our good-news story. It was scandalous but that was how that now-defunct Sunday tabloid used to operate. They were intent on ambushing us and we found out a team of 'Screws' journalists had been despatched to the north-east with the explicit instructions to 'get some shit' on us. That had nothing to do with anyone from Old Trafford and, as I have said, it might sound like sour grapes, but why did they come after us and not Manchester United? Why did we have that going on in the background, and not them?

All I can say is that the best team won the league. We drew

1–1 at Forest, where we were clapped off again by the home supporters, and when we took on Tottenham Hotspur in our final
match there was still a faint chance that Manchester United
might fall at the last hurdle. We were even sent a replica of the
trophy, just in case, but the real one went down the road to Middlesbrough because that was where everyone knew it would be
needed. David May scored first at the Riverside and the next
update, letting us know Andy Cole had made it 2–0, wounded St
James' Park. Ryan Giggs added a third and they were home and
dry. Our game finished 1–1 but that was immaterial.

What it proved to me was that Alex would do anything to
win, whereas the same could not be said of me. There was a line
I would not cross because if I had been wired the same way I
might have added some mischievous spin to the fact that Bryan
Robson, a Manchester United legend, was now Middlesbrough's
manager. I wouldn't have dreamt of questioning anyone's professional commitment, let alone a man of Robson's standing,
and that was where Alex and I differed. In his world it was an
anything-goes mentality, and it didn't seem to bother him if out-
siders disliked those tactics. It was maybe why he won so much
as a manager, including thirteen Premier League titles, and I
didn't.

That said, I wouldn't want anyone to get the wrong impression. The newspapers tried to portray us as enemies but that was
never true. We worked together as television pundits during
Euro '96 and never even discussed it. What was the point? He
had chucked in the grenade, in his own style. The reaction was
me all over and that was it, finished, as far as I was concerned.
Would I want to go for a drink with him? Not really. And would
he want to break bread with me? Probably not. We are very different people, but I do have the utmost respect for him, and when
he asked me a few years later to do him a favour on behalf of a
charity venture in Scotland, I was happy to help. We might not
see everything the same way, but life moves on and I was
delighted he recovered so well from the brain haemorrhage he

suffered in the spring of 2018. Do I hold a grudge? Absolutely not.

When everything was done at the end of the 1995–6 season, I was absolutely drained. Terry says he could see how badly it scarred me – but I think it scarred us all. For ten days I sat at home in the north-east thinking everything through, wondering whether I had taken the club as far as I could and torturing myself with thoughts of all the shots that had struck the wood-work or all the goalkeepers who seemed to reserve their best performances for us. There was an emptiness about finishing second. It didn't even mean qualifying for the Champions League in those days and, even with my stamina, it took an awful lot out of me. A part of me wondered whether it was time to leave New-castle. I wasn't sure we would ever get a better start to a season, or if we had it in us to go to all those places where we had come away with three points and do it again. My mind was in a whirl, and that was the first time I told the board that maybe it would be better if I stood aside. I was offering to quit, not threatening to do so, but the job can suck you in sometimes and it was probably exhaustion as much as anything else. The pressures of football management had left me feeling guilty even having a day off. I needed a rest before I was ready to give Manchester United another run for their money.

The arrival of Alan Shearer from Blackburn was the biggest motivating factor because if the greatest scorer in the country, with thirty-one goals the previous season, had ended up at Old Trafford, then we, and everybody else, might as well have announced them as the 1996–7 champions before a ball had even been kicked in anger. Alex Ferguson was desperate to make it happen. He did everything he could to convince Alan that Man-chester United would be a better move for him than Newcastle and, deep down, I wonder if my former player ever thinks of all the trophies he could have accumulated if he had chosen Old Trafford. I'd like to think not, however, and that it was enough for a man with his upbringing to wear those black and white stripes for a decade and surpass the scoring record of Newcastle's other football god, Jackie Milburn. Alan pined for the glories that would have accompanied a move to Manchester, but he also understood, as a born-and-bred Geordie, that the only way for it to be truly meaningful would be with his hometown club. He didn't manage that but, in another sense, I am sure he would say there was no greater feeling than representing his own people.

Our first meeting was in Huddersfield, and the smokescreen was a Bryan Adams concert at the McAlpine Stadium. Alan had tickets for the gig but arrived strategically early, and we met at a terraced house owned by a friend of his agent Tony Stephens. None of us wanted anything to leak out, and Alan had taken a leaf out of my book by wearing dark glasses and a baseball cap to avoid being recognised.

I had always liked what I had seen of Alan even before I got to know him. Now I had met him in the flesh, my admiration only increased. Arthur Cox always used to say to me, 'He's just like you, you know. He has his own mind, his own thoughts, and if he doesn't agree with something he'll let you know.' Alan was very much his own man, albeit in the framework of a team. He had natural presence, gravitas, call it what you will, and it didn't need long to realise he would be a leader in the dressing room – potential captaincy material – as well as being such a formidable provider of goals.

The key was persuading him to devote the best years of his professional life to Newcastle and, once he had indicated that was exactly his intention, a follow-up meeting was arranged at a farmhouse owned by David Platt, another client of Tony Stephens, near Crewe. This time, I had Freddy Shepherd, Douglas Hall and Freddie Fletcher with me. Alan had told Blackburn he wanted to go and the best two teams in the country were doing everything they could to land the England striker. It was amazing all this was happening and not a word had leaked out.

By that stage Alan had spoken to Ferguson, but I knew we must have the edge when the player walked in, shook my hand

and told me he had only one condition when it came to Newcastle. 'I don't want to know about the financial stuff,' he said. 'That's all down to Tony and I trust him to handle that side. All I would ask is that I can wear the number nine shirt.'

I looked him in the eye. 'You've got it.'

Everything was going according to plan until Douglas rang Jack Walker, the Blackburn owner, to confirm we would meet the £15 million asking price and the message came back that we could forget it unless we produced the cash in one lump sum rather than, as was the norm in big-money transfers, various instalments. It sounds like chickenfeed now but, in 1996, it was a world-record transfer and the kind of deal that had people asking whether football had lost its mind. It was a massive outlay, and when Douglas came off the phone, cursing at what he had just heard, I sank back in my seat, wondering whether that was the moment a great player slipped through our fingers.

It turned out Blackburn had made the terms even more difficult for Manchester United, insisting the fee was £20 million because Walker apparently had a grudge against the Old Trafford club due to a previous transfer wrangle. All that mattered was that the player was ours as long as we could raise the money. Douglas was quickly on the phone to his father and, yet again, Sir John came through for us. It was exhilarating – exhausting but exhilarating. Newcastle, the club that once tried to stop me signing a player for £90,000, had agreed the biggest deal in football history.

After that, I had to keep my part of the bargain, and that wasn't straightforward when Les Ferdinand was the proud owner of Newcastle's number nine shirt. Andy Cole had found it difficult in his first full season at Old Trafford, with thirteen goals. Les, on the other hand, could not stop scoring for us and became the Professional Footballers' Association Player of the Year. Nobody was going to be as prolific for us as Andy, but Les wasn't far away, scoring twenty-nine times. He was prodigious in the air – 'Les's Leap', I called it – and his athleticism had given the team a new dimension. The number nine shirt in Newcastle was iconic. Les had grown attached to it and, in that position, I would have felt exactly the same.

We were due to fly to Bangkok on a pre-season tour when I took him to one side in the airport to explain I would not be boarding the plane because I was in the process of signing Alan Shearer. I quickly assured Les I had no intention of removing him from the team, let alone selling him, but when I mentioned we needed his shirt he was taken aback. Typically, his first reaction was to agree, but when I slipped away, leaving him with a long flight to think about it properly, his views hardened. By the time I joined everyone in Bangkok he had decided he was not going to let it go without a fight.

That was the only time Les and I crossed swords before common sense prevailed and he agreed to take the number ten shirt. That, in turn, put Lee Clark's nose out of joint, and could anybody be surprised my hair was getting greyer and greyer? Les even asked for number ninety-nine at one stage. Lee settled for number twenty and, once all that was sorted, I had to sound out our captain, Peter Beardsley, because Alan's other request was to take over penalty duties. The season started with the Charity Shield against Manchester United. We lost 4–0 and the press took great pleasure in questioning whether Alan had joined the wrong club.

I was never the kind of person to go into depression after defeat. That, however, was a hard one to take. But we quickly shook it out of our system, and when we trounced the champions 5–0 in October we were back where we liked to be, enjoying the view from the top of the table. Alan's signing was, I hoped, a game-changer, and it was never going to be a problem for us to score goals when we also had Les and Peter, as well as Faustino Asprilla's intricate skill, plus two wingers in David Ginola and Keith Gillespie who had a tremendous amount to offer.

Keith was brave, fast as a whippet, and the fact that he did not let his personal problems affect what was happening on the pitch indicated his strength of character. Over the years, he has been very honest about the gambling issues, even calling his book *How Not to Be a Football Millionaire*, but he was so convincing in his denials when I first confronted him I gave him the benefit of the doubt and went back to my sources to tell them the rumours were incorrect.

There were certainly no clues he was in any trouble from the way he was playing, and I was still in the dark until a journalist from the *Sun* informed us a story was being printed the next day. That was when Keith and his agent turned up at my house to confess that the young Irishman owed a five-figure sum to a bookmaker who, in turn, had passed it on to a local debt collector. I was disappointed Keith hadn't levelled with me in the first place but, above all, I wanted to help, and when I spoke to the bookmaker I arranged to reduce the debt if it was paid straight away. The club advanced Keith some money and I made it clear to him, as I did all my players, that he knew how to get hold of me if he had any problems. It saddened me to find out that his gambling habit, like all addictions, was not an easy one to kick. Keith tells the story of one game against Tottenham when I put my arm around him and said, on current form, he might well be the best player in the country. What I didn't know was that, two days earlier, he had lost £47,000 in one afternoon, then blown another £15,000 the following day trying to win it back.

Ginola was one of those players the fans could put on a pedestal, with his flowing hair, Hollywood-handsome looks and an uncommon ability to wrong-foot opposition defenders before putting the ball on the centre-forward's head. I loved watching him play but I did have to explain to him that we did things differently in England after one of his first away games when, halfway home, a plume of smoke started wafting down the bus. It didn't smell like normal cigarette smoke – it was stronger, more pungent – and when I walked down the bus I found our new signing stretched out on the back seat, puffing away on his Gauloises with his feet up on the chair in front. It was hard not to

16. Holding the German championship trophy for winning the Bundesliga. This was the first time in nearly twenty years that Hamburg had won the domestic league.

17. Giving Maggie an impromptu peck on the cheek before we flew off to the 1980 European Championship. Mind, that doesn't mean I had any affection for her policies.

18. Collecting the Golden Boot for being the top scorer in the First Division during my final season at Southampton.

19. Celebrating scoring for Newcastle against QPR on my debut at St James' Park.

20. Almost two years later, myself and the rest of the Newcastle team pay homage to our fantastic supporters for what was my final league game as a player at St James' Park.

21. Enjoying my retirement with Jean and the kids in Spain.

22. Signing autographs on my return to Newcastle as manager.

23. The infamous 'I will love it' interview.

24. Saluting the fans after the last game of the tumultuous 1995–6 season.

25. With Mohamed Al Fayed at Craven Cottage for the announcement that I would be joining Fulham as chief operating officer.

26. Receiving a champagne shower during victory celebrations for Fulham clinching the Second Division title and, crucially, promotion.

27. Giving a very young-looking Steven Gerrard his first England cap.

28. Consoling Germany's Lothar Matthäus, who we beat 1–0 at the 2000 European Championship. However, due to our loss to Romania neither team would progress to the knockout stages.

29. With the championship trophy for winning the First Division title (now the Championship), which secured Manchester City's place back in the Premier League.

30. Newcastle fans unveiling a banner in January 2018 protesting against Mike Ashley. They are using one of my quotes from after my second spell as manager.

laugh when he held open the packet to offer me one. But the stench was so appalling I had to stop the bus and he finished his cigarette in the layby, with all the lads looking out of the window, wishing he would hurry up because I had promised everyone fish and chips at Wetherby, a ritual for our away trips down south. Ginola finished chugging away in his own time. And then, no kidding, once he had stubbed that one out, he sparked up another one straight away.

As for Asprilla, he was another interesting character. We signed him from Parma and I dread to think what he made of the weather when he landed at Teesside airport, peering out from a fur jacket with those huge brown eyes in the middle of a north-east snowstorm. I had a glass of wine with him over lunch at the team hotel, and when I asked if he would like to go on the bench for our game at Middlesbrough that afternoon, I explained it was purely so he could get a feel for it. It was never my intention to bring him on, but midway through the second half we were losing 1–0 and in need of some inspiration. I gambled. I put on Tino and his trickery turned the game on its head, setting up Steve Watson for the equaliser and creating enough mayhem for Les to stick in the winner.

Not that it was always like that with Tino. I had to take him off in one game because of his lack of endeavour (though it was only once). He was banned after an off-the-ball clash with Keith Curle of Manchester City and the newspapers had a field day about his partying lifestyle, his relationship with a 'porn queen' and his apparent habit in Colombia of pulling out a gun and spraying bullets in the air. Tino had got himself in trouble with the police by firing a gun during the New Year celebrations in his hometown of Tuluá. The fall-out from that incident had followed him to England and that meant we never saw him on Thursdays because he was on probation and had to report to the Colombian embassy in London once a week.

Asprilla's scoring statistics for Newcastle, nine goals in forty-eight appearances, are not going to knock anyone over, and when he signed for us I'm sure a lot of people were thinking, *Do they really need another player?* His time-keeping could be pretty dubious too – '*Tarde, muy tarde*, Tino,' I'd shout, dusting off my old Spanish – but he was another one whose strengths out-weighed his weaknesses and, similar to Batty, I never understood why so many people outside Newcastle wanted him to carry the can for us throwing away the league. Asprilla should never have been made the scapegoat. They loved him to bits on Tyneside and still eulogise about his Champions League hat-trick against Barcelona in the 1997–8 season.

By then, of course, I had gone. Everything started to acceler-ate after our defeat to Blackburn at Ewood Park on Boxing Day 1996, and I have to be honest with myself and say that, for the first time, I was not enjoying the job. I no longer had the same enthusiasm going into training and that, I must clarify, had noth-ing to do with the players. It was because the people at the top of the club were preparing to float Newcastle on the stock market and, as a rift grew behind the scenes, it had started to feel as if we were no longer all on the same wavelength.

Financially, that flotation meant a £1 million bonus for me and, though I had to wait almost a year for it, the club did even-tually stump up the money. It was still only a tiny fraction of what the directors made and, yes, I can understand why people say the proportions were way out of line. But good luck to them – I don't begrudge them a penny after all the success we enjoyed together and the way they backed me in the transfer market. It was noth-ing to do with money why I left. It was the simple fact that the manager-and-board working relationship had broken down and I didn't like the way, behind the scenes, Newcastle had changed.

It didn't help that the club had appointed a financier called Mark Corbidge to broker the flotation as joint chief executive. Corbidge had arrived from NatWest Markets in November 1996, full of his own importance, and was quickly in and out of St James' Park, leaving within three months of the flotation going through and taking a £400,000 pay-off. Nice work if you can get it. He turned out to be the main architect of my departure, and the man who gave me the ultimatum of signing a new contract or packing my belongings.

The politics were never-ending in my final season and I was down for all sorts of reasons after that visit to Blackburn. We hadn't won in seven league games, including a defeat to second-from-bottom Coventry, and we had dropped from top of the table to sixth position. All the euphoria of thrashing Manchester United had vanished. We still had it in us to turn everything round but when I spoke to Freddie Fletcher it was the first time he expressed doubts about whether I could take Newcastle to the next stage. I appreciated his honesty.

The upshot was that he convened a meeting with Freddy Shepherd, Douglas Hall and Mark Corbridge, which gave me the chance to get a few things out in the open. I felt that the board had taken their focus off the team. I didn't feel as though the people at the top were pulling in the same direction as me any longer. It had left me feeling isolated and, if the board weren't happy with the way things were going, I would rather know. I was under pressure to sell players to recoup the Shearer money, and that was another issue when we had only a smallish squad anyway of twenty-one professionals. It had become a totally different organisation – suddenly the flotation had taken over everything. At times, I was doing well if I could even get hold of one of the directors. There were lots of things that didn't feel right.

Once I had shared my thoughts, I was asked to wait down-stairs, and when Freddie Fletcher appeared an hour later he told me they had listened to my views and maybe the best solution would be for me to have a dignified departure at the end of what we all hoped could still be a marvellous season. And he was right: it was best for everyone. 'Shake my hand,' Freddie said, 'wait until the end of the season and then go.'

When we went back upstairs to inform everyone, I suddenly felt reinvigorated, as if a weight had been lifted from my shoul-ders. We were still in Europe and had rediscovered our form in classic Newcastle style, walloping Tottenham 7–1 and Leeds 3–0. We still had an awful lot going for us. I now had four months to roll up my sleeves, go out on a high and put right what had gone wrong the season before.

Except two things then happened. First, the details of a confidential meeting were leaked to the *Sunday Mirror*. That was a betrayal, particularly as I hadn't even had the chance to speak to Terry about it at that stage. Secondly, it was obvious my position was an integral part of the flotation document and our new agreement was not ideal for a club that wanted to launch on the stock market in the strongest position possible.

The background to all this was that I had verbally agreed a ten-year contract the previous summer but never signed the paperwork. Then, on 7 January, I was told that the directors needed to see me urgently at Sir John's house. When I asked who was coming, I was told the chairman was in Spain but all the other board members would be there, plus the club's lawyer. The alarm bells immediately started ringing. Why did the board want a lawyer present? I could see the warning signs and went through to tell Jean that my time at Newcastle might be ending abruptly.

When the meeting started, Mark Corbidge came straight to the point, telling me I had to sign the contract that was on the table and guarantee that I would see it through or the only alternative was they found somebody else. I was being asked to forget the handshake with Freddie Fletcher, and it was very clear who was in charge of this discussion. Corbidge hardly knew me and I am not sure I would even recognise him now if we were stood at the same bar. Yet here was a man who had been at the club five minutes and he was doing all the talking. 'You either sign it or you go,' he said – as blunt as that.

I turned to Freddy Shepherd, Douglas Hall and Freddie Fletcher, and I could see they were not going to intervene. 'Maybe now you can see my point,' I said. 'He doesn't even know me. You do – and you know what my answer is going to be.'

Douglas did eventually find his voice. 'This is ridiculous,' he said. 'We want you to stay until the end of the season, and you want to stay, and yet we cannot do it.'

'You're not running the club now,' I said, nodding in Corbridge's direction. 'He is running your club. He's telling you what you have to do and you are all dashing round doing this for the float and doing that for the float. Where was he when we nearly got relegated?'

And that really was it. Everything seemed very cold and calculated, but Newcastle did have that hard-faced nature towards the end. It pained me, for starters, to see how many people were let down when the club started looking at the flotation. Sir John's plan until that point had been to set up a single, overarching organisation called the Newcastle Sporting Club and make it the 'Barcelona of the north'. He brought on board the basketball, ice hockey and rugby union clubs, but that went by the wayside once the football club took a different direction. A lot of promises were broken and a lot of people disappointed. It wasn't fun seeing people treated that way.

I felt the same after so many loyal Newcastle fans took out the £500 bonds that supposedly guaranteed ten-year season tickets. I had been asked to promote that offer – Terry and myself even bought a pair of season tickets each – because the club knew the fans trusted me. The brochure was headlined 'The next 10 years guaranteed', and the deal included having your name put on your seat. Newcastle later abandoned everything to earmark the relevant seats for corporate entertainment, and the fans who had splashed out their hard-earned cash were told they would have to move to a different part of the ground or pay through the nose to stay where they were. Season tickets that cost £383 or £498 were hiked to £1,350. It was a scandal. The prospectus Newcastle issued to potential investors highlighted the 'high-quality revenue streams' gained from the bond scheme and Platinum Club tickets at £3,000 per time. I would never have been involved if I had known what would happen. But that, again, felt symptomatic of the way the club had started to operate.

I can imagine Alan Shearer felt let down that the manager who had brought him to the club had gone within six months. I knew the fans, lacking the full story, would be horrified. But I had to go, and this time there was no call from the man who had rung me four years earlier to say we were the only two people who could save the club. The chairman clearly didn't think it necessary to get in touch and, though I will always hold Sir John in high esteem, he did have a habit of disappearing in difficult moments. Our houses on the Wynyard estate were only 300 yards apart but there was no contact for seven weeks until I decided it was getting ridiculous and rang his villa in Spain. I told him life was too short to fall out and I would always be grateful to him for giving me the opportunity to manage Newcastle. He sounded flustered. 'I've been meaning to ring you,' he said, 'but Mae and I have been so busy furnishing the villa.'

When I walked home, now an ex-Newcastle manager, Jean was shocked about how quickly it had all happened. Death does come quickly, I told her, especially in football. My concern was my family. Laura and Sarah were teenagers now. 'Get packed,' I told them. 'We're going on a holiday. We might be going skiing or it might be America.' We set off to Heathrow, driving through the night, and when we couldn't get four seats together on a flight to Florida, we jumped back in the car and headed for France via the Channel Tunnel.

We were on the M25 when the announcement was made at 11 a.m. and Radio 5 Live suddenly became Radio Keegan for the day. It sounded like uproar in Newcastle, and I was glad we had escaped the madness. My departure was the lead item on the news and all sorts of people were invited to have their say – supporters, players, journalists; even the prime minister, John Major, and the Labour leader, Tony Blair. 'People are saying that Kevin leaving is like the Queen dying,' one guy from the supporters' association said, 'but it's worse than that.'

The coverage was incredible, completely over the top – but when was it anything else with Newcastle United on Kevin

Keegan's watch? I felt sorry for the fans and I didn't leave New-castle with any real animosity. I had had some of the times of my life with that football club, but now it was time to take stock and recharge my batteries. I was still young, at forty-five, and who knew what the future might hold? Newcastle's statement had specified I would not be back in football for the foreseeable future, but I had no idea where they had got that from, or how they had the presumption to put that out. Those were their words, not mine.

15

LONDON LIFE

This time around, I didn't stay out of football too long. It was Fulham, in the old Third Division, who tempted me back and, knowing what I do now, I am being perfectly serious when I suggest I would have been happier staying at Craven Cottage rather than leaving within two seasons to become the new England manager.

The bottom line, of course, is that it is very hard for anybody to turn down the chance to manage England, so I can understand if people find it difficult to understand why I was so torn. Fulham were seventh from bottom of what is now League One when I joined the club in September 1997, eight months after my last game at Newcastle. I hadn't gone that low since my Scunthorpe days and, if we fast-forward to February 1999, when Glenn Hoddle's dismissal left the England job available, I was preparing for matches against the likes of York City, Notts County and Lincoln City. England were trying to qualify for Euro 2000, whereas my next engagement for Fulham was a trip to second-from-bottom Wycombe Wanderers.

That, however, is a rather simplistic view, and doesn't take into account the project we had under way at Fulham or the ambitions of the chairman, Mohamed Al Fayed, to create a dynamic and successful team with a five-year plan and a stack of money. I was never a football snob and dropping into the lower leagues didn't bother me if it was only a temporary measure. With Fulham, we had too much going for us to be down there

long. We were top of the league, on our way to a second promotion in three years, and it was only a matter of time before we
were a Premier League club.

That was why I was so reluctant to commit myself fully to
England when the Football Association made its first approach. I
didn't want to leave Craven Cottage and I made it very clear that
the only circumstances in which I would accept the job were in a
part-time capacity – meaning I carried on at Fulham but took
charge of England for their next four games. That would take
them into the summer and at that point, I said, they should bring
in somebody else.

I doubt the FA was happy with the idea, and I know many
journalists were outraged that England should have to suffer the
ignominy of a job-share. But I didn't budge. I was happy at
Fulham. I had a chairman whose ambition was to take the club
into the top division and we were the best team in our league
by a country mile. Not only that but I was convinced we could
make it back-to-back promotions the following year. We had a
confident team, money to spend, and we were going places. Of
course I dearly wanted to manage England, but I was in my forties and there was plenty of time for that opportunity to come
around again. It's hypothetical now, perhaps, but I'm pretty sure
if I had stayed at Fulham and the club had continued its upward
trajectory, it wouldn't have been the last time I was offered the
England job.

Initially, I joined Fulham as chief operating officer and when
I first took the call, completely out of the blue, from one of Mr
Fayed's representatives, inviting me to a meeting with the club's
billionaire owner, I had no idea a role at Craven Cottage was even
on the agenda. The message I received was that Mr Fayed had
heard about my Soccer Circus project, liked the idea of a football-
orientated theme park and wanted me to go down to London to
discuss the possibility of him being involved. That in itself was
tremendously exciting because, in my time since leaving Newcastle, I had thrown myself back into the idea of getting Soccer

Circus up and running. I had all sorts of plans and drawings, and I was convinced it could take off now I had the time to give it my full attention.

Instead it became apparent Mr Fayed wanted me to consider his own project. His view was that I could do for Fulham what I had done for Newcastle, even though, in my mind, the two clubs were chalk and cheese. I had no burning desire to get back into management. But it was when Mr Fayed suggested I could take a role higher up that I started to think seriously about whether this was the way forward. I could tell Mr Fayed was serious and I knew enough about his background, as the owner of Harrods, to know that when he did something, he did it properly.

After that, I am not sure we ever discussed Soccer Circus again. I was being offered the chance to have almost complete responsibility, bringing in the staff I wanted, finding and appointing a new manager, while operating with the kind of budget that would make Mr Fayed's ambitions, and mine, perfectly feasible. It was a different path for me but, once I started working it all out in my mind, I saw it as a terrific opportunity. I liked the idea of having success at a small, unpretentious club that had achieved little in the past. And when I thought about it, I had effectively been working as a chief operating officer a lot of the time at Newcastle anyway, heavily involved in transfer business and always in the thick of everything.

The 1997–8 season was already under way, and there was a huge amount of work to be done because the manager, Micky Adams, had already been moved out. Micky had led the team to promotion from the old Fourth Division the previous season. He was popular with the fans and if I had been appointed any earlier there was no way I would have let him go. Yet Mr Fayed wanted someone for an elevator-like progress through the leagues. It was my job to find that person and, in my view, the right man was Ray Wilkins.

I knew Ray from our time together in the England team. He was intelligent, he knew the game at the highest level and I had always got on well with him, which was important if we were going to be working together. He had had a tremendous career, including spells at Chelsea, Manchester United, Milan and Glasgow Rangers, and though his time as player-manager of Queens Park Rangers had not worked out, he ticked the boxes for me. Ray was only forty-one when we offered him the role – there was plenty of time for him to make a success of himself as a manager.

Ray had been doing a bit of coaching with Crystal Palace, but he wanted another stab at management and liked what we were proposing. He brought in Frank Sibley, an experienced coach, as his assistant, and it filled me with optimism when I saw their work on the practice ground. Ray was a fine coach and had a lovely way of interacting with players who were a long way behind him technically. Some managers, if they have been elite players, can get frustrated too quickly, but Ray never seemed too exasperated, even though, age aside, he was probably better than any footballer we had.

Unfortunately it also became clear in the following months that there were parts of the job in which Ray was not so strong. When I asked Ray in his first week if he had a list of players he wanted me to check out, now I was overseeing the club's transfer business, I assumed he would have lots of names in mind. He had been around the London football scene for years; he had been doing bits of television and radio, regularly watching matches, and I was sure we could turn that to our advantage. Instead, the message from Ray was that he wanted me to locate the players and didn't have a great deal to contribute on that front. I would have gone anywhere to watch a player he had recommended, but the only one was Leon McKenzie, who we took on loan from Crystal Palace. Ray then used him so sparingly that Alan Smith, the Palace manager, got the hump with us and the player went back to Selhurst Park.

We also had a number of players who were clearly not up to scratch for a club with our ambitions; they needed to be moved on and, in some cases, paid up. It was never easy telling a player he was no longer wanted, but it was part of the job and often kinder that way than stringing people along. As far as I was concerned, it was for the manager to break the news. But a week after saying he was going to do it, Ray came back to me and admitted he had not got round to it yet. The following week, I brought it up again and he said it had slipped his mind again. Ray could be very disorganised and forgetful. In the end, I had to ask if he wanted me to do it.

None of this was the end of the world. I had hired Ray, I was desperate for it to work and it disappointed me that I was blamed in some quarters when he left the club towards the end of his first season. It has been suggested that Ray was sacked because of an argument with me over team selection, and that he and I then had 'frosty relations'. But that's nonsense – and there was nothing of the sort. Ray was a good person. He died too early, aged sixty-one, and the turnout at his memorial service was a measure of his popularity within the sport.

We never had a row in all the time we were together, and the only occasion I can remember any issue between us was before a game at Gillingham when the team stayed overnight and Ray and his coaching staff went out for a Chinese meal, leaving the players behind, because he didn't think the food at the hotel was very good. I thought that was a bit off and told him that if the food was not good enough for the staff it shouldn't have been considered good enough for the players either.

Again, no big deal. I liked Ray and the only reason he lost his job was because Mr Fayed didn't think he was the right man and, I suspect, never did. The chairman had spent big and set the team a target of promotion, but Fulham had not taken the division by storm in the way we had hoped and, perhaps, expected. We lost our last three games to slip from third to sixth, only qualifying for the play-offs through goal difference, and that was when Mr Fayed summoned me to Harrods to give me his thoughts, in the bluntest possible way, about Ray's first season.

Those audiences with Mr Fayed could be surreal sometimes,

if you can picture us surrounded by the biggest collection of teddy bears you have ever seen. He had dozens of them in the boardroom, including rare antique ones from the 1930s and 1940s. I would pull up a seat around this huge table and the entire place was filled with cuddly toys. It always used to make me laugh that we were discussing important business with so many beady eyes on us – but not on this occasion. Mr Fayed was straight to the point. 'He has to go,' he said. 'Then you have to take over as manager because you appointed him.' He didn't even ask me to think about it.

Ray, a proud man, was bitterly disappointed, but I tried to be straight with him and we saw each other many times in the following years without any lingering issue. I think Ray knew, deep down, that we had underachieved that season, but it wasn't pleasant for him or me, and he found the timing particularly difficult, just before we played Grimsby in the play-offs. I didn't feel entirely comfortable assuming control in those circumstances, and if Mr Fayed was hoping it might spark a dramatic improvement from the players, it didn't work out that way. We drew 1–1 in the home leg, lost 1–0 at Blundell Park and the biggest spenders in the history of third-tier football had to make do with another season at the same level.

It was a tough first year. Fulham might have been situated in one of London's more affluent areas, amid fashionable wine bars and expensive Georgian properties, but it was an under-developed football club in an anachronistic ground and that, funnily enough, seemed to be exactly how a lot of their supporters liked it. The offices at Craven Cottage were virtually derelict and had to be rebuilt. There wasn't a proper club shop, and the players were training on a couple of pitches at an old BBC sports ground in Motspur Park, then taking their own kits and boots home to clean. The club had suffered years of financial issues before Mr Fayed took control, and there were all sorts of stories, from years gone by, about unpaid bills being stuffed behind the safe.

It wasn't a modern club, though that was actually part of the charm. Fulham didn't have a flat-pack Ikea-style stadium with four shiny stands and everything built to perfect symmetry. It was all a bit higgledy-piggledy and, in the nicest possible way, it took you back in time, with its old-school values, the river, the Grade II listed stand (the oldest in the country), the antique wooden seats and the red-brick frontage. Craven Cottage had a fabulous location on the bank of the Thames, just a short stroll from Putney Bridge tube station, and I am struggling to think of a more picturesque scene in English football. The only problem on the walk through Bishops Park, with pensioners sitting in the rose gardens and families throwing bread to the ducks, was that the kids playing football were invariably wearing the shirts of Chelsea, Arsenal and Manchester United.

The crowd at Fulham did not make the same noise as Newcastle's but, to be fair, very few places did. Yet I have lost count of the number of people who have told me over the years how much they loved visiting Craven Cottage. It felt more real, less overwhelming, than Tottenham or Arsenal. It was safer and more homely than Chelsea or West Ham and typified, perhaps, by the fact the tannoy announcer was the old disc jockey 'Diddy' David Hamilton, best known from the years at Radio One in the 1970s, when the people playing the records were almost as famous as the pop stars themselves. When Fulham did make it to the Premier League, he was removed from the role because of the club's desire for something fresher. There was such an outcry, including a 'Diddygate' campaign in the press, he had to be reinstated.

Even when we wanted to modernise Craven Cottage, we were stopped from doing so because of possibly the most 'Fulhamish' reason ever. The plans were all drawn up and everything looked ready to go until a team of conservationists discovered there was a rare species of snail inhabiting that part of the Thames. There had already been concerns raised because we had bats in the rafters of the Riverside Stand, but it was the discovery of the *Pseudotrichia rubiginosa*, otherwise known as the 'hairy German snail', that did more than anything to keep Craven Cottage as it was. I can't pretend my snail knowledge is too hot, but apparently it was one of the most endangered molluscs in England and we had to shelve our plans for that side of the ground. I have known a few hairy Germans in my time, but that one was a particularly difficult opponent.

A lot of Fulham fans were suspicious about Mr Fayed when he started talking about wanting to create one of the stronger teams in London. His decision to sack Micky Adams upset a lot of people, and many supporters were worried that his real motive for buying the club was to relocate the stadium and put housing on the land. Over time, the fans started to realise that Mr Fayed had a genuine affinity with the club. He would walk across the pitch before games, wearing a Fulham scarf and waving to the fans, and I think he saw it as a bit of escapism if you remember what was going on in his private life. The car crash in Paris that killed his son, Dodi, and Princess Diana, was only a few weeks before I joined Fulham. It cast a long shadow over the club, and Mr Fayed has stated many times that he suspected they were killed by the security services. He had all this going on in the background, and he was already a high-profile and often controversial figure because of the cash-for-questions affair, plus the furore about his attempts to qualify for a UK passport and the government blocking his application for British citizenship. It was difficult to imagine the kind of strain he must have been under, and the immeasurable grief as a father who had lost his son in the most appalling circumstances. Yet he was always there, every Saturday afternoon, when we had a game.

I liked him from the start. He always listened, he understood football more than people realised and he never tried to interfere with team matters. Yet it was an unusual set-up. In one game I was watching from the directors' box when someone in the next row suffered a heart attack and everyone jumped to their feet to see what was happening. In all the pandemonium, at least ten bodyguards in dark suits – I had assumed they must be directors or guests – appeared out of nowhere. They thought it was an assassination attempt and were rushing around to make sure Mr Fayed was not in danger. It was like a scene from a film and I came to realise that was just the norm – wherever Mr Fayed went, there was always security in the background. Nobody ever realised because they were experts at blending in.

Then there was the time, in a home match against Wigan Athletic, when we were close to sealing promotion as well as setting club and divisional records for accumulating 101 points and – this might surprise a few people – twenty-four clean sheets. By Christmas, we had already accrued fifty points. We knew we were going to win the league. My first season since taking over from Ray had gone brilliantly, and the only issue for me was to keep the lads motivated and make sure we did not allow complacency to creep in. I wanted to go up in a way that sent a message to the rest of English football.

I was about to start my team-talk along those lines, when Mr Fayed marched into the dressing room with a big grin on his face, followed by a tall, rake-thin guy who looked a bit like Michael Jackson. He was in a black hat, with a long black coat and mirrored sunglasses, and I did briefly wonder whether it was one of those lookalikes you could hire for the day. He smiled shyly. Then I heard him say 'hey' and it dawned on me that, crikey, this was the *real* Michael Jackson. Mr Fayed introduced everyone properly. 'Watch your arses, boys,' he announced.

It was pointless trying to continue with my team-talk – the players weren't listening to a word – so I walked the King of Pop through the corridors of the old Stevenage Road Stand to make him a cup of tea in the players' lounge. The walls were decorated with black and white photographs of games from the 1920s and, stopping to look at the huge crowds, our guest of honour seemed fascinated by the fashions of the time. 'That's cool,' he said, 'all these guys like the same hats as me.' Then it was time for him to walk across the pitch, holding up a Fulham-branded umbrella to shield him from the sunlight, while the crowd did a double-take and a couple of people on the old Putney End shouted for him to moonwalk. Not your average day, that one. But we did win 2–0 and that left us needing only one more victory to go up.

We ended up winning the league by fourteen points and Mr Fayed put on a banquet at Harrods for everyone to celebrate. We also knocked two Premier League sides out of the FA Cup, beating Southampton 1–0 after a replay and winning 2–0 at Aston Villa in the fourth round. Manchester United, the eventual winners, knocked us out in the fifth round, but there was only one goal in it – scored by Andy Cole – and that was the team Alex Ferguson led to the Premier League title and the European Cup that season. We held our own against the best side in Europe, with 8,500 Fulham fans in the crowd, and when we left Old Trafford I was even more convinced we could win promotion the following season, too.

I was not surprised at our success, because the bottom line was that we had out-spent everyone in our division over the previous two seasons. Yes, it was still an achievement to win promotion by such a clear margin, but it would have been dreadfully disappointing if we hadn't gone up. Ray had been sacked the previous year for not managing it, and I would have deserved the same if we had been stuck in that division any longer.

To put it into context, Fulham set a new transfer record for that level of the game when Chris Coleman arrived from Blackburn Rovers for £2.2 million. We had already smashed our transfer record by signing Ian Selley from Arsenal for £500,000. Ian broke his leg after only three games – I heard the snap from the halfway line – and Mr Fayed had reservations at first about Coleman because the player had needed surgery on a ruptured Achilles. In the end, though, Mr Fayed sanctioned the kind of deal that was virtually unheard of in those days. Coleman was so impressed by our ambitions that he dropped down two divisions to join us.

That gave me someone at the back with a bit of stature. Paul Bracewell, who had been one of my first signings at Newcastle, had already joined us from Sunderland. Paul Peschisolido, who signed for £1.1 million from West Brom, gave our attack the speed and directness I wanted, and we also spent £700,000 on the goalkeeper Maik Taylor from Southampton, plus £600,000 on Paul Trollope from Derby County and the same again for Steve Finnan, who arrived from Notts County and must rank as one of my greatest all-time signings, with a splendid career ahead of him. Around that, we also brought in the likes of Barry Hayles, Rufus Brevett and Geoff Horsfield plus, of course, we still had some of the lads we inherited – in particular Simon Morgan, who proved to me he was far too valuable to discard.

Philippe Albert signed on loan from Newcastle, which was a great coup, and Peter Beardsley also joined us, at the age of thirty-seven. Peter was new to London when we signed him on loan from Bolton Wanderers. I lent him my car one afternoon to pop out for a sandwich, but he wasn't used to driving in the narrow streets around Craven Cottage, with the cars tightly parked on both sides. When he came back he looked a bit embarrassed and asked if I wanted the good news first or the bad news. I asked him for the good news. 'It was a lovely sandwich, gaffer,' he said. The bad news? 'Is there a repairs garage round here?' I looked at my car, and the wing mirror was dangling off.

When I arrived at Fulham the supporters were still harking back to Johnny Haynes and George Cohen or the times, in the 1970s, when Bobby Moore, George Best and Rodney Marsh brought some stardust to the club. I saw it as my job to bring the club some modern-day heroes, just like I had done at Newcastle. I wanted to see how far a club of that size could go, and it was incredibly difficult to give up that challenge when the chance arrived to take the England job. Ultimately, though, it was very difficult to say no, and keep saying no, when England came calling. So it was another manager, Jean Tigana, who led Fulham into the Premier League once my part-time role with England became a full-time one. The critics had laughed at Mr Fayed when he said he wanted Fulham in the top division within five years. He did it in four, and he was still there when the club reached the 2010 Europa League final at, of all places, Hamburg's Volksparkstadion. I have never been the type to dwell too much on what might have been but, as I have said, there were times when I wished things had worked out differently. I would have liked to experience those kind of adventures with Fulham for myself.

As it was, the England job became too difficult to resist. The morale of the national team was depressingly low after Glenn Hoddle's departure, and I was constantly being told I was the leading candidate from a shortlist of one. All the time, there was the pressure from the media that it was wrong to have a part-time England manager, and the bandwagon started rolling even more forcefully after my first match of the job-share – a Euro 2000 qualifier against Poland. England badly needed to win to get their qualifying campaign back on track and it ended 3–1, with Paul Scholes scoring a hat-trick. I had given Scholes some shrewd, albeit recycled, advice. 'Go out there,' I said, 'and drop some grenades.'

Mr Fayed declared I could be his 'gift to the nation' if I wanted to go. That took me by surprise because I had thought he was totally against losing me. The FA had been chasing me from the start and, though I was not going to dance to the tune of the press, the Poland game had given me a taste of it. The crowd at Wembley had given me a marvellous ovation. The team rose to the challenge and, though I didn't enjoy my time overall with England, there was no doubt that when things did go well it could be exhilarating.

I knew I was on to a good thing at Craven Cottage but, patriot that I was, I was seduced by the idea that I could succeed where others had failed with my national team. My mind was filled with exciting thoughts about what it would be like to go to Euro 2000 and actually win the damn thing – or, even better, the World Cup in Japan and South Korea two years later.

It turned out I was kidding myself, but everyone is entitled to their dreams. I had plenty, and it was not until later, when reality hit home, that I was reminded why so many other England managers had described the job as a poisoned chalice. By then, however, I had passed over my ambitions with the small, homely club from the banks of the Thames. My time with Fulham was over and I was on to my next adventure, blissfully unaware of the struggles I was going to encounter. On 14 May 1999, I became England manager with no strings.

16

THE POISONED CHALICE

I can never hold anyone other than myself responsible for my shortcomings in the role of England manager – and I am certainly not going to start looking for excuses now – but it is a good job the sport, as a whole, has never had its hands tied by the bizarre restrictions that were imposed on me when I signed my contract with the Football Association.

I had fully expected I would be allowed to bring in my own people, so it was certainly an eye-opener when my first request – that Arthur Cox should be installed as my full-time number two – was rejected on the grounds he was too old.

Too old? Howard Wilkinson, the FA's technical director, explained they did not want anyone over the age of sixty. Yet if the same rules had been in place when Alex Ferguson was managing Manchester United, the most successful manager in the business would have been ushered out of Old Trafford with seven Premier League titles rather than thirteen, and missed out on twelve major honours, including a second European Cup. Bobby Robson would never have been allowed to manage Newcastle a second time. Vicente del Bosque would have been finished in management ten years before he won the World Cup with Spain, and the miracle of Leicester City's league championship would never have happened because of some brainbox's decision that Claudio Ranieri, at the age of sixty-four, was past it. I had never heard such a load of cobblers in my entire life.

As if that wasn't absurd enough, Arthur was actually fifty-nine when I was appointed full-time in May 1999 and didn't turn sixty until later that year. Howard himself stayed in football until well into his sixties. As for the average age of the gentlemen who made up the FA committee, let's just say most of them had reached the point of life where it takes longer to rest than it does to get tired. Howard was an experienced football man, and I thought he would understand I had a valid point. Plainly, I mis-judged the man. He refused to budge, sticking to his line that it was against the FA's rules until, funnily enough, things turned sour for me and everything changed to suit Sven-Göran Eriksson, the next manager. Sven also wanted to bring in his own number two and the man he identified was Tord Grip. How old was Tord Grip? Sixty-two.

I say this with a smile, but I wish I had been stronger at the time. I should have told Howard that I couldn't be expected to do the job properly if I wasn't allowed to bring in my own staff. The FA did allow me to appoint Derek Fazackerley, who was a fine coach and had been a trusted colleague at Newcastle. Yet the best I could get for Arthur was a part-time deal, and that left me won-dering from day one whether I had the FA's full support. Arthur was still squeezing every drop out of footballers in the Premier League until he was nearly seventy and, as far as I know, Howard never sought to impose any age restrictions when he became chairman of the League Managers' Association.

Nothing can be done about it now, of course, and when it comes to analysing my time as England manager, let me reiterate that I will always look in the mirror first. The buck stopped with me. That's perfectly understood, believe me – but I'm not seeking excuses when I say that working for the FA confirmed my worst suspicions about the people at the top of the sport.

My other request was to bring in a couple of people to scout the opposition teams and help me monitor the form of our own players. I mentioned this in my first meeting, but the official in charge of the scouting department cut me off mid-sentence to tell me the set-up was fine as it was. He was obviously put out by what I was suggesting and his entire tone was, 'Kevin, we'll tell you which people are going to which games, not the other way around.' Again, I let it go. But I was taken aback by his brusque manner and I asked Howard afterwards what he had made of it. 'Oh, don't worry about him,' came the reply, 'he's getting near his pension now.'

That, in a nutshell, was the FA. There were some good people working hard behind the scenes who wanted to move the organisation into the twenty-first century. Otherwise, it was an old boys' network that was completely set in its ways and appeared to be stuck in a time warp.

Some of the committee members seemed to regard their roles, with all the perks of travelling round the world in five-star luxury, as honorary positions. At FA meetings they reminded me of the people you might find running the seniors' competition at your local golf club. The septuagenarians in their FA blazers would stay in their expensive hotels, have a few drinks on expenses and get up for their full English breakfasts. A taxi would take them to FA headquarters in Lancaster Gate. Then, partway through a mid-morning meeting, it was quite common to see them shuffling out, explaining they had to catch a train home. We might be only halfway through the agenda but their day was done.

Taking the England job, I was quickly discovering, was like entering a jungle. My first press conference was at the London Metropole Hotel and, as far as I was concerned, my cross-examination had been a success. Everyone seemed happy. I smiled my way through the questions, talked in glowing terms about the players and shook the hands of the journalists who I had not worked with before. The press had been in overdrive to declare me as the saviour of English football and I didn't get the sense anyone was unhappy about my appointment. More fool me. At the end of the press conference, Monte Fresco, who was probably the most famous sports photographer in the country, asked if we could have a word in private. Monte, who had principles, wanted to let me know about a conversation he had eavesdropped. 'I'm not going to tell you who it was,' he said, 'but I've just overheard two journalists talking and the tone of it was, "Let's get this bastard out as soon as we can."'

I had known Monte a long time, I trusted him, and I knew he would not tell me something of that nature unless it was true. I was grateful for the heads-up but it saddened me that there were journalists with their knives out for me before a ball had even been kicked. I had always enjoyed talking to journalists and, as the football writers in the north-east can testify, I bent over backwards at times to accommodate them. Some of the nicest guys I've met in football have been pressmen. With England, however, there was a movement against me from day one and purely, I suspect, because there were four or five of the more influential football journalists – 'the Number Ones', as they called themselves – who realised they weren't going to get any inside info or preferential treatment as long as I was in charge.

When Terry Venables had been manager, he had taken Fleet Street's big hitters under his wing, adopting the view that if he kept the main guys happy it didn't really matter what appeared in the less popular newspapers. It was clever on Terry's part, and he used that relationship to his advantage. Terry's record with England was stronger than most, including that memorable ride to the Euro '96 semi-finals, but if he did run into difficulties he knew he could rely on backing from his newspaper allies. They supported him, they stuck by him and they felt an affinity with him because he gave them the inside track. He looked after them; they looked after him.

A lot of managers – Don Revie, for one – have played that game, but it wasn't a tactic I favoured. Even if an old friend such as Bob Cass, a journalist I had known for years, rang for a 'steer' I would politely remind him I didn't operate that way. Bob, God rest his soul, would know even before he picked up the phone it wasn't my style. He would still have a go but it was never going to happen. I didn't go off-the-record. I didn't mark people's cards and I didn't think I should break that policy just because I had taken the role of England manager.

As a consequence, I used to walk into every England press conference knowing I had enemies whose objective, behind the smiles and superficial niceties, was to get rid of me. Some managers might have felt pressured into adapting, purely to suit the journalists, but I never considered changing my principles. My view was that I would live or die by the team's results. And that, ultimately, is why I lasted only eighteen months. The results finished me, not the newspapers. But I'm sure some of Fleet Street's finest enjoyed dancing on my grave. Not everyone, but a good few.

In the end, I had stopped enjoying the job. In fact, that began a long time before I set off on the lonely, unforgiving walk from the England dugout to the tunnel at the old Wembley, listening to the vitriol of the supporters after losing 1–0 to Germany in our first qualifying match for the 2002 World Cup. As soon as I started walking through the grey drizzle, I knew that when I reached the dressing room it would be to tell the players I was finished. I was pained by the deteriorating results, by the way I had fallen short as a manager on the international stage, and by my inability to get the team playing as I wanted. As difficult as it was to accept, the job had been beyond me, and when I announced I was resigning I didn't duck the truth. 'I'm blaming nobody but myself,' I said. 'I wasn't good enough. I don't feel I can find that little bit extra you need at this level to find a winning formula.'

I gave it my best shot. I worked hard and tried my best to bang the drum for the English game. But I had also come to realise it wasn't the job it was cracked up to be. I didn't enjoy dealing with the FA. I didn't like the way I had so little time with the players. I didn't like the long, frustrating periods between games when the job could feel soulless and it wasn't easy knowing how to fill my time, sometimes bored rigid. I didn't like all sorts of things. I was better suited to being a club manager where I could have daily interaction with my players and time to work on things properly. As great an honour as it was, England didn't suit my style of management.

Although I never said it so bluntly at the time, there was such a dearth of English players that there were some weekends when I would go to watch a Premier League match and take my seat thinking, *What am I even doing here?* Let me give you the example of Arsenal's game against Chelsea at Highbury on 6 May 2000 and a meeting between the second- and fifth-placed sides in the Premier League. Aimé Jacquet was two seats along from me on the same row. We were preparing to name our squads for Euro 2000 and can you imagine how demoralising it was to tot up the number of Englishmen on the pitch and realise the manager of France had more players out there than me?

Of the twenty-two players, six were English. Four were in Arsenal's colours: David Seaman, Lee Dixon, Tony Adams and Ray Parlour. Dennis Wise and Jody Morris were playing for Chelsea, and when the game kicked off I was running through a list of questions in my head. Did I need to watch David Seaman to know he was England's first-choice goalkeeper? No. Was I going to learn anything about Tony Adams I didn't already know? Probably not. Was there anybody else I should be watching closely? Not really.

Then I looked across to Aimé Jacquet and wondered if he had made the same calculation. Patrick Vieira, Emmanuel Petit, Gilles Grimandi and Thierry Henry were all in Arsenal's starting line-up. Franck Leboeuf, Marcel Desailly and Bernard Lambourde were playing for Chelsea, and Didier Deschamps came on as a substitute for the last half an hour. Arsenal won 2–1, with Henry scoring twice, and as I set off home I asked myself what I had learned. Not a great deal, was the answer.

I've picked out one match but there were many others, and the frustration I experienced at Highbury that day was a regular theme when I was watching some of the leading Premier League teams, working out which games to attend and trying to second-guess how many English players might be involved. It was on my watch, for instance, that Gianluca Vialli, then the Chelsea manager, did something that nobody else had done in 111 years of league football, by putting out a side that didn't contain a single Englishman. Other clubs were heading the same way, and when I looked down the fixture list it wasn't easy knowing where to go on weekends. I used to set off to some places and I'd be thinking, *Oh my God, I'm going to watch one player here.*

Even when I went to see Manchester United, where there was David Beckham, the Neville brothers, Paul Scholes and Nicky Butt, it could still feel unsatisfactory. 'Is this going to be another wasted trip?' I'd ask myself on the drive to Old Trafford. 'Do I know these players already? Yes. Do I need to see how well they play, good, bad or indifferent, to know I'm going to pick them anyway?'

I would still go, because everyone expected the England manager to attend those games and, yes, sometimes there were little things I could pick up. Yet there were many occasions when it felt like a complete waste of time. I was going to some games for appearances' sake, and when I looked at the players on the pitch there wasn't any obvious reason why I was there. Many times I had the same thought that I wasn't going to learn anything I didn't already know. So what was the point of being there?

What you quickly come to learn with England is that it is only a great job if you have the right players. I inherited some brilliant old pros at a time, unfortunately, when many of them were coming to the end of their international careers. Six of my players in a squad of twenty-two for Euro 2000 were aged thirty-two or above. If I could have turned the clock back three or four years, they would have been more than good enough. We had the Manchester United lads, who were definitely good enough, but some of our older players were only just hanging in there and, though we had younger ones coming through, they weren't quite ready. I gave the teenage Steven Gerrard his debut, along with Frank Lampard and Gareth Barry, but at that stage they had not developed into the players we saw in later years. It was a question of timing and, at that moment, it just wasn't right.

We scraped into Euro 2000, lucky to get past Scotland in a two-legged play-off, and it was startling to see how quickly we lost our way in our first game against Portugal. After eighteen minutes, we had a 2–0 lead through Paul Scholes and Steve McManaman. But then we collapsed. Luís Figo and João Pinto made it 2–2 before half-time. Nuno Gomes completed the Portuguese recovery after the interval and, though we still had plenty of time to save ourselves, we didn't have the wit or creativity to find a way back. Portugal played football as I liked to see it played. As a neutral it was fantastic. Unfortunately, I wasn't a neutral.

We beat Germany in our next game, courtesy of a second-half header from Alan Shearer. That result made us feel a lot better, even if it was against the poorest German side for many years. We didn't play brilliantly but we were the better side, and that set up our final group game against Romania, when we came from behind to lead 2–1 at half-time and then threw it away again in the second half. A draw would have been enough to put us into the quarter-finals but, at 2–2, Phil Neville gave away the decisive penalty. It was the eighty-ninth minute, Shearer's last game in an England shirt, and we were on our way home. All that optimism, all those dreams – and it was all over in eight days.

The press was merciless, of course. I tried not to take the abuse personally but it wasn't easy shutting it all out. I hoped my tormentors might stop to consider whether it was necessary to add such venom to their words. I wondered if they ever felt any remorse about their poison-pen attacks. But they never did. It was relentless, and the pressmen never seemed short of telephone numbers when it came to former players who could weigh in with their own dismissive remarks.

Maybe, in hindsight, it would have been better if I had resigned after Euro 2000. I did consider it but, once I started thinking about the next assignment, qualifying for the 2002

World Cup, I still had the appetite to do the job. Despite everything, it was still an incredible honour to be in that position and I never lost sight of that fact. I wanted to have another go, reach another major tournament and make sure we did better next time. I was still backing myself. Yet the minute that game against Germany ended – the last match at the old Wembley – I knew that was it for me.

If I could turn back the clock to my first game in charge, we were cheered off the pitch after a 3–1 win against Poland and the walk to the tunnel was euphoric. Eighteen months on, the abuse was incredible. I was empty. I didn't feel wanted any more and, for the first time in my managerial career, I felt I wasn't up to the job. I had been built up as the populist hero because of the way I wanted football to be played. But I had created that football at Newcastle by finding pieces of a jigsaw, buying players and piecing it all together. With England, that wasn't possible.

The crowd was vicious and, as I entered the dressing room, I already knew it would be the last time I addressed the players. Some of the lads – Tony Adams and a couple of others – tried to talk me out of it. If they had known me better they would have understood it wasn't negotiable. 'I can't go on like this,' I told them. 'I'm not getting the results. I want to thank you for what you've done but I'm done now.' It wasn't a long conversation.

David Davies, the FA's executive director, came in and we went into the room, adjacent to the changing area, where there was the bath and the toilets. The press loved that: 'Keegan quits in toilets!' But where else could we go? The corridor outside was crawling with television reporters. The dressing room was full of wrought, emotional players and we needed somewhere quiet. I told David I couldn't face it any more. I knew I would be branded a quitter. I knew it would be a permanent regret and that all kinds of hell would be unleashed in the press, but I didn't see any point carrying on. I was honest. 'It's a step too far for me,' I said. And that was it. Jean drove me home and Howard Wilkinson was put in charge for our next qualifier.

I walked away with the worst win percentage of any England manager – eighteen games with seven victories, seven draws and four defeats – but, in my defence, those numbers ignore the fact I deliberately chose the toughest opposition available for our friendlies. Argentina and Brazil were two of the games I picked. France was another one, in my penultimate game, when Michael Owen's late equaliser got us a draw against the European and world champions. Maybe if I had picked easier opponents, my win ratio would have been much better. Instead, I didn't see any advantage in meaningless friendlies when the alternative was taking on elite teams who would provide us with a proper challenge. We had only one 'knock-over', against Malta, but that tends to be forgotten when people look back at that era – along with the fact, for all the raw disappointment of Euro 2000, we were sixty seconds away from the quarter-finals.

One thing I should clarify is that I didn't have any problems with Alex Ferguson, or any of the other Premier League bosses, and there were none of the club-or-country issues that can make the job of England manager even more complicated. Despite what everyone thinks about Fergie and myself, I can't recall one phone call from him complaining about anything to do with his players. They always turned up and Paul Scholes, in particular, played extremely well for me.

As difficult as I found the FA sometimes, I also enjoyed my dealings with Adam Crozier when he came in as chief executive, and Michelle Farrer, who worked with a succession of England managers and later became director of team operations. It was just a pity not everyone was so helpful. I tried a couple of times to persuade the relevant people to change their minds about Arthur Cox but it never got me anywhere.

As for the media, it wasn't fun when some of the more influential writers wanted me to turn on a spit of public ridicule. Equally, it wasn't a surprise. I wasn't the first to suffer that way, I won't be the last, and at least I had been tipped off that I would have to be on my guard during press conferences. The best analogy

I could make was that it was like being a cricketer standing at the wicket with a bat in my hands and waiting to face a new over. There were six balls coming my way. The first was going to be gently tossed up – 'How did training go today?' – and I could smash it out of the ground. The second was another easy one – 'Any injury updates, Kevin?' – and again I could deal with it, no problem. But now I had been warmed up the next question would be a little bit harder. In the next over, I knew a googly would be coming and a couple of bouncers whizzing past my head.

One memory is of a red-top journalist, a regular on the England beat, being taken aback when he asked for an interview and I pointed out that it was only a few weeks earlier that he had savaged me in print. I didn't like the smile-and-stab culture. For that, I was portrayed as 'sad, sullen, spoilt and suspicious'. I was vilified and lampooned as a tactical no-hoper. Then the people crucifying me would expect me to be all sweetness and light the next time I saw them.

Nor did it help that on the night before the Germany game my team selection was leaked to the press. That wasn't a nice feeling, knowing someone inside the camp had let it out, and I hope whoever was responsible felt proud of themselves. Those kinds of details should be sacrosanct, but someone blurted it to the newspapers and that gave our opponents the advantage of knowing precisely how we were going to line up.

I suppose that game will always be remembered for my decision to play Gareth Southgate in midfield and, sure enough, the newspapers could barely disguise their scorn when they found out. What these so-called experts ignored was that Southgate actually began his career at Crystal Palace as a midfielder. He had captained the club in that role and, though he later made his reputation as a centre-half, I didn't think it was beyond him to switch to a position he had already filled with distinction.

The idea that it was the first time he had ever occupied a holding midfield role was a complete nonsense, and more a reflection of the journalists' knowledge than mine. I wanted some experience for the position – the idea being that Southgate could stick close to Mehmet Scholl – and I still find it difficult to understand the contrived fuss that selection caused. It wasn't Southgate's fault that a long-distance free kick from Dietmar Hamann skidded past David Seaman for the only goal of the match. Yet, as always with England, the whole thing was blown up to ridiculous proportions.

The job was difficult enough without having to deal with the unrealistic expectations. I always wanted to think positively – I genuinely thought we could win Euro 2000 – but I never lost sight of reality or underestimated our opponents. I remember being really upset with Ray Stubbs after we drew 0–0 against Poland in Warsaw and he went on the BBC to talk about it being a terrible result. I have worked with Ray. He was a fine broadcaster and I enjoyed his company, but that felt typical of the media's attitude that we should automatically win every match. If we ever dared to lose we were slaughtered. Then if we won the next game we were back to being world-beaters again and lauded as 'England's bravehearts'. I would read the newspapers thinking, *Blow me, we weren't that good, were we?* Everything was black or white, never grey.

What I could not tolerate was the story that appeared on the front page of the *News of the World* a few weeks after my resignation, carrying the headline 'Keegan's £40,000 Bet Shame' and alleging that I had instigated high-stakes betting nights with my players during Euro 2000. It was a pack of lies, and so damaging I felt compelled to take legal action, suing for libel and eventually winning damages and a public apology. It took a long time to come to court, with all the stresses that inevitably incurred, but there are certain times in life when you cannot let people walk all over you, and that was one for me. I simply couldn't accept such a distorted version of events.

As anyone who has been involved with England can testify, there have always been card games in that environment. It was like that when I was an England player and it was still the same culture when I went back as manager almost twenty years later. If you speak to any of Alf Ramsey's players from 1966, they will all say the same. It was something I inherited, in line with a succession of England managers. The money was nothing the players couldn't afford and nowhere near the fanciful amounts that particular tabloid wanted its readers to believe.

Indeed, the only person who lost a few quid was the manager. We used to have race nights using tapes of obscure races from America and Hong Kong. The tapes would be sealed and the idea was to place bets without anybody knowing in advance who had won. I got cleaned out one night when I was acting as the bookmaker, and it was only a few years ago that I discovered the true story behind my losses. Apparently the players had carefully opened the tape, found out the winners and then expertly sealed it back together. To avoid suspicion, they didn't pile in with big bets when it came to the first couple of races. And muggins here didn't have a clue until I found out Ray Parlour was triumphantly telling the story on the after-dinner circuit. It was a proper sting – clever, I have to say.

Those nights were a bit of fun and I wouldn't want to portray my time as England manager as one long struggle against adversity. Overall, though, how can I look back at that period of my life with anything but regret and disappointment? I found it very difficult, and I sympathise with anyone who takes the job nowadays. Arsenal versus Chelsea? These days you might be lucky to find three or four English players in the starting line-ups. How many in a Manchester derby? Four or five, perhaps? Watford versus West Ham? Maybe even fewer. There are only a sprinkling of English players left in the Premier League and the frustration is compounded by how little time you get with them once it comes to the international fixtures.

Imagine what it feels like, as England manager, if you have a game coming up on a Wednesday night and when the players arrive on the Saturday evening, after playing for their club sides, there might be only half the squad reporting for duty. The rest are playing on the Sunday because television usually wants the big games, and if those are 4 p.m. kick-offs then you might be getting ready for bed by the time they arrive last thing at night. You see them for the first time on Monday morning, and you can't do much in training because so many players are recovering from the previous day. It's Tuesday before you can all train together properly, and how much preparation can you get through when the game is the next day? After games, there is no time to work on anything because the players immediately go back to their clubs. Then it might be three or four months before you see them again. You are like ships passing in the night, and then it is the weekend and, once again, you know that whatever game you attend you might be wondering, an hour in, whether it was a wasted trip.

For a short while in the summer of 2018, with Gareth Southgate now managing the team, the World Cup opened up with all sorts of exciting possibilities. England made it to the semi-finals before losing to Croatia and maybe it wasn't a coincidence that the improved performances coincided with the press being more supportive than any other time I can remember.

Sadly, I didn't have that luxury. It was tough. I really thought it would work but it didn't take long to see the reality. I really thought we could build something but, leaving Wembley for the final time, I just wanted to get away for a bit, clear my thoughts and avoid the inevitable savaging on the back pages. I had failed and it wasn't a nice feeling. But I knew it was the right decision to quit and, deep down, there was a measure of relief as well. It had reached the point, in my heart of hearts, where I didn't think England would qualify for the World Cup unless there was a change of manager. I needed a break and then I wanted to get back into club management, where I could start enjoying my work again.

17

BLUE MOON

When Manchester City offered me the opportunity to return to football management six months after I had given up the England job, I knew even before I walked through the doors of Maine Road that there were players within the dressing room who needed to be made aware that bending the elbow, contrary to what they appeared to believe, was not actually a legitimate form of exercise.

We were moving into an age when most sensible players understood the importance of taking care of themselves. Unfortunately for City, there was still a hard-drinking clique at the club, who seemed intent on living in the era when that kind of behaviour was considered the norm. Everyone in football knew their reputation, and the chairman, David Bernstein, brought it up on the first occasion I spoke to him about the job. There were players drinking to excess, showing a lack of respect to their profession and failing to understand basic responsible conduct, and it was my job to put a stop to it.

It was a major problem, and in my first team meeting I knew it had to be confronted straight away. I told the players I was aware of what was going on, that I knew who was involved and that the only way the club could hope to get back into the Premier League would be if things changed. It was going to be different on my watch, I said, so they could either fall in line or get drunk on the wages of another team.

It needed decisive action, and my first move was to sacrifice one of the players, Mark Kennedy, whose name kept cropping up as a repeat offender. That wasn't straightforward because Mark was technically the best player we had. But this wasn't anything to do with his ability; it was because I wanted to break up the gang of boozers and give them something to think about. I didn't like losing a player of that quality, but Mark was someone I could get decent money for – Wolves were offering £2 million – and I wanted to send a strong message to the other players that, 'Crikey, if he can get rid of him, we'd better take this guy seriously.' It put down a marker.

At first, though, the message didn't seem to get through. We finished training one day in pre-season – one of my first days working with the players – and I was house-hunting in Hale, to the south of Manchester. I had a look at some apartments with the property developer and then we decided we should go for lunch to discuss my options. I had never been to Hale in my life, but we had the choice of at least a dozen restaurants in the centre of the village. The one we chose was called Up & Down, and the same could be said of my heart-rate when I walked through the door to find a group of my players with a bottle of champagne at their table. Steve Howey was one, with Jeff Whitley and a couple of others. The usual suspects, from what I had been briefed. All looking guilty as hell.

I walked to the bar rather than creating a scene, chose a table on the other side of the restaurant and, without acknowledging the players, sent over another round of drinks with the barman, purely to make a point. I was livid. We had just started pre-season training, they were meant to be working on their fitness, and we had already had a long discussion in which I made it clear there would be serious problems if they didn't abide by a new code of professionalism. They weren't drunk but they were on the way. We had barely finished training and it just underlined what I already knew. *These lads don't care*, I thought. In my mind I was already thinking I had to get rid of them.

Steve Howey was panicking. 'I've not been drinking, boss,

honestly,' he started babbling as I made my way out. Steve knew me better than the others because of our time together at Newcastle, and he understood the importance I placed on discipline.

'We'll talk about it tomorrow,' was all I said.

The next day I hauled them in and Steve had enough common sense to hold up his hands, accept he was out of order and apologise straight away. I read them all the riot act. I told them their attitudes had to change and that they had better listen this time, otherwise they would be out the door.

Yet it would be an exaggeration to say the penny dropped straight away. Nicky Weaver was a crowd favourite at City, but another one whose career in Manchester featured too many lost nights. One story that got back to the club was of Nicky, worse for wear, walking into a kebab shop, going straight to the front of the queue and upsetting so many people that one of the other customers took a swing at him. Another time, we got a letter from one supporter telling us that Nicky had been seen, blotto again, throwing up into a dustbin in Cheadle High Street after watching an England game in one of the pubs.

Jeff Whitley, who has since admitted having alcohol issues, did not last long beyond my first season, and it took over a year before Richard Dunne, another serial offender, started to heed all the lectures and warnings. Dunne ended up proving me wrong, just at the point when it seemed I had no choice but to cut him free. It was only when I threatened to sack him that he agreed to get professional help and, though it was a close call, I'm glad I persevered with him. But he certainly pushed his luck.

The culture of the club had to change, but one of the problems was the lack of leadership in the dressing room. In a successful club, the senior players tended to keep everyone in line, not the manager. At Liverpool, Tommy Smith, Ian Callaghan and Emlyn Hughes would intervene if anyone needed telling. At Newcastle, we had Brian Kilcline. I didn't see anyone for that role at Manchester City, though. The closest was Andy Morrison, who had a reputation for being a bit wild, but I couldn't get him in the team. Nobody else was willing to step up to the plate and I needed someone who could lead by example.

That was why I made Stuart Pearce one of my first signings. I needed a player who would sort out the dressing room and Pearce, coming to the end of a long and distinguished career, was perfect for the role. We signed him on a free transfer from West Ham and, even at the age of thirty-nine, he was still a formidable player. 'You see him?' I would say to the others. 'That guy broke his leg playing for his last club and tried to run it off. That's commitment, that's dedication. Remember that – and don't come crying to me the next time you have a grazed knee.'

His influence was immense and, after all the traumas that accompanied my time in charge of the England team, it was re-assuring to remind myself that my talents were better suited to club football. Not that I had ever properly doubted myself, or allowed myself to wallow in self-pity. England had been a difficult and, ultimately, chastening experience, but was I going to let it dominate my life for ever? It was done, there was nothing I could do to put it right, and I wasn't embittered by the experience. I had to move on. City had given me the opportunity to start enjoying football again and I was going to take it.

We didn't too badly either. When we won promotion in my first season it was as champions of the First Division (now the Championship) and playing with a style to make supporters quicken their step on the walk to the stadium. We finished ten points clear. Our goals tally, 108, was the joint highest in City's history, equalling a record from 1927. The team won thirty-one games and accumulated ninety-nine points, setting two more club records, and Shaun Goater was the first City player since Franny Lee in 1972 to score more than thirty times in a season. England was somebody else's problem now. I was happy to leave Sven-Göran Eriksson to it – and good luck to him.

To begin with, City were the classic Jekyll and Hyde team. On our good days we were capable of scoring goals against anyone. On the bad days, however, we had a fragile mentality, and there were too many players who caved in if our opponents got on top. The team I inherited from Joe Royle had been relegated from the Premier League in eighteenth position, eight points adrift of safety, and shipped four goals or more on six different occasions. Stuart Pearce would never disappear when the pressure was rising dangerously close to intolerable. The others, I wasn't so sure about.

It certainly wasn't easy knowing what to make of a team that, in one run of games, lost 4–3 at Coventry, won 6–2 at Sheffield Wednesday, beat Walsall 3–0 at Maine Road and then crashed 4–0 to Wimbledon in our next home game. We also lost 4–0 at West Bromwich Albion during my first few months. Afterwards I sat on the coach with Arthur Cox, gloomy as hell, and told him the job might be harder than I had envisaged. My new employers had taken the sensible view, unlike the FA, that Arthur's vast experience and knowledge could be a huge asset. I was glad to have him alongside me because every manager needs the right people around him. And on that occasion I was very down. 'We are going to struggle even to finish in the top six with this lot,' I said.

After that, however, everything started to click. We played some beautiful football and it was no coincidence that our improvement could be traced back to the arrival of the player I would nominate, without a moment's hesitation, as the best signing of all my years in management.

Ali Benarbia was certainly the most technically gifted player I ever managed. He was also the luckiest signing I ever made because, the truth was, I had never even heard of him when his agent, Willie McKay, rang out of the blue to say he was picking up a player from Manchester airport and taking him to Sunderland for a trial. Willie had strong links with a number of players in France. He wanted to know if he could drop into the training ground before setting off to the north-east and, truthfully, I wasn't certain I wanted an agent hanging around while all my players were there. 'Come and have some lunch,' I said. 'But you will have to sit in the corner, out of the way, because – no offence – but I don't want an agent among my players.'

He turned up anyway and I will never forget the look on Arthur Cox's face when my colleague knocked on my office door that afternoon. 'Do you know who that is with Willie McKay?' he wanted to know.

I couldn't understand why he was interested. 'Some lad called Ali,' I said. 'He's on his way to Sunderland for a trial and hoping to get fixed up. But I don't know anything about him.'

Arthur closed the door and took a seat. 'When you left Newcastle, can you remember our next game in Europe was against Monaco?' he asked. 'That lad sitting in the corner of the canteen destroyed us that night, single-handedly. Forget Thierry Henry, forget Emmanuel Petit and everybody else they had in their side – that lad Bernabia put in the kind of performance, when we went to their place and they beat us, that I had never seen from anyone. We couldn't get near him.'

That was all news to me because, once I had severed my ties with Newcastle, I had done my usual thing of retreating from football. I didn't watch a single minute of Newcastle's 3–0 defeat at the Stade Louis II and the name wasn't even remotely familiar. I had no idea Benarbia had scored two of Monaco's goals that night.

I knew from the way Arthur was talking that I had to investigate, and when I went into the canteen to ask Benarbia if he was enjoying his salmon, the first thing that struck me, apart from the fact he spoke good English, was how all our French players were coming up to him, embracing him, kissing him on the cheek. Straight away, I could see the respect they had for him.

My next stroke of luck was that Peter Reid, the Sunderland manager, didn't turn up for the game where Benarbia was having his trial and, by that stage, I had already asked Willie if the player wanted to train with us later in the week. We arranged a practice match and it seemed too good to be true that Paris Saint-Germain could possibly let this player leave on a free transfer.

Were they insane? Benarbia was an island of composure. He played by the principle that giving away possession was a sin, and he measured his passes so beautifully that the player receiving the ball never had to fight for it. He reminded me of Alan Ball because of his ingenuity with the ball at his feet. Alan had a wonderful knack of making space for himself with his movement and intelligence. Benarbia could do the same. He would go one way, then shift his body, and suddenly he was gone, two yards away from his nearest opponent.

We got him for a snip, signing him on a short-term deal for the rest of the season for £2,000 a week in wages, with a £250,000 bonus if we went up, and then we let him fly back to France to get his belongings. He returned to Manchester on the Friday morning and I put him straight in the team for our game against Birmingham the following day. Nobody really knew who the hell he was, but he was so mesmerising on the ball that, after twenty minutes, he went to take a corner and everyone inside Maine Road gave him a standing ovation. City's supporters had spent years harping back to the days of Colin Bell and all those wonderful players from the 1970s. Benarbia was as good as any of them and the crowd adored him. I did, too. He was my bit of luck.

The issue for me was whether I dared to partner him in midfield with Eyal Berkovic and, as always, it never frightened me to take the exciting option. The critics said that tactic would leave us too lightweight in the muck and nettles of the First Division and, early on, there was some friction between the two players. That, however, was very one-sided. Ali was one of the nicest guys you could ever meet, whereas Eyal could be surly and withdrawn. He felt threatened by the new arrival and didn't exactly welcome Ali with open arms, for the simple reason he suspected he might take his place.

Unfortunately, that was Eyal in a nutshell, and might explain why his career featured so many fall-outs with his managers, myself included. Everything was black and white with him – he either liked you or he didn't. Everything had to be done around him. He wanted to be indulged and, if everything wasn't exactly to his liking, he had a tendency to take it badly and throw a strop.

Eyal should have been playing, and excelling, at a higher level. Instead, he had left a top-division club, West Ham, to join Celtic, then clashed with their manager, Martin O'Neill, and ended up in the second tier of English football. He was definitely a Premier League player but his attitude stopped him going as far in the game as he should have. He always ended up falling out with everyone and, rather than understand that he might be the common denominator, his verdict was always the same: that his managers were rubbish. He would leave under a cloud, then go to the newspapers and tear you to pieces.

There were certainly some difficult players to manage in my City years, if you think I later brought Nicolas Anelka to the club, and also had strong personalities such as Peter Schmeichel and the likes of Robbie Fowler, Steve McManaman and David James. They all had their own demands and egos, and it was unquestionably the most challenging dressing-room environment of all my club sides. I stayed at City for just under four years. At times, it felt more like ten. It was an exciting club to manage but a tough one that could sap your energy.

Benarbia, on the other hand, was a dream. At one point, I wanted to experiment with Shaun Wright-Phillips, a right-winger, as an attacking full-back, and I was unconcerned if other people couldn't understand the logic. Shaun was only nineteen, one of the smallest footballers in the league, and one of my own coaches asked how I expected a kid of five feet four to deal with far-post headers against players a foot taller than him. That didn't worry me unduly. My thinking was that Shaun could get the ball inside his own half, then bomb down the line to set up counter-attacks. I was never frightened to gamble. And, besides, I had a stubborn streak that meant I wanted to prove people wrong.

On the first occasion we tried the new set-up, we came in at half-time and Benarbia went over to his teammate. 'Shaun, when

I come for the ball, give me the ball, I will not lose it. And then you go, just go. You fly, my friend . . .'

Shaun was new to the role and worried about leaving the right-back spot open. 'I will not lose it,' Benarbia reassured him. 'Just go. You go, and I will find you.'

From that day, Shaun grew to trust him completely. He would play Ali the ball and then hare up the wing in the safe knowledge the return pass would be exactly where he wanted it. Shaun was eventually sold to Chelsea for £21 million. It was a huge amount of money for the time and, trust me, Benarbia played a significant role in making him such a valuable player.

We didn't look back once we hit the top on 12 March, staying there until the end of the season and winning eleven of our last thirteen games. They were exciting times and I could see great things in the future, bearing in mind we had only one more season at Maine Road before moving into the stadium that was being built for the 2002 Commonwealth Games.

It was the deal of the century – a stadium that cost £110 million being given to us for virtually nothing – but it wasn't easy for a lot of supporters, and I could understand why it caused so much heartache. I could remember playing for Liverpool at Maine Road in the 1977 FA Cup semi-final against Everton and I'd also played there against some of the great City sides. It had charm and warmth, colour and noise. Upstairs, there was that wonderful old English football-club hospitality where you could get a pie and a pint. Downstairs, there was always someone to greet you at the front door with a smile. Everyone always used to say that from the moment you walked into Maine Road, you were made to feel welcome.

It had been their home for eighty years and fans would often come up to me, close to tears, saying they didn't want to leave. The reality, however, was that Maine Road was holding City back. It felt like a stadium from another era. None of the stands was the same height, and I always remember that if you went down the tunnel and turned right there was the old ticket office where they used to count the takings. It was full of junk and rubble during all my time at the club. It had been that way for years.

I used to drive across Manchester to see the new stadium going up, and it was so exciting to think it would eventually be ours. I knew it was the right thing to do, but there was a bit of apprehension because, historically, it had always been difficult for any football team to acclimatise to new places. All of a sudden we were going to be in a dressing room we didn't know, in a stadium where we had never played. I did worry that our home advantage would pretty much be wiped out.

All the same, the deal that David Bernstein agreed with Manchester City Council was too good to turn down. The stadium had been paid for by taxpayers and lottery revenue, and the only rent we would have to stump up was a percentage of ticket sales once our attendances went above 32,000, the capacity of Maine Road. It was an incredible offer, and if it hadn't been for that chain of events, all sparked off by the Commonwealth Games coming to Manchester, City wouldn't be the club they are now, owned by Abu Dhabi's royal family with a very different set of ambitions to when I was manager.

In my time, it was still the era when you could understand why Joe Royle used to talk about a virus in Manchester known as 'Cityitis'. The time, for example, when we signed a three-year shirt-sponsorship deal with a company called First Advice. We had all the shirts printed and the team pictures taken. We put the shirts in the club shop and First Advice went bust within a year. With City, there was always something going wrong. 'Oh my God,' you'd say, 'surely not?' Then the people who had followed the club all their lives would let you in on the secret. 'It's Manchester City, mate, happens all the time.'

When I was at Newcastle the fans were always too optimistic. City's fans were too pessimistic, but they had a lovely, self-deprecating sense of humour. They had this saying – 'Typical City' – whenever anything went wrong and, though my natural inclination was to try to be upbeat, I did wonder sometimes why the club suffered so much misfortune.

The classic story is when we signed a French striker by the name of Alioune Touré and, after one league game, he was ruled out for the season with deep-vein thrombosis. It was City's fault – the club hadn't checked his medical records when he arrived from Nantes. He was on medication, and when we got on the bus for a trip to Portsmouth he didn't bring his tablets because he had no idea it was a six-hour journey. His leg flared up and that was the last we saw of him.

Christian Negouai, another of our French contingent, also had a chequered time in Manchester, including landing himself in trouble by missing a random drugs test. It was an innocent mistake but an embarrassing one. Christian didn't speak very good English, and failed to comprehend he wasn't supposed to drive off on the morning the drug-testers arrived at the training ground. When I rang him he cheerfully announced he could be back by four that afternoon. I asked him where he was. 'Liverpool airport,' he explained. 'My mother is visiting.'

Negouai received a £2,000 fine from the Football Association and must have lost a fair bit of money during his time in Manchester. He came to see me one day to say he was in trouble with the police and kept getting letters telling him he was being prosecuted for speeding. 'How many letters?' I asked, and he dropped a huge wad of paperwork on my desk. He hadn't realised there was a traffic camera as soon as you drove out of our training ground in Carrington. Every day he was pulling out, revving up to 50 mph in a 40 mph zone and getting flashed. There must have been seventy speeding notices, all from the same camera.

It was amazing sometimes to think of the trials and tribulations that could trouble you as manager of Manchester City, but it was worth the occasional hassles when, in my first season, we were recreating the kind of excitement I remembered from my time at Newcastle.

Shaun Goater was our most prolific striker, which shows how

much I knew because, when I took the job, I was convinced he would be one of the first players I had to move out. I watched him in our first few training sessions and couldn't see the attraction. Was he quick? Not particularly. Did the ball stick to him? No. How was his touch? Hit and miss. Overall verdict? We could find better.

Shaun proved me wrong. No matter who he was playing against, he kept finding the back of the net. His first touch could let him down but when he hit the ball – and sometimes he didn't even hit it right – it kept going past the goalkeeper. He scored thirty-two times in our promotion season and, even at the age of thirty-one, he was always seeking advice, hanging back after training for extra shooting practice and asking me if there were parts of his game I wanted him to work on.

Paulo Wanchope was another one who could either bewitch or bewilder you and, again, there were times when I watched him in training and found myself wondering why the club had ever signed him. His limbs were all over the place, like a high-jumper in the wrong sport, but that long, loping stride made him a difficult and effective opponent. He had a knee injury in my first season at City but still contributed thirteen goals. Darren Huckerby had the most productive year of his professional life, scoring twenty-six times. Our midfielders chipped in with decent totals – Kevin Horlock, Ali Benarbia and Shaun Wright-Phillips with eight each, and Eyal Berkovic seven – and it was the first time since 1957–8 that City scored more than a hundred goals in a season.

As for the old punk rocker with the captain's armband, Stuart Pearce's contribution could probably be summed up by the time he suffered a hamstring injury that would have kept out most players for at least a fortnight. Two days later we were all training on a freezing winter's morning, wrapped up in bobble hats and gloves in what felt like minus ten degrees, when he emerged through the mist wearing nothing but a pair of underpants and a towel wrapped round his head. That's why they called him Psycho.

Stuart played forty-three times for us that season – his last year as a professional footballer – and he had the opportunity for a perfect send-off when we won a late penalty in our final game at home to Portsmouth, three days before his fortieth birthday.

Dave Beasant was in Portsmouth's goal and in ordinary circumstances he would have been trying everything to keep it out. These, however, were not ordinary circumstances. It was the last kick of the season, four minutes into stoppage time, and we were already winning 3–1 against a team that knew, whatever happened, they were finishing in seventeenth position.

It wouldn't have made any difference to either team if that penalty went in but, if you can put yourself in Stuart's boots, it was the final act of a playing career spanning twenty years, getting on for 750 appearances, seventy-eight England caps and those two penalties – the failed attempt in the World Cup semifinal against Germany in 1990 and the redemptive effort in Euro '96 against Spain – for which he will always be remembered.

He was on ninety-nine career goals, and now he had the opportunity to make it a century with the last kick of his entire career. More than that, one more goal would see us establish a new club record of scoring 109 times in a league season. Darren Huckerby was our regular penalty-taker whenever Paulo Wanchope was not playing, but it had been agreed beforehand that Stuart should get the honour. The newspapers had been building it up before the game and it seemed like everybody, even the opposition goalkeeper, would have been happy for him to score.

As our skipper walked up to place the ball on the penalty spot, Beasant wandered over to have a word. 'Listen,' he said, 'I'm not going to move. I'm going to stand perfectly still, so just put it either side, no sweat.'

It was a gift and our biggest crowd of the season, 34,657, was on its feet, waiting to see if Stuart Pearce, one of the legends of his era, could deliver a fitting finale to a marvellous career. What the fans didn't realise was that all he had to do was get it on target, left or right, and it was going in. Then he came forward, pulled back that formidable left foot and I'll never forget what happened next. He blasted it over. And Beasant, true to his word, never moved an inch. Remember that saying? Typical City, yet again.

18

CITYITIS

After winning promotion back to the Premier League, my message to Manchester City's supporters was that they had suffered too many false dawns and that, if I had my way, this time it would be different. The expectation level of the club had to go up. I knew what was possible. I had done it before at Newcastle and I desperately wanted to think we could fasten our seatbelts for the same kind of adventures.

Unfortunately there were other people at the club who had different objectives. The chairman, David Bernstein, preferred a more conservative approach. David was a lifelong Manchester City fan and he was always cautious about spending lots of money in case it didn't work out and potentially plunged the club into trouble.

He knew what I meant, and I knew what he meant. I could understand his point of view and, even now, I don't necessarily think he was wrong. David had been prominently involved in setting up that incredible deal for the new stadium. He was a chartered accountant, a shrewd and intelligent man, and I knew from his very nature that he would be reluctant to take the same financial risks as Sir John Hall at Newcastle.

At the same time, I did feel David ought to have shown more ambition and that, in his determination to play it safe, he didn't fully appreciate that his cautious approach could eventually work against City. I could envisage problems further down the line if we tried to do it on the cheap and that, ultimately, was how it panned out. We had different ideas about the way to run the club and, in the end, our relationship did become strained. David's heart was in the right place, but it had reached the point where I felt as if he was trying to stop almost everything I was proposing.

The classic example was when I set up a deal to sign Robbie Fowler from Leeds and David went behind my back to try to change the terms. We had already shaken hands on a £6.5 million fee – myself and the Leeds chairman Peter Ridsdale – and my understanding was it had the support of everyone in City's boardroom. Those were the days when managers took a more hands-on role in transfer business and I had negotiated a fair price, in line with the board's thinking.

We had been talking about Robbie for a while, and we were convinced the former Liverpool striker could score a lot of goals for us, providing he stayed fit. Then David phoned up Leeds, with the player already on his way to Manchester, and said City would pull out unless the fee came down by £500,000. That was poor. It showed a lack of trust in me and made it look as though I had been acting without the club's authority. At the very least, he should have consulted me, whereas the first I knew about it was a flustered call from Peter Ridsdale saying, 'I thought we had an agreement.' We managed to save the deal, but David's late inter-vention caused me a lot of embarrassment. He should never have gone behind my back that way.

David left the club amid all sorts of boardroom politics about finance and structure and, though I wasn't part of that, it was becoming clear we couldn't work together any more. His view was that we were spending big money. Mine was that we weren't spending enough. We both had valid points and, even if it didn't end particularly well between us, I did always understand his priority was to do the best for City.

When he took over from Francis Lee in 1998, City were a volatile, unstable club on the way to being relegated to the third tier of English football for the first time in their history. Only four clubs – Leicester, Grimsby, Birmingham and Notts County – had been promoted or relegated more times, and when he offered me the job I wanted to know his ambitions if the club reached the Premier League. 'That would be the fifth season in a row we've either gone up or gone down,' he said. 'I'd like to stay in the same division for two years rather than yoyo-ing all the time.'

Once we were promoted, David's view was that we should be satisfied with a period of consolidation. His objective was simply to stay up and, if that was the sum of his ambitions, it would have been better to have given me a two-year contract from the start, with the instructions to get the team promoted, keep them there and then take a bonus and walk away. As it was, I had a five-year contract and I wanted to take the club higher and higher. 'We've got to keep marching on,' I'd say. I didn't like the word 'consolidation', and I tried to explain to David that if we started thinking that way, other teams would jump ahead of us. That was precisely what happened. It was always a source of frustration for me because, on the one occasion we did push the boat out, signing Nicolas Anelka for a club-record fee, we saw what a difference a player of that quality could make.

Anelka cost £13 million from Paris Saint-Germain. Everyone advised me to steer clear of him, and I lost count of the number of people who warned us he would be difficult and said his brother, Claude, who doubled up as his adviser, was a nightmare to deal with.

We had just been promoted, however, and at the back of my mind there was always the nagging sense that I would need to upgrade my strikers once we reached the Premier League. Darren Huckerby, for example, was sensational a league below, but we needed an extra touch of class for the higher level. Signing Anelka was, I hoped, a statement of intent.

The statistics don't lie, either. Nicolas stayed with us for two and a half years and his record of forty-five goals in ninety-eight appearances gave him a superior scoring ratio at City than at any of the other stops – Arsenal, Real Madrid, Liverpool, Chelsea and all the rest – on his playing career. There was only Chelsea where he played more games and, despite everything that was said about him in Manchester, he was a Ferrari of a footballer. Even though you didn't get it in every single match, or he wouldn't always do it for the entire ninety minutes, he could turn a game single-handedly. He and Thierry Henry must have been the two quickest footballers I had ever seen – and it would have been a hell of a race.

It would be stretching the truth, though, if I said that I found Nicolas easy to understand. He was a divisive character who didn't always endear himself to the other players or help foster a spirit of togetherness. If training started at 10.30 a.m., the players would usually go out at twenty past to have a chat and do some stretches. Nicolas would prefer to stand in the doorway by himself. He would wait and wait and wait and, finally, when it reached 10.29 a.m. he would walk out, alone. He didn't want to mix. There were players he wouldn't even acknowledge – not even basic pleasantries – and that was always going to cause problems.

Robbie Fowler, for one, didn't get on with him, which didn't surprise me. The truth was, very few people did. Nicolas was fine, for example, with Ali Benarbia but he wouldn't give Eyal Berkovic the time of day. We didn't have any cliques at Newcastle, which was one of the reasons we did so well, but I couldn't say the same about City, and Nicolas helped to create that unhealthy atmosphere. Nicolas was part of a French coterie. If he was annoyed with someone he wouldn't insult them in English, he would do it in his own language. The other French speakers might laugh and the English lads would find it annoying and want to know what he was saying.

I took the view that if we signed a player with Anelka's reputation, we would have to accept him, warts and all, as long as he did the business every Saturday, and for the most part his performances made it worthwhile. Equally, if I had to pick out two players from my time in management who had everything, ability-wise, but should have done a lot more with it, I would say

I had them both at City at the same time. One was Eyal, the other Nicolas.

Nobody knew what to expect from Nicolas from one day to the next. On a Friday afternoon, we would arrange a practice match and Nicolas, if he fancied it, could run rings round the centre-halves. When Richard Dunne and Steve Howey trudged in at the end I almost felt sorry for them. Then one of them would pipe up, 'Well, he won't do it tomorrow.' And they might be right. Nicolas could be sensational, but there were other times when he just wasn't in the mood and I could never find out why. I tried every tactic possible. I asked him questions, I put my arm around him, I coddled him, I shouted at him, I praised him, I hugged him – none of it worked. The more I tried, the more stubborn and reclusive he became. Did anyone ever truly work out Nicolas Anelka?

Our other recruits that summer included Sylvain Distin, who arrived for £3 million from Paris Saint-Germain and went on to become an important player for City. Marc-Vivien Foé joined on a season-long loan from Lyon, and Peter Schmeichel signed on a free transfer from Aston Villa to take over from Nicky Weaver as our first-choice goalkeeper.

Schmeichel was a match-day player – give him that shirt and he came alive – and still a formidable presence even if, at the age of thirty-eight, he was no longer the same goalkeeper who had broken Newcastle's heart in his Manchester United days. In training, though, he didn't want to do goalkeeper practice, he just wanted to play in the five-a-sides and see how many goals he could score. He was the only goalkeeper I had ever worked with who didn't want to be near his own net. 'I've always trained like this,' he told us. Our goalkeeping coach, Peter Bonetti, found it bewildering, and the other players hated it, because when they passed the ball to Schmeichel it usually bounced off his shin and never came back. 'Bloody hell, gaffer,' they would shout, 'get him out of here, will you?' But we let him train that way because, at that stage of his career, after all those years at Old Trafford, it didn't feel right to try to change his routine. Then we would get to Saturday and he would be immense.

It was a balancing act and, as I've already explained, I had more high-maintenance players at City than any other team I managed. There was always something going on, especially when Joey Barton started to break through, and there wasn't a great deal of leniency in my mind when Richard Dunne turned up for training one day, after all the warnings I had given him, and I realised he was hungover from the night before.

I could smell the booze on him but, to be honest, all it needed was a pair of eyes to see he was worse for wear. As far as I was concerned, that was him finished at City. We were barely a month into the new season and, yet again, he had crossed the line. I told him I was going to ban him for two weeks, fine him as much as I could and recommend that the club sack him.

If that sounds excessive, remember this was far from his first warning when it came to alcohol consumption. He was on thin ice already with me because, not long before this latest incident, he had received a warning for missing a training session. To turn up dishevelled and drunk was the final straw, and when Gordon Taylor, the chief executive of the Professional Footballers' Association, came to see me at the training ground, I was determined to rip up the player's contract and find somebody else who deserved the shirt. Gordon's job was to look after the members of his union and he wanted me to give Dunne one last chance. 'He's had loads of chances,' I told him. 'He's had the same lecture a thousand times, he's had his chance, and he's not the sort of player we want at our club.' Yet Gordon was persistent. He practically begged me to change my mind, and eventually I was persuaded to offer one final ultimatum whereby we both made it clear to Dunne, in the strongest possible terms, that he either sorted himself out or he was on the scrapheap.

Once that was decided, I came up with a strict new regime for Richard whereby he had to arrive at eight o'clock each morning and train three times a day. 'When I say "last chance", I mean "last chance",' I told him. 'Don't say sorry to me ever again, don't ever tell me it was someone else's fault, don't ever give me any more excuses. Last chance is last chance.'

If I was really honest, I didn't think he had the discipline to see it through. Richard had started his career at Everton and I had already ordered him to move away from his old drinking pals in Liverpool because of the kind of excesses that had led me to fine him, Nicky Weaver and Jeff Whitley after some typical non-sense at a nightclub in the city. I was saddened and infuriated by the way Richard was leading his life. *Why am I even wasting my time?* I was thinking. *This lad's a nuisance, a liability. I'm not the first person who has tried this with him, and I probably won't be the last.*

I drove him to a clinic just outside Manchester, but my under-lying suspicion was that leopards didn't change their spots. He didn't want to go. He was adamant that it wasn't necessary. Once he had been seen by the professionals, though, I started to see a dramatic change in his attitude. Richard brought down his weight by almost two stones. He stopped drinking and I watched, full of admiration, as he pulled himself back from the brink. He gave everything to getting properly fit, and when he came back into the team he was twice the player.

That made him a highly effective defender because even when he was unfit he was an accomplished, sometimes excellent, centre-half, who read the game well and had deceptive pace. People used to laugh at the idea he was quick because he was so big – the Honey Monster, they called him – but he was never a slouch. Now he was leaner, quicker, and finally showing signs that he had the dedication to be a top professional.

Not that his return to the team was entirely seamless. In one game against Arsenal at Maine Road, we lost 5–1, and Thierry Henry gave him such a chasing that Richard turned to the dugout towards the end of the first half to ask, utterly dejected, if he could be taken off at the break. He was playing at right-back against the reigning champions and the first three goals all came down his side. Henry was skinning him every time, and at half-time we gave Richard his wish, for his own sake as much as the team's. It was a painful lesson but the personal embarrassment he suffered in that game was another reminder that he needed to buck up his ideas.

Richard could be so accident-prone and liable to personal calamity that I have to confess I had some reservations about him in his early years. He was a prolific scorer of own goals, for starters, finishing his career with the unwanted honour of having scored ten times for the opposition, more than any other player in the Premier League era.

The bottom line, however, was that once he realised he had to dedicate himself to the sport, he proved me wrong and won my respect and admiration. Richard grew to understand that a professional footballer cannot take liberties with his body. He knuckled down and achieved the outstanding feat of winning City's Player of the Year award four years in a row. Later in his career he had four seasons at Aston Villa in the Premier League. He captained QPR when they were a top-division club and seventy of his eighty caps for the Republic of Ireland came after that near-sacking in 2002. In total, he made over 650 career appearances, and I will always think of him as a prime example of why a manager should never give up on someone too quickly. What a waste if he had been lost to the sport.

We finished ninth in our first season back in the top division, but it was difficult to look back on that period too fondly because we also had to deal with the tragedy of what happened that summer when Marc-Vivien Foé collapsed and died while playing for Cameroon in the Confederations Cup. Marc, who was twenty-eight, had a heart condition, hypertrophic cardiomyopathy, that meant he was up to five times more susceptible to go into cardiac arrest during exercise than a non-sufferer. Nobody knew he had this condition, and in eighty per cent of cases there are no warning signs. It was a terribly sad story – one of the saddest, saddest things I've ever had to deal with in football –

and a genuine tragedy in a sport that sometimes overuses that word.

Marc was exactly what we needed during his season on loan from Lyon – he wasn't technically brilliant but he was big, strong and physical, and nobody got past him easily. He was happy to cover the ground and he could score a few goals, especially from set pieces. He played thirty-eight games for us and scored nine times, including two in a 3–0 defeat of Sunderland on 21 April 2003 – the second one being the last-ever goal by a City player at Maine Road.

More than anything, he was such a nice, caring man. He used to send money back to Cameroon to look after his relatives, as well as funding his own academy, and he had at least a dozen people staying with him at his house in Manchester.

I had a go at him after one game because he hadn't done particularly well, and I was surprised that he wouldn't look at me. He just kept his head down, avoiding eye contact. 'Marc,' I said, 'when I'm speaking to you, can you show me the respect of looking at me?' He lifted his head but he still didn't want to look me in the eye.

After training the next day, he knocked at my door. 'Can I please explain, Mr Keegan?' he asked. 'In Cameroon, if you're speaking to your manager or someone in authority, it is a mark of respect not to look them in the eye. I wasn't being disrespectful, I was actually being respectful.' It was my fault – I should never have imagined he would have been discourteous in the first place.

I went to his funeral in Lyon and there was a charity match to raise money for his family. We retired City's number twenty-three shirt in his honour. It was difficult to understand how someone who seemed so fit and strong could die that way. I was watching that Cameroon game on television and I knew it was bad as soon as he went down. It was like a tree falling. There was nobody around him at all and you would never see a player go down that way, not even putting out his hands to break the impact, unless it was serious. I was out of my seat, shocked by what I had seen. Then I went through to see Jean and told her I feared the worst. I desperately wish I had been wrong.

That was the summer we left Maine Road for what was known then as the City of Manchester Stadium, now the Etihad, and when we tried to put our minds back on football I did have misgivings about how the following season would pan out. I knew the fans would automatically think, after a ninth-placed finish, that we should be top-six candidates in the first year of the brave new world. I wanted to believe the same, but I also knew that if our rivals were showing more ambition than us in the transfer market, it was more likely we would drop back or, at the very best, stay where we were.

We also needed a new talisman. Ali Benarbia had found the pace harder in his first season in the Premier League. He was thirty-four, and he came to see me in the summer to say that if he wasn't going to play in every game – I had given him only forty-five minutes of a pre-season friendly against Mansfield – it might be better for him to find somewhere else. We said goodbye to our brilliant Algerian and, after that, we never struck gold again in the transfer market.

That summer, Trevor Sinclair was our most expensive signing, at £2.5 million from West Ham, and our lack of spending started to bite. We went out of the Carling Cup to Spurs and our brief dalliance with the UEFA Cup, having qualified through the Fair Play League, ended ignominiously against a small Polish outfit called Groclin Dyskobolia.

That left the FA Cup, and when we went to Leicester City in a third-round replay, having drawn 2–2 at our place, Trevor walked down the bus to push a little piece of folded-up paper into my hand.

'There you go, gaffer,' he said, with a knowing wink.

When I unfolded it, there were eleven names written down in formation – Leicester's team to play us that night.

It turned out he had a mate in the Leicester dressing room

and had rung ahead to find out how our opponents would line up. 'Crikey,' I joked, 'I take it you've given them ours as well.'

He grinned. 'Yeah, I have actually, gaffer.'

I could laugh about it afterwards – we won 3–1 – but I didn't find it particularly amusing at the time that one of our own players was leaking our line-up to the opposition.

Nor was I feeling particularly jovial when we were drawn against Tottenham in the fourth round and, having drawn 0–0 at our place, found ourselves 3–0 down after forty-three minutes of the replay at White Hart Lane. That trip to north London came in the midst of a long, miserable run when we did not win a single league match from 1 November until 22 February. It was live on television and, as the players sloped into the dressing room at half-time, I knew it was going to be a challenging team-talk, to say the least. We looked drained of confidence. We had players who were treading water, going through the motions, and Spurs could have scored six, maybe even more. Nicolas Anelka had gone off with an injury and I knew I had my work cut out. 'That isn't good enough,' I started. 'You'd think they had two or three more players than us—'

'Well, they've definitely got one more,' someone interrupted. 'Joey Barton's just been sent off – he's told the referee to fuck off as we were coming down the tunnel.'

My team-talk had to change completely from that point. Three down with ten men, it was turning into a nightmare. I was thinking it could get really ugly – *Oh my God, guys, just don't embarrass us here* – and the thought did occur as I walked back to the dugout that if Spurs scored seven or eight I was probably out of a job.

My anxiety wasn't eased when they hit the crossbar with virtually the first attack of the second half. But then we scored one of our own through Sylvain Distin and finally we started to show a bit of character. Paul Bosvelt, our Dutch midfielder, got another one back in the sixty-ninth minute and, crikey, it was game on. It was an incredible turnaround. When Shaun Wright-Phillips clipped in the equaliser to make it 3–3, it did briefly flash through my mind that we had an important game coming up against Birmingham that weekend and didn't want to be exhausted because of extra time. But there were still ten minutes to go and suddenly we had all the momentum. Our ten men were going for a winner, working their socks off, doing all the things we didn't do in the first half. We were like men possessed. And then, in the dying seconds, a cross came in from the left and it was Jon Macken with the header over the Spurs goalkeeper, Kasey Keller. I'd signed Macken from Preston North End midway through the previous season. He was the third most expensive player of my time at the club, costing £5 million, and he struggled for a long time with the weight of his price tag. That header, however, was a goal that City's supporters will never forget.

Our victory that night will always be remembered as one of football's great comebacks – 'They have made the impossible possible,' as Martin Tyler said from the commentary box – and when we boarded the bus back to Manchester that night we were all thinking we had a great chance of winning the FA Cup. Then we drew Manchester United in the next round and lost 4–2 at Old Trafford, despite Gary Neville being sent off in the first half for headbutting Steve McManaman. The draw wasn't very kind to us.

Unfortunately for Joey, that red card at White Hart Lane was a prime example of the way he used to let himself down sometimes. Joey was desperate to be an elite footballer, eventually winning an England cap, but when I was his manager at City, it was sad to think that just about all his highlights – if that was the right description – came off the pitch.

The first time I saw him, he was playing for City's under-19s and Arthur Cox asked me what I thought. Joey had spent the entire match running around kicking people, flying into silly tackles and trying to pick a fight with the opposition.

'He's a thug,' were my exact words.

But Arthur saw a decent player. 'I think he's got something,' he said.

Maybe we were both correct and the truth was somewhere in the middle. I would also say it was difficult not to like Joey, and I did enjoy his company once I got to know him. If you spent time with Joey on your own, you could have an intelligent conversation. He was bright, articulate and a lot of the stuff he said made sense. He just had another side to him. He could be a liability and, in the worst moments, he was dangerous.

In my time with City there was the infamous incident at the Christmas party when Joey stuck a lit cigar into the eye of another young player, Jamie Tandy, amid all sorts of drunken idiocy. What he did that night was stupid and reckless and an embarrassment for the club – but that was Joey. He always had that capacity to lash out and think of the consequences later.

I had started to realise he was going to be a regular visitor to my office when Asa Hartford, one of City's coaches, came in one day to say he had heard from a friend in the police that Joey was in trouble.

'Apparently he's been in a car that's smashed into a car showroom in Chorley and almost wrecked the place,' Asa explained. 'And it gets worse. He's jumped out of the car and legged it. The police want to speak to him about leaving the scene of a crime.'

With a sense of foreboding, I brought in Joey.

'Tell me the truth here, Joey, were you in Chorley last night?'

I could have strapped a polygraph to him and I'm sure he would have given nothing away.

'Chorley?' he replied, with an expression of childlike innocence. 'No gaffer, I don't know anyone in Chorley.'

'Are you sure?'

'Absolutely.'

'You didn't have an accident?'

'I don't drive, gaffer.'

'You weren't drinking?'

'Never drink, gaffer.'

He gave a performance that Robert De Niro would have been proud of and, more fool me, by the end of this little act I was willing to give him the benefit of the doubt.

When I saw Asa later that day I told him it must be a case of mistaken identity. I was aggrieved on Joey's behalf. 'The police want to get their facts right. Joey tells me he doesn't drive, he doesn't drink and he wasn't anywhere near Chorley last night. I don't know who was in that car but it certainly wasn't him.'

The next day, a police officer turned up at the training ground with the CCTV from the car showroom and we sat down to watch the tape. The cameras showed all the shiny new cars lined up inside the showroom and, yes, you can probably imagine where this story is going. All of a sudden, a blue Vectra appeared out of nowhere and came hurtling through the front window. There was glass everywhere, alarms going off and at least three cars damaged. Then, through all this chaos, guess who jumped out of the car, turned on his heels and was out through the smashed window like a greyhound? The only mitigation was that Joey wasn't driving. It was one of his mates behind the wheel and Joey in the passenger seat.

Joey ended up in court for that one, and when I managed him again at Newcastle, in my second spell in charge at St James' Park, he was sent to prison for giving two people a vicious beating – one a boy of sixteen – on a night out in Liverpool, again involving alcohol. His violence that night predated my appointment, but I had to deal with the fall-out and supplied a reference for the court case. Newcastle had been playing a Boxing Day game at Wigan and the manager at the time, Sam Allardyce, had left Joey out of the squad. Joey went into Liverpool in a rage, got drunk, beat this kid up and ended up getting six months.

It was in his DNA unfortunately. One year we went to Doncaster for a pre-season friendly with Manchester City. I was so pleased to go back to my hometown club and help raise a few quid for them. We took a good following and everything was very good-natured until, for some unfathomable reason, Joey flew into a senseless tackle and sparked a brawl between the two sets of players. The home fans wanted to lynch him and I had to take him off because the referee told me that, if I didn't substitute him, he would be sent off instead.

With any other player, you wouldn't expect these problems but, with Joey, there was always something going on inside that confused, angry mind. He would do it in training, too. He was too good not to include but, in another sense, he was bad for the club. The last thing I wanted was a player trying to hurt a team-mate, but there was always that danger with Joey because his competitiveness went to ridiculous levels. He would get upset about a tackle and then he would go looking for revenge. I couldn't change him, and no one after me was able to change him either, judging by the mess he made of his teammate, Ousmane Dabo, in a training-ground beating that landed Joey in court again. In the end, you just had to accept he got a kick out of hurting people. That was Joey. Then the last time I saw him he couldn't have been more charming. 'I just wanted to thank you for all you did for me,' he said. Jean thought he was lovely.

There were other issues, too, with various other players at City. Robbie Fowler did score goals for us but still had fitness worries. Steve McManaman started well after his free transfer from Real Madrid but fell away. We signed Daniel van Buyten, a Belgian international centre-half, on loan from Marseille, but he was injured after six games. Peter Schmeichel retired after one season and David Seaman, another great of the goalkeeping profession, arrived on a free transfer from Arsenal to replace him. Seaman then suffered a bad injury that meant we had to pay him up after only half a season. David James was next to arrive, for £2 million, but City were never in a position where we could spend the kind of money to take on Manchester United, or even the clubs on the next rung down.

Our first season in the new stadium finished with us in six-teenth position and, as I had suspected, it was difficult trying to adapt to our surroundings. The financial restraints had continued even after David Bernstein's departure and, after a decent start to the season, we went on a dismal run where we won only one out of eighteen league and cup matches. We didn't make sure of survival until there were two games to play and, after that, we couldn't get the season over quickly enough.

We were in a rut, and the drift continued into the 2004–5 season, just as I had predicted it would if we were unwilling to take some calculated risks in the transfer market. We weren't moving forward any more. The players were becoming increasingly difficult, as often happens when a club is struggling, and perhaps I was losing a bit of my old spark. Jim Cassell, the academy director, asked me to speak to the youth-team players one day. I went through all my motivational lines – 'This club's a big club . . . you have to up your game . . . you need to give us everything.' Then I looked over and a young Ishmael Miller had fallen asleep in the front row. Inspirational stuff, gaffer!

There was always humour at City, but my time at the club had gone stale and when we got to March I announced I would leave after the final game of that season. I had a contract until the summer of 2006 but we weren't in great shape. It was easy to blame the new stadium, but there were other factors. We hadn't pushed on with our playing staff. The club had underachieved for too long and I was exasperated because it felt as if we were going nowhere. We had become also-rans. All we were trying to do was stay in the division while other teams were overtaking us.

Anelka had gone to Fenerbahçe in the January transfer window, and our only signings in my final season were free transfers – Danny Mills from Leeds and a back-up goalkeeper, Ronald Waterreus, from PSV Eindhoven. We had lost our firepower. The chairman, John Wardle, had said we weren't going to buy any more players and I couldn't see any point continuing. We were twelfth, we had consolidated. I wanted more for the club and more for myself. Consolidation was what David Bernstein had wanted – it wasn't necessarily what I wanted.

After that, it was not a huge surprise when John suggested it might be better to bring forward my departure rather than it turning into a long goodbye. Despite my occasional frustrations, John and I had a strong working relationship. It was me who helped persuade him to take over from David Bernstein, having previously been deputy chairman, and nobody should ever forget that if it hadn't been for John and his business partner, David Makin, City wouldn't be where they are today. They saved the club when the previous regime moved on in the late 1990s. They put in millions, and it was their money, as the founders of JD Sports, that bailed out the club after Thaksin Shinawatra's take-over led to financial problems a few years later. Yet they would never ask for thanks because that wasn't their style.

Indeed, David Makin preferred to sit in the stand with the fans rather than watch games from the directors' box. We scored in one game, and when he realised the goal had been disallowed, he swore at the referee and one of the stewards chucked him out. It's a great story. Most people in that position might point out, 'Hang about, I'm the major investor in this football club.' But nobody knew what David looked like and he never sought publicity. You would struggle to find a photograph of him anywhere.

I always had a lot of respect for him and John and I'm glad that I left on good terms. I would like to have achieved more, but I enjoyed those four years and they must have quite liked me because I lasted longer at City than any manager since Tony Book in the 1970s. None of the managers who has followed me has stayed any longer.

Jean and I liked the area so much we made the north-west our home. I am often asked to name which club gave me my happiest memories – Newcastle or Liverpool – and I always say I don't want to choose one above the other. But I like to throw in Manchester City's name, too.

19

MY BIG MISTAKE

It was Terry McDermott who sounded me out about returning to management at Newcastle and, at first, I didn't find the idea hugely appealing. In fact, my response was to knock back the idea straight away. As far as I was concerned, that chapter of my life was closed. I wasn't a great believer in going back to a former club and I had already had two spells at Newcastle, as player and manager. The idea of a 'third coming' was not one, to begin with, that I embraced.

At the same time, it was amazing how quickly I got the bug again. The time I had been away from football was fulfilling but I would be lying if I said I hadn't missed it. I missed the banter, the camaraderie and the euphoria of getting on a coach when your team had won away from home. It can be strangely addictive, football. Terry, who was still on the coaching staff, had planted a seed, and when Chris Mort rang to introduce himself as Newcastle's executive chairman and ask if I would meet him in London, I agreed on condition that Mike Ashley, the owner, was there, too. It was a completely new regime. I wanted to meet the man at the top and, as soon as I got off the phone, I started looking through Newcastle's squad and their fixture list. Mentally, I was tuning in straight away.

We drove through the middle of the night. Jean went shopping while I headed into an 11 a.m. meeting with the Newcastle hierarchy and the first impressions were encouraging. Mort was a lawyer for Freshfields and had been seconded to Newcastle to

replace Freddy Shepherd after Ashley's takeover in 2007. He and
Ashley shook my hand and then I was introduced to Tony Jimenez, who I was told was a property developer who would be
taking an executive position to help with transfer business. I had
never heard of him but he talked a great game. He had contacts
all over the world, he said, and a particularly strong network in
South America, where he felt we could get ahead of our rivals.

They were sizing me up as well. They wanted to know whether
I would be willing to work with a director of football when it
came to identifying players in the transfer market and I made
it clear that wouldn't be a problem. Three possible names
were floated as candidates. Terry Venables had already been
interviewed. Monchi, the director of football at Sevilla, was
on the shortlist, and the person they seemed really keen on
was Dennis Wise. I told them I was comfortable with that
arrangement as long as I had the final approval about the players
we signed. Wise was young in football terms, at forty-one, and
not particularly experienced for that specific role but I didn't
see that as a problem. He could learn. I had the feeling he was
their main target and he would probably have been my pick of
the three candidates, too. He was managing Leeds at the time.
He obviously knew the inner workings of the sport and I could
remember picking him to play for England. We had always got
on fine.

Ashley talked some more about his plans for Newcastle,
explaining that he envisaged an exciting future for the club but
pointing out he was 'not another Roman Abramovich', which
struck me as fair enough. But it was Jimenez who did most of the
talking, telling me he knew people in Brazil, Argentina, Chile,
Uruguay and all these other places, and that he would use his
contacts to find me brilliant young players. He was clearly a very
confident guy.

I was liking everything I heard, but when it came to discussing my contract, knowing what I do now, perhaps I should have

realised it was never going to be straightforward with these people.

My view was that the contract had to be a minimum of three years. I didn't have a set figure in mind for the salary but I had an idea of the going rate. I certainly hadn't gone down there to make any excessive demands but I had never anticipated they might deliberately low-ball me by offering £1 million a year. I found out later it was a deliberate ploy to try to get me on the cheap.

To be clear, I know very well that the money in football must seem outlandish to many people, and I am not asking for sympathy when it is such a high-earning business. Yet I didn't want to be taken for a ride either. Newcastle's offer was a third of what the previous manager, Sam Allardyce, was earning and the same amount I had been on at St James' Park ten years earlier.

They had also inserted a clause that meant I would be entitled to £1 million – one year's pay – if they decided to sack me. They told me it was a three-year deal but, from that perspective, it actually worked out more like a rolling twelve-month contract. I was on my own at this meeting, with no agent or financial advisers, but I wasn't born yesterday. 'That's not a three-year deal then,' I said, 'that's a one-year deal.'

'No,' Mike said. 'It still works out as three years.'

'Not if you decide to get rid of me,' I pointed out. 'It's a twelve-month contract that way.'

I was starting to feel uneasy, taken aback by the tactics they were using. Had they really got me all the way down to London to try to pull a fast one? It wasn't what I was expecting and, after going back and forth in this manner for several minutes, we had reached a stalemate. I politely made my excuses. 'Look guys, it's been nice meeting you but it's not for me. I'm not going to move my family back to the north-east, buy a house and everything else, on these terms.'

I hadn't even got down the stairs before my phone rang. It was Chris Mort and he wanted me to go back. 'Why don't we try again?' he said. 'Don't head off, let's have another go at working it out.'

I was willing to give it a second go, but first I wanted to be absolutely certain my suspicions were justified. I met Jean for a coffee and rang a good friend, Neil Rodford, because I knew he would be clued up about what the average Premier League manager was earning. Neil had been managing director at Fulham when I was at Craven Cottage and he confirmed what I had already suspected. It was a fiasco.

When I went back to see Ashley and his colleagues, everyone seemed keen to put a difficult start behind us. The second meeting was a lot more straightforward and they made it clear they did understand, after all, that I was entitled to earn the same as the previous manager. The contract was £3 million a year and the clause was changed so I would get £2 million as compensation if they wanted to get rid of me. We got down to business, and when the paperwork was signed it was an exhilarating feeling. Everything had happened incredibly quickly and I was just as excited, if not more, as when John Hall offered me the job in 1992.

Before I knew it, we were on a private jet to the north-east. Newcastle had an FA Cup third-round replay that night against Stoke City, and when I took my seat in the Milburn Stand I was reminded of the alluring qualities of St James' Park. It was special when I last managed there. It was even bigger and better now. The players rose to the occasion, winning 4–1, and as I looked around the stadium, with all that incredible noise and fervour, I dared to imagine what was achievable.

In my view, anything was possible. Mike had taken control the previous summer, buying the club for £135 million and wiping out huge debts in the process. He was clearly a man of immense wealth, a billionaire who told me he wanted to make Newcastle great, and he had developed a huge business portfolio since making his fortune with the Sports Direct empire. I had the football knowledge. He had the money and, I hoped, top-notch people around him. It felt like the dream ticket and the perfect opportunity to fulfil the grand ambitions I nursed for Newcastle. *This guy is going to help me take this club to where it's never been,* I thought. *We're going to win something this time, we're going to get this place rocking again.*

Newcastle's supporters had been denied happiness for so long and that hadn't been put right since I was last at the club. But the passion, dreams and expectations on Tyneside hadn't changed. They still had the same love, yearning and loyalty. They wanted to win something, see good football, enjoy their Saturdays. I'd been there before, I understood. Plus there was unfinished business. I knew what it felt like to relinquish a twelve-point lead at the top of the league and watch another team win the title. Manchester United, once again, were the champions of England, but I was convinced Newcastle could go one better than last time.

My excitement intensified the following day when I was shown round the training facilities and saw how far the club had progressed behind the scenes. When I left Newcastle in 1997 we were still training on the sports fields at Durham University. Eleven years on, Newcastle had a purpose-built training ground. The pitches, the gyms, the food, the treatment rooms – it was all on a different planet to what I could remember. Newcastle had some fine players and were twelfth in the Premier League, which was a much better starting position than the side I inherited in the Second Division in 1992. Plus it was lovely to hear the northeast accents again and see some familiar faces. The physio, Derek Wright, was still there. The kit-man, Ray Thompson, was another one. On match-days, it was still Kath Cassidy, an institution at St James' since the early 1960s, serving tea in the press room. It felt like I had come home.

I knew it was important to build a relationship with Jimenez. I was intrigued by this guy and wanted to know how a property developer had found himself in such an influential role at one of England's top football clubs. He certainly talked well, but was there any substance to it? I wanted to know more about him but there wasn't a great deal of information forthcoming. All I could find out was that he was mates with Mike Ashley and Paul Kemsley, who was the vice-chairman at Tottenham Hotspur, and that the three of them used to watch England games together at Wembley.

I did a bit of digging. Jimenez used to tell people he was involved when Juande Ramos was interviewed for the job of Tottenham Hotspur manager. Jimenez had also worked as a football agent, but his only deal of any significance seemed to be Celestine Babayaro's transfer from Chelsea to Newcastle four years earlier. Otherwise, there wasn't much else when it came to his involvement in an industry where he now presented himself as an expert. Jimenez had risen without trace. Yet I did find out he had a background, of sorts, in football. It turned out this Newcastle executive – a man given the title of 'vice-president (player recruitment)' – had previously been a steward at Chelsea's home games. That was where the link with Dennis Wise, formerly a Chelsea player, came about, and how he had befriended some of the players at Stamford Bridge. It wasn't the most glittering CV I had ever seen.

That wouldn't have mattered too much if Jimenez could walk the walk, as well as talking the talk, but it wasn't long before I began to suspect there might not be a great deal of substance behind the big promises.

Arthur Cox, my long-term ally, had joined me on a deal until the end of the season, with the instructions to go round the whole club and let me know where we could improve. Arthur and I had been in the game virtually all our lives and, with our experience, it was never going to be easy to pull the wool over our eyes. We could suss when someone was trying to blag it and, at our first meeting with Jimenez, we didn't have any confidence in what he was telling us. Arthur was looking at me out of the corner of his eye. Terry McDermott was getting the same bad vibes. We were all thinking the same: *Either the game has really changed or this doesn't sound right.* Jimenez was having to prove himself in front of proper football people and, straight away, cracks were appearing.

He wasn't short of self-belief and wanted us to know we should think of him as Mike Ashley's eyes and ears. The clear instruction was that we should always go to him, and never the club's owner.

'So, if we're talking to you, Tony,' Arthur asked, 'it's as if we are talking to Mike Ashley?'

'If you talk to me, it *is* Mike Ashley.'

We had another meeting a short time afterwards, this time with Mike involved, and I was still trying to work out whether my suspicions about Jimenez were correct, or whether I should give him the benefit of the doubt. Jimenez started going through the same spiel about having access to young players from South America who nobody else knew about, bringing them to Newcastle and turning them into multi-million-pound assets who would take us to the next level. What he didn't seem to understand was that players from these countries would need work permits to move to England and, to qualify, they needed to have appeared in a significant percentage of their country's senior international matches over the previous two years. If they were young players, as Jimenez kept saying, the chances were they wouldn't fall into that category. Everybody in football knew a system was in place. Everybody, perhaps, except Tony Jimenez.

As he went through all his plans I had one simple question. 'How are you going to get these players into the country?' I asked.

Anyone with even a semblance of football knowledge would have known what I meant, but his expression was of a man who thought it was the daftest question he had ever heard.

'We'll fly them in, of course,' he replied.

Looking back, it's a wonder I did not burst out laughing. At the time, however, there was nothing amusing about this exchange. I was still new to the Ashley regime, still trying to memorise the names of the staff and desperately wanting to believe the best of the people running the club.

'Fly them in?' I said, trying to keep calm. 'I meant, how are you going to get them in without a work permit?'

Jimenez blinked dumbly. He didn't know what I was talking about, and that was the killer moment. I was trying to establish if he could deliver on his promises and I knew now that the answer, emphatically, was no. He didn't even appear to know the rules. This guy boasting about all his amazing contacts, this former Chelsea steward who I was supposed to be relying on to help me find players, didn't have a clue. I knew at that point that I was working with amateurs and I looked at Mike Ashley and held out my arms as if to say: What the hell . . . ? And the moment I did that, I guess the relationship with Jimenez was broken. After that meeting, I never had any confidence in him again and he might say the same about me, too. I'd caught him out, embarrassed him, shown him up for what he was. I'd undermined him in front of the boss. He wasn't going to forget that lightly.

After that, I came up against a wall of incompetence, deceit and arrogance; you really couldn't make up some of the things that happened at Newcastle under this regime. It was a tragicomedy. Jimenez had positioned himself as a football expert but it turned out this bewildering character – the man in charge of Newcastle's recruitment, no less – admitted during discussions about potential transfer targets that he had never even heard of Per Mertesacker.

Can you believe that? Mertesacker had made his debut for Germany four years earlier. He was recognised as one of the outstanding players in the 2006 World Cup and had been an ever-present for his national team when they reached the final of Euro 2008. He was one of the best defenders in Europe and would go on to win over 100 caps for his country. Yet Jimenez didn't have the foggiest who he was.

I tried my hardest to retain a sense of humour and, somehow, I could laugh on occasion at the absurdity of it all. But there were other moments when it made my head ache to think what they were doing to a famous old sporting institution. It was an incredible story, but a sad one, mostly – and I had never known anything like it at any other football club.

The club's transfer business, for starters. To be clear, I had been more than happy to agree with the club's vision about bringing in younger players. I had made it clear I liked that idea, but I had also inherited a struggling team, in the bottom half of the league, and we needed players for the present as well as the future. 'Let's build from the top and bottom,' I told them. 'Lay the foundations, but don't forget your roof is leaky, don't forget the roof needs fixing, too.'

Jonathan Woodgate was a player who would have dramatically improved the team. He had just won the north-east Player of the Year award at Middlesbrough and was a popular figure at St James' because of the eighteen-month spell on Tyneside that had earned him a move to Real Madrid a few years earlier. His time at the Bernabéu had been blighted by injury issues, but he rarely missed a game for Middlesbrough and we knew he was keen to come back to Newcastle. He was mates with Steve Harper, our second-choice goalkeeper, and they had been texting one another.

Woodgate had been speaking to Spurs, but our information was that he would choose us if we matched his wages and the £7 million fee. We then found out that Middlesbrough weren't keen to sell their best player to one of their north-east rivals and that we would have to pay a little extra on top. That, however, wasn't unusual. Woodgate was a classy player and, if we could keep him fit, I told the board he could solve our centre-half problem for the next four years.

The response was lukewarm. They thought he was too old, too injury-prone and they had heard rumours he was a drinker. Then we had the opportunity to speak to the player, and Jimenez informed me, very matter-of-factly, that he didn't want me in the meeting.

It didn't make sense. One of my strengths was being in a room with a transfer target and letting him know that if he joined us it was going to be special. I had done it with Alan Shearer when he had already spoken to Alex Ferguson about moving to Manchester United. Rob Lee was going to Middlesbrough until I sat down with him. I persuaded David Ginola that Newcastle was the place to be. I could go on and on – and I would have fancied myself with Woodgate as well.

I also knew how important it was, in the player's mind, for the manager to be there rather than leaving it to a club official. Arthur Cox knew it, too. 'If you leave it to Kevin, that player will sign,' he said. But Jimenez was adamant he didn't want me there, and the truth, I suspected, was that he never wanted Woodgate at Newcastle. The deal collapsed and the player moved to Spurs instead.

This was all within the first two weeks of my appointment, and it was deflating to realise that working with this regime might not be quite as advertised. I also had to make sure I kept Newcastle in the top division and, though I never seriously thought we would go down, we did stray dangerously close to the relegation quicksands. We were only three points above the drop zone at one point and we didn't win any of my first eight games until a 2–0 defeat of Fulham set us on a six-match unbeaten run.

Michael Owen was a key performer in our resurgence, and it never particularly bothered me that he had used his autobiography to scrutinise my shortcomings as England manager. We got on well. Mark Viduka was a hell of a player when he was fit, and Obafemi Martins, the other attacker in a front three, had the speed and trickery to go past people. Behind them we had Nicky Butt and Joey Barton before, Joey being Joey, he went to prison for beating up the kid in Liverpool. Shay Given was in goal and it seemed strange to me that Newcastle had endured such a difficult season. There was the nucleus of a decent team.

At the same time, lots of little things were not right. Nigel Pearson, one of Sam Allardyce's assistants, had taken charge of the team for the Stoke cup tie. I had started calling Terry 'Black Box' because of the way he survived all the managerial changes.

Steve Round was also on the staff, but it was difficult to keep a count of all the other coaches and different fitness gurus. I knew Sam liked to have a large staff, but it took me aback when I arranged to see everyone on my first morning and there were twenty-five people crammed into one room. I didn't need that many people around me. I wasn't prepared for the sheer numbers, and it did create problems on away games when we literally didn't have the space to include everyone. We didn't have enough seats on the bus, or enough rooms in the hotels, and that meant I not only had to pick a first-team squad for every match, I had to choose which members of staff should be involved and which should be left out. I got a knock on the door after one game – 'You've left me out, gaffer, I can't believe I'm not in the team, what's going on?' That was one of the masseurs, believe it or not. We had five in total, including a Chinese masseur for reasons that were never properly explained. But he didn't last long.

Similar to my time at Manchester City, we also had a lot of strong personalities and challenging egos. Michael Owen had his own fitness trainer, who was allowed to come in because of the player's injury history. I could understand why the club wanted to make an exception for their record signing, but then another player, a supposedly big-name player, came to see me and said that if Michael was getting preferential treatment, he wanted his guy to be allowed in, too. It wasn't the biggest problem, but I could have done without it.

My mood wasn't helped either by what happened in our final game of the 2007–8 season. We were playing at Everton, and when we got off the bus to walk to the dressing room, I noticed Abdoulaye Faye, our Senegalese centre-half, had a suitcase with him. At half-time we were 2–0 down and it was the worst performance he had put in since I rejoined the club. I wanted an explanation. 'What the hell is the matter with you today?' I asked him.

I wanted to see he was hurt, angry even, and determined to

put it right in the second half. But he didn't look bothered in the slightest. 'I'm tired,' he said.

I had heard enough by that stage. 'You've got your case with you?' I asked.

'Yes, I'm going home straight after the game – back to Africa.'

'Off you go, you're subbed pal.'

Faye did go. He took his case, ordered a taxi, and I presume he went straight to the airport while the rest of his teammates went out for the second half. He had been one of our better players for the previous four months, but I couldn't tolerate that kind of attitude. We sold him to Stoke that summer and he finished his first season in the Potteries as their Player of the Year, but I never regretted my hard-line stance. 'He won't be here next season, will he?' Terry asked after the game. Terry once told me that he always knew if I was really mad with someone because I would call them 'pal'. We both knew the answer to his question. 'He won't kick a ball for me ever again,' I said.

The bigger problem was that Dennis Wise had been confirmed as the club's director of football within a couple of weeks of my appointment. I had envisaged we would work together closely, but it wasn't long before I realised that the likeable guy I used to pick for England – a chirpy little character who had never given me any problems – was going to stick very closely to Jimenez and, in turn, keep his distance from me. Jeff Vetere, who was previously a scout for Charlton Athletic and West Ham, was also appointed in a senior position. Vetere, whose official title was technical director, also aligned himself to Jimenez, and I saw and heard very little of him. An us-and-them situation was developing and the disagreements behind the scenes were already beginning to take their toll.

At one point I took a call from Luka Modrić's agent to ask if I would be keen on signing the player from Dinamo Zagreb. Modrić had already been speaking to Spurs and his agent was honest enough to explain the move to White Hart Lane was likely to happen. Yet it was clear there might still be a chance to gazump that deal, otherwise the agent would never have bothered getting in touch. 'Mr Keegan, I'm a massive fan of yours and I'd very much like to discuss it with you,' he said. Dinamo Zagreb wanted £16 million and the wages were quite high, but it was still within our budget and, at twenty-two, Modrić had his best years ahead of him. He was exactly the kind of player I wanted to see in a black and white shirt.

His agent flew up from London and this time it was me inviting Jimenez to be part of it, rather than him cutting me out of the loop. It was an opportunity to sign one of the outstanding young footballers in Europe and, to begin with, I was making decent inroads. I explained what a great club Newcastle was, how the supporters would adore Modrić and how we were looking for someone to spark us off.

Then Jimenez piped up. 'Can I come in here?' he said. 'I don't think Luka is good enough for the Premier League. He's too lightweight. He's decent, but he's not good enough.'

Terry was also in the meeting and we just stared at each other in disbelief. The agent looked shocked. 'What do you mean?' he asked. 'Are you saying my player is not strong enough? Luka's a very strong boy, I can assure you.'

'That's exactly what I mean,' Jimenez continued. 'My view is that he's too lightweight for English football, he's too small.'

It was an awful moment and, ten years on, it needs only a cursory glance at Modrić's achievements to realise what a nonsense it was. Even back then, however, it was laughable. Too lightweight? Croatia had played England that season on possibly the worst Wembley pitch since the 1970s, and Modrić passed the ball as though he was playing on a bowling green. In torrential rain, he glided across the pitch. He ran his heart out. England lost 3–2, meaning they failed to qualify for Euro 2008, and Modrić played everyone off the park. He was brilliant. 'Have a look at the video,' I told Jimenez afterwards. He had killed the deal. There was no way back and Modrić ended up at Spurs with Woodgate.

Paul Kemsley, Ashley's long-time associate, must have been delighted how everything was working out.

I was left to wonder if there was another reason why Newcastle didn't appear to want a player I had identified and, if so, why the relevant people couldn't just tell me straight. Maybe they thought the fee was too high and it would have been difficult to sell Modrić for a profit further down the line. Yet that would have been another mistake. Modrić decorated Tottenham's midfield for the next four years and when he left for Real Madrid it was for £30 million, almost twice what Spurs had paid for him. He is now a four-time Champions League winner. He was named the best player of the 2018 World Cup after captaining Croatia to the final and, looking back, I don't think he would have been a bad player for Newcastle.

I felt I was being tested to the limits by Jimenez and getting zero backing from Wise when I needed his support. If Dennis had taken it upon himself to say, 'Look, Tony, this is difficult for me, but trust Kevin, he knows about football', it might have stopped the rot. But he didn't. They were friends and Jimenez somehow had a hold over him, as the man who had brought him to the club. Dennis was surprisingly weak when, as a footba man, he should have taken my side. He went along with it far t easily.

It didn't help either that Derek Llambias, another of Ashle allies, had arrived towards the end of the season, preparing take over as managing director once Chris Mort's secondme from Freshfields ended in the summer. Llambias ran casin and met Ashley at his club, Fifty, in Mayfair. He was another o who had been parachuted into Newcastle with no football bac ground.

The first time I met him was at the Capital, the hotel Knightsbridge where the Queen's mother used to stay, and I couldn't have been nicer. I was with Jean. We had a cup of tea ar Llambias clearly wanted to make a favourable impression. 'I come and work with you, Kevin . . . I want to learn from you . .

you've been in the game such a long time . . . it will be an honour to work with such a legend' – all that sort of stuff, blowing smoke up my backside.

Then, as soon as he took over, all the superficial niceties went out of the window and I had the misfortune of seeing, close-up, the real Derek Llambias. Like had attracted like. He was another Jimenez – arrogant, aloof, full of self-importance. It was difficult even to have a conversation with him. I couldn't trust him and, rather than make the situation any better, he made everything worse. After fifty years in football, I can honestly say he was one of the more unpleasant characters I have ever had the misfortune of encountering.

Llambias was cold and calculated and not to be trusted. He thought Chris Mort was 'weak' and didn't regard Dennis as the brightest of people. Llambias was another one, like Jimenez, who didn't want me ringing Mike Ashley. Yet there were times when I felt I had to ignore their instructions. I wasn't sure if Mike knew what was going on. We never had a board meeting where official minutes were taken. It wasn't that kind of professional operation, and I wanted to ask the owner if he was aware what was happening at his own club. Jimenez found out one day and went absolutely berserk. The power had gone to his head. 'You don't ever ring Mike Ashley, you come through me if you want to get to Mike Ashley. Do you hear? Everything comes through me. You do not go to Mike Ashley.'

All the time, the divide was growing. Bafétimbi Gomis, a Senegalese striker, had been scoring a few goals for Saint-Étienne and was one of the players Jeff Vetere had recommended. Saint-Étienne had a Ligue 1 game at Paris Saint-Germain, so Terry McDermott and myself flew over to check him out.

We took our seats at Parc des Princes and the game was about to kick off when we realised Jimenez and Wise were three rows behind us. It was awkward, to say the least, and another sign of the deteriorating situation between us. They knew we were going to be there, but we didn't have a clue they would be. They hadn't felt it necessary to tell us.

It didn't help that Gomis was very poor. Vetere had apparently done some scouting in the past for Real Madrid, but I would rather trust my own eyes, and there was nothing to suggest Gomis was good enough for the kind of team we were trying to build. The ball kept bouncing off his shins and, twenty minutes in, my phone bleeped with a text from Dennis. 'He's having one,' it read. 'Shall we go home? Jeff Vetere is shit.'

At least Dennis had a sense of humour. 'Looks like Didier Drogba, plays like Dracula,' I replied.

We stuck it out until the second half but I presumed once we flew back to England that our interest in the player would be finished. I was mistaken. I was asleep at home one night, past midnight, when my phone rang. At that late hour it always used to give me a jolt if the phone went. All sorts of things flashed through my mind, but it was Llambias. He was with the others and, judging by the background noise, it sounded as if they were in a bar.

'Kevin, just to let you know,' he announced, 'we've put in a bid for Gomis.'

'Pardon?'

'Ten million euros.'

It felt like a dream, but it was actually more like a nightmare. 'But I don't want him,' I said, 'I don't want him.'

I could hardly hear him. Wherever they were (they claimed later it was an Indian restaurant), it sounded as if they were having a big night. I didn't get much sleep, and first thing in the morning I rang the Newcastle secretary, Lee Charnley, to ask if the club had put in a bid to sign Gomis behind my back.

He didn't sound too convincing but tried to put me off the scent. 'No,' he said. 'If we'd bid for any player, I'd know about it – and I can assure you we haven't.'

A couple of hours later he rang back and, as I suspected, he had been lying. 'Look, Kevin,' he said, 'I'm sorry but the truth is, yes, an offer has been made.'

I didn't blame Charnley for the lack of honesty. He was in an invidious position and I could understand why he felt unable to tell the truth. But I was still shocked by what he was telling me and only marginally cheered by the news that the bid had been rejected. As far as I was concerned, the club had gone back on our agreement that I would have the final say when it came to signings. It was a betrayal. They had broken the golden rule and I wasn't sure I wanted to work with these people a day longer. 'I don't think the club can do this,' I told Charnley. 'I'm going to have to check my contract because this is outrageous.'

The next day, Llambias came back on the phone to apologise and promised it wouldn't happen again. At least he was willing to say sorry – but only, I found out later, because Mike Ashley had ordered it. I told him I was grateful for the apology and wouldn't hold it against him as long as it was a one-off.

Nothing changed, though. I was being ostracised. They didn't want my input when it came to transfers. They kept me out of the loop when it came to contract talks with Michael Owen, Steven Taylor, Nicky Butt and others. They didn't even tell me who they were appointing as our academy director. Richard Money had previously been the manager of Walsall and I didn't think it was a bad appointment. It just came out of the blue, with nobody asking for my opinion or thinking I might want to know.

I tried my best to protect my players, but it was another blow to the club's self-esteem when the board decided to ditch the suits we used to wear to games. The players liked those suits. We were representing Newcastle and they were proud to have the club's badge on their jackets. But the people at the top thought we could save a few quid. I tried to argue that it was important, but they didn't listen and the message came back that if the players wanted to wear suits they would have to stump up the cash themselves. After that, everyone wore tracksuits and trainers.

Then there was the time Steve Harper, who was on the

players' committee, wrote to the board to point out that the bonuses had not gone up for six years and asking if they could be adjusted during the summer, in time for the 2008–9 season. I didn't know anything about it at first, but Steve came to see me a couple of weeks later to say the club hadn't even had the decency to reply. When I raised the issue with Llambias, he waved his hand dismissively. His view was that we should wait six or seven weeks into the new season before deciding whether to address it. It was Lee Charnley who let him know there were rules in place to stipulate bonus sheets had to be submitted before the season began. Our new chairman, from the world of blackjack tables and roulette machines, didn't have a clue.

The problems had started from virtually day one, and I had to be honest when I spoke to Alan Shearer about the possibility of him joining my backroom staff. Alan and I talked a couple of times. I had a lot of respect for Alan, who was now retired from playing, and I told him, for his own sake, he was better off steering clear until the club was run differently. I was protecting him. Another time, another place, it would have been marvellous to have him with us, but I wasn't even sure the people running the club would let me bring him in anyway. If they had turned it down, as I feared, how would that have looked? 'Alan, you don't want to come here,' I said, 'not now, not with these people and the way they are. It's not right here, trust me.'

When I took the job I was told we should target ambitious signings. Thierry Henry was one. He wasn't getting a regular start for Barcelona and I thought there was a possibility we could coax him back to England. David Beckham, who was at LA Galaxy, was looking for a move back to Europe, and we were told Frank Lampard was having problems at Chelsea and would be interested in moving to Newcastle. People might think they were unrealistic targets and, of course, there was no guarantee whatsoever we could have signed any of them. But if we had had that defeatist attitude at Newcastle in my first stint as manager, we would never have landed Alan Shearer. These were the sort of

category-A players, with Mike's backing, I felt we could realistically go after. The roof of St James' Park would have come off if I
had fetched Thierry Henry to Newcastle.

Instead, none of my recommendations ever seemed to happen, for one reason or another. We had missed out on Jonathan
Woodgate, we had lost Luka Modrić and various others and,
though I was trying to remain positive, I was getting more and
more exasperated. We finished twelfth and I told myself we
could start again over the summer and relaunch the club in my
first full season. I loved the club and I wanted to stick with it. But
I wasn't kidding myself. I had gone back to Newcastle with high
expectations and, within a matter of weeks, it was a case of feeling, *My God, we're going nowhere here.* They had painted such
an exciting picture and, barely a month in, I knew it couldn't
work, that they weren't going to bring in who I wanted; that they
were going to bring in who they wanted and if I wanted to stay
I was going to have to put up with it.

It takes the heart out of you when you are being treated that
way. It saps your confidence. It demoralises you and leaves you
with the awful feeling that your own colleagues are taking you for
a fool. It was a mess and it was obvious that, if it continued that
way much longer, it was going to end badly.

20

TRIALS AND TRIBULATIONS

The final straw at Newcastle came when the club went behind my back to sign two sub-standard players as a multi-million-pound favour for a pair of mysterious South American agents, a deal that aroused so much concern in my mind that I always found it difficult to understand why the Football Association never felt it warranted a proper investigation.

Yet there were plenty of other occasions when it felt like Tony Jimenez and Dennis Wise, the two executives who were supposed to help me assemble a team capable of challenging at the higher end of the Premier League, were orchestrating a campaign to undermine me in just about every possible way.

As we approached transfer deadline day, early in the 2008–9 season, it was disconcerting to learn the club wanted to sell James Milner to Aston Villa against my wishes. I didn't want to lose Milner, for the simple reason he was one of our more consistent players. James was a highly competent footballer who would go on to win over sixty England caps and I wanted to build a team around players of that nature. He could play either side, he could operate behind the strikers, he was a fit boy and, though his final ball needed a bit of work, he could chip in with a few goals. He was twenty-two – a young player, just like Newcastle wanted – and it baffled me that they seemed so keen to sell him to another Premier League club.

We did, however, need to build some bridges, because Milner was unhappy about a couple of issues, not least the fact he was one of our lowest-paid players. He had put in a transfer request and the club had agreed not to publicise it, only to break that arrangement by announcing it on their website. It was all a bit messy, but I was sure Milner would stay if he felt he was being treated fairly. He wanted a £7,000-a-week pay rise and I was certain he would sign a new contract if we could stretch that far.

Instead, we had a conference call in which Jimenez announced that he had given his word to Martin O'Neill, the Aston Villa manager, that the move was going to happen. Villa, he said, had made a £12 million bid. It was terrific money, I had to concede, but I was potentially losing one of my better players and I tried to argue against it until Wise jumped in to announce there was a good chance we could get Bastian Schweinsteiger from Bayern Munich as Milner's replacement.

That was a different story altogether. Milner was a talented player, but not important enough that we couldn't swap him for a footballer with Schweinsteiger's gifts. Schweinsteiger was only twenty-three, but had already established himself in the heart of the Bayern Munich midfield and had just helped Germany reach the final of Euro 2008. He was developing into a great player, a truly great player, and someone whose know-how, football intelligence and leadership qualities would have made him the answer to a lot of our problems. According to Wise, a deal with Bayern was already pretty far down the line. I liked what I was hearing and gave it my seal of approval.

Milner's transfer duly went through and, though I was sad to see him leave, I was sure we would be getting an upgrade in Schweinsteiger. Except it suddenly went quiet on that front and, somehow, it all seemed a little too good to be true. I started to feel uneasy. Could I really trust these people, after everything I had learned in the previous few months, to pull off a deal for one of the best players in Europe?

We were playing at Arsenal the following day and, when we arrived at our hotel in Canary Wharf, I decided to ring Karl-Heinz Rummenigge, the Bayern chief executive, to find out if we had made a bid for Schweinsteiger or if, as I was beginning to suspect, it had all been a smokescreen to ease through the Milner transfer.

I spoke to Karl-Heinz in German, exchanged a few pleasantries and explained why I was ringing. I was half-expecting him to say he had no idea what I was talking about. But he just started laughing down the phone. 'Kevin, we did receive an offer,' he said. 'It was for five million euros. We just laughed when we saw it. Kevin, what are your people thinking of? We wouldn't sell Bastian Schweinsteiger for fifty million euros. We are a big club.'

Newcastle were supposed to be a big club as well. We were also a laughing stock. 'Five million euros, Kevin,' Rummenigge repeated. 'We killed ourselves laughing.' I left him chuckling at the other end of the line and rang off.

I felt like an idiot. It was the equivalent of offering Barcelona £10 million for Lionel Messi a couple of days before the transfer window closed. It was humiliating, and it made us look like amateurs – which was exactly what we were. I had lost James Milner, a future England international, as part of this fiasco. Key players were going out, nobody was coming in, and I had just had one of the greats of European football laughing down the phone at me. It was one of the more embarrassing phone calls I had ever made.

We had at least found a new centre-half in the shape of Fabricio Coloccini, meaning we had a replacement for Abdoulaye Faye, even if our new £10 million signing wasn't my first pick when we started going through the list of possible options. Jimenez and Wise always had this obsession about wanting South American players, and came up with Coloccini or another Argentine, Nicolás Burdisso. If it was a straight choice between the two, I preferred Burdisso because he was stronger physically and more experienced at the highest level, as a three-time Serie A winner with Internazionale. Instead, Coloccini arrived from Deportivo de La Coruña. Jeff Vetere had seen more of the two players than me and I was happy to go with his recommendation.

I still felt we were light in that department. We needed a

leader at the back and we knew Liverpool had told Sami Hyypiä he could leave for a knockdown fee of £2 million. We also knew he was keen on a move to Newcastle because he had been texting Michael Owen, who was previously his teammate at Anfield. Hyypiä wanted a two-year contract at £40,000 a week, which seemed reasonable, and when I recommended him to the Newcastle board I thought they would see him as a huge asset. 'We can get a really solid guy here,' I said. 'He might be coming to the end, but he knows his way around English football, he's worn Liverpool's colours with distinction and he's the kind of organiser we need. If we put in that offer, he will come.'

That was a 9 p.m. conference call. What I didn't realise when I rang off was that Tony Jimenez, Dennis Wise and Derek Llambias then had a second conference call, this time without me, and agreed to put in a £1 million bid, rather than £2 million, and not tell me. It was another demoralising blow, but not entirely a surprise. They must have known a bid that derisory would be rejected. Stoke City then came in with a £2.5 million offer and, behind the scenes, the various executives at Newcastle were delighted because that meant we had no chance even if we doubled our bid.

Why did they do it? All I can think is that they didn't want a player who was thirty-four and, for some reason, they didn't feel able to tell me the truth. I thought Hyypiä would be an inspirational player for Newcastle, but the club didn't like the idea, I suspect, because we wouldn't be able to get our money back in the transfer market further down the line. They didn't understand the value of having a player with Hyypiä's experience for two years. They didn't appreciate what a young centre-half such as Steven Taylor could have learned from him, and the benefits of being able to tap into the Finn's knowledge and leadership qualities. They just didn't get it, full stop. They also seemed utterly determined to keep me out of the loop. A few days later, we had a League Cup tie at Coventry and a transfer meeting was scheduled for the following morning at the Forest of Arden hotel in Birmingham. Instead, Derek Llambias told me after the game that he had called it off, explaining that Jimenez was away on urgent business. That was completely made up. He just didn't want to explain why the Hyypiä deal had collapsed.

Jimenez texted me at one point saying he was working on deals for Steve Sidwell from Chelsea as well as three players from France – Stéphane Mbia, Mamadou Sakho and Stéphane Sessègnon – and possible loans for Royston Drenthe from Real Madrid and Eiður Guðjohnsen from Barcelona. There was talk of Karim Benzema from Lyon and Samir Nasri from Marseille. On other occasions David Bentley (Blackburn), Jermain Defoe (Portsmouth) and Aaron Lennon (Tottenham) were on the wish list. Peter Crouch, then at Liverpool, was another one.

They put forward another six names at one stage and I had to point out five were African players. We had already lost Obafemi Martins, Geremi, Abdoulaye Faye and Habib Beye for a month at the previous African Cup of Nations, which was poor planning. The tournament was held every two years and I explained that, if we weren't careful, we might lose over half our team on the next occasion.

Apparently we also tried to sign Fabian Delph from Leeds, though I didn't know about that one either. Unfortunately, I didn't know a lot of things that were going on at the club. Diego Capel, a winger at Seville, was supposedly on their list. Then there was Maxi Rodríguez at Atlético Madrid, Miguel from Valencia, Pablo Aimar from Real Zaragoza and Mousa Dembélé from AZ. And on and on. Crikey, you have to laugh. How many of these players did the club actually sign? At one point I was told that Mike Ashley had given Jimenez three out of ten for his trans-fer record. He was being generous. Jimenez also talked about going for Joleon Lescott, an England international. Except he used to call him 'Julian'. I probably shouldn't have been surprised. Remember, this was the guy who had never heard of Per Merte-sacker, for heaven's sake. We did bring in Danny Guthrie, who had been on loan at Bolton from Liverpool, and we also signed

Sébastien Bassong after a tip-off from an agent I knew. Bassong was twenty-one and cost £500,000 from Metz. 'I don't think he is good enough,' Jeff Vetere announced. Well, Bassong won Newcastle's Player of the Year award in his first season, and moved to Tottenham for £8 million the following summer. Those were the sorts of deals I knew I could pull off if the club trusted me.

We also brought in Jonás Gutiérrez to give us an extra bit of pace. Gutiérrez, an Argentine, was famous for pulling on a Spiderman mask to celebrate his goals. He was known as 'El Galgo', the Greyhound, and took advantage of the Webster ruling, meaning he bought himself out of his contract with the Spanish club and we didn't have to pay a transfer fee. Mallorca lodged a compensation claim for £12 million, but we ended up paying under half that amount. I imagine Mallorca were furious with us.

What I didn't realise, with the transfer deadline approaching, was that Newcastle were trying to get other players out behind my back. Joey Barton, back in the team after serving seventy-four days in prison, rang Terry at one point to ask why the club were trying to shunt him out to Portsmouth on loan. Michael Owen was offered to Liverpool and, soon afterwards, we were hearing reports that the entire squad had been put up for sale. The players must have wondered what the hell was going on and the manager, I'm embarrassed to say, didn't know anything about it. I was being completely undermined. Players were being sold, players were being touted out. It was one thing after another.

Everything reached a head on the weekend of that Arsenal match, trying to prepare for one of the toughest games of the season while also having to deal with the growing knowledge that the people who were supposed to be my colleagues were taking me for a ride. I was already feeling sore because of the Schweinsteiger farce, and it was on the morning of the game that Dennis Wise rang to ask me to go online and check out a Uruguayan player called Ignacio González. Dennis said he had heard great things but admitted he had never actually seen him play. Further enquiries revealed that nobody, in fact, from Newcastle had ever seen this guy kick a ball.

Nor did it say much for the player that Dennis had texted me the wrong name, and my initial search on the internet came up with nothing. I had to go back to Dennis to find out the correct spelling. But I did as he asked. I logged on again, typed in González's name and eventually found him. I looked at his background, his age and what he had done in his career, and it didn't need a great deal of investigation to realise this player would be out of his depth in the higher echelons of the Premier League. The only possible way to justify our interest was that González had played fourteen times for Uruguay. That, however, felt like a deception when I looked more closely at his international record, and it turned out he had managed only one ninety-minute appearance. In all the other games, it was five minutes here and there, half a match perhaps, or he would start and then end up being substituted. They weren't the statistics of a top player.

I also noted he had played for the same club, Danubio, until he was twenty-six, and it crossed my mind that any player of that age in Uruguay would have been snapped up already if he was any good. González had gone on loan to Monaco, then a mid-table team in France, earlier in the year and flopped. He made five appearances in six months and didn't finish ninety minutes once. We were coming to the end of August and he had played fewer than 200 minutes since Christmas. He didn't speak a word of English and, for the life of me, I couldn't see any reason why Newcastle might be attracted to him.

When I rang Dennis to explain it was out of the question, he seemed determined to change my mind. González, he said, was a 'great player' and our contacts in South America meant we had the chance to get him on a season-long loan. He was adamant we should give him a go and suggested that if I clicked on YouTube I might find some footage to change my opinion.

YouTube? I came from an era when managers chose players on more than a few carefully edited clips on YouTube. I wanted to know a player's character. I wanted to see how hard he worked, whether he had a good positional sense, what his concentration was like. Those were things you didn't get from sixty seconds online. I didn't want to sign a player, any player, on the strength of YouTube. With a bit of clever editing, some of the worst footballers in history could be made to look like world-beaters on an internet showreel.

I couldn't believe what I was hearing from Dennis – an experienced football man – but I did log on to YouTube and eventually found a short video showing González's career highlights. It looked as if he was playing in a local park in some of the games. It was shocking quality – grainy, dark, shaky footage – and my patience was wearing thin. I rang Wise back and couldn't have made myself any clearer. 'You've got to be kidding,' I said. 'Do you seriously think that video is going to impress me?'

This was all a few hours before we were due to play Arsenal and the normal etiquette would be to leave the manager alone on the morning of a match. That day, I lost count of the number of calls that went back and forth. I had a team-talk to prepare and a huge game coming up. We had started the season well and we wanted to give Arsenal a run for their money. Yet we had all this going on in the background.

I wanted an explanation as to why it had been presented to me that a deal for Schweinsteiger was on the cards. But when I rang Jimenez there was no shame, no apology, and not even the faintest hint that he knew he had let me down. Instead, that was when he threw Xisco into the mix and told me the club were about to sign a second player I had never heard of.

'You can't do that,' I said. 'No player can come in without my say-so, you know that.'

'Wait and see,' he replied, and then he hung up on me.

It was difficult to take it all in. They had gone behind my back before, with Bafétimbi Gomis, but they had promised me they would never do anything like that again. Stupidly, I had believed them.

It wasn't long before my worst suspicions were confirmed and I had a tip-off that González and Xisco had already arrived in England. One was in London, I was told, and the other was in the north-east. The two deals were going through, and it didn't make me feel any better to learn about the amount of money the club intended to throw away in the process.

Xisco alone was costing £5.7 million as well as a salary of £60,000 a week. He was twenty-two, which was a better age than González, but when I checked out his background it was unremarkable stuff again. He had been at Deportivo de La Coruña 'B', the club's reserve set-up, and then moved up to the seniors, playing forty-four times in three years. It had earned him a call-up to Spain's under-21s, but it was still absurd to expect him to play in front of 50,000-plus people at St James' Park. Xisco had previously been loaned to UD Vecindario, a team from Gran Canaria that played on an artificial pitch at a 4,500-capacity stadium in Spain's lower leagues. He made twenty-seven appearances for Vecindario in 2006–7, the only season in their history when they competed in Spain's second division. They finished bottom, seventeen points adrift.

González had been offered a lower salary, at £26,000 a week, but that still worked out close to £1 million over the season, and a very strange deal had been cooked up whereby he was actually signing for Valencia, a big club with their own network of agents, and within twenty-four hours we were getting him on loan. What was all that about? It was an unusual arrangement, to say the least, and I didn't like the look of it one bit.

What I didn't know was what Mike Ashley made of it. Did he know these deals were being arranged behind my back? Did he care? My head was spinning and I did what I was told I should never do. I took out my phone and rang the owner.

He answered straight away and seemed happy enough to hear from me. 'Hi, King Kev.' Mike always called me King Kev, or sometimes he would refer to me as 'the most honest man in football'. I think, deep down, he respected the fact I had integrity.

He didn't seem to know anything about the González loan, but he said – if it would make me feel any happier – he would pay for it out of his own pocket rather than the club's transfer budget. He didn't seem to realise why I was so aggrieved, and he certainly didn't look too concerned when we went into that game against Arsenal and the television cameras picked him out in the away end with a pint of lager in his hand. Twelve seconds was all it needed for the entire pint to disappear down his throat. 'Is he in a rush?' the television commentator asked.

We lost 3–0 and when I came home, utterly demoralised, I was already thinking that was it for me. I was sick of them; sick of the way they were riding roughshod over me, sick of being treated like dirt, sick of the attitude where they clearly thought, *Oh, don't worry about the manager, he'll come round in the end.* I had had enough.

The next day I rang Mike again. 'I'm just with someone,' he said, 'but I'll get back to you.' The phone went dead and he never rang back. He did that to me a few times at Newcastle.

I waited a full day and then I texted him a message. 'The most honest man in football treated like garbage.'

When I spoke to Wise on the telephone that day, it was the first time he explained the real reasons why the González loan was being done. Dennis explained it was a favour for two agents – Paco Casal, a Uruguayan, and Marcelo Lombilla, an Argentine – who had helped us get Coloccini and Gutiérrez, and that if we took the hit on this one occasion and agreed to 'park' González, they would look upon us favourably in the future.

'You don't even have to play this guy,' Dennis said. 'We want to keep the agent sweet. If you don't want the player to train with you, you can put him in the academy. And if you don't like him, we can get rid of him in January.' Mike had been filled in and the owner's view was that González didn't even have 'to set foot in St James' Park.'

I thought Dennis was kidding at first. He liked a laugh and I genuinely thought he might be joking. When I realised he was actually being serious, I knew immediately that I couldn't have anything to do with a deal of that nature. I wanted to save the club from the possibility of being investigated. I wanted to protect the people around me and I wanted to look after my own reputation. I didn't like the word 'parked', and I dreaded to think of the repercussions if what the club were doing reached the newspapers. It would have been a scandal and, as far as I was concerned, it was not one I could defend.

Dennis called it a 'favour'. A favour? As favours go, it was going to cost Newcastle a fortune. Both players were going to earn seven-figure salaries, and in Xisco's case it was upwards of £3 million a year. Paco Casal pocketed €250,000 from Valencia as his slice of the deal. It must have been the easiest money he had ever made and, laughably, González's loan deal had an option to buy him for £8 million at the end of the season.

Newcastle were not breaking any rules, but it looked terrible, and left us open to all sorts of questions. The club weren't buying these players for orthodox reasons; it was to do a favour for two agents, one of whom was getting a six-figure sum for setting it up. I felt that it was fundamentally wrong at every level and various people were getting rich off the back of it. On the one hand, Newcastle were putting up the price of season tickets and telling fans it was a necessary expense if they wanted the club to bring in top signings. On the other hand, they were bringing in two players, spending the best part of £10 million in transfer fees and salaries, as a 'favour'. It turned my blood cold.

Transfer-deadline day was twenty-four hours away. I had a small squad, by their own admission, and now I had a player coming in over my head to keep two agents sweet. Not because he was a good player or because he was going to get in my team. I had never been asked to 'park' a player in my life and this wasn't a kid of fifteen or sixteen we were talking about. This was a man of twenty-six. Maybe Dennis, when he was a manager, would have done it. But I wouldn't. 'I have my pride and my dignity,' I told him. 'I do not want to be associated with this deal. It stinks.'

They asked me to go to St James' Park to talk it through, and when I arrived at the ground the club photographer came over, completely oblivious to what was going on. 'Oh, Kevin, great timing, we've got the two new signings here, can we get a picture of the three of you?' There was no way I could let that photograph be taken, but I did feel sorry for the two players. They had just been shown round the stadium and they must have thought their new manager didn't want to know them.

I knew it was over. But I wanted an explanation and I asked Dennis at that meeting if he would have agreed to this kind of 'favour' when he was managing Leeds. I told him I could ask the same question to a hundred managers and none would have put up with it. Can you imagine, I asked, what Alex Ferguson's reaction would have been at Manchester United if two players had been signed behind his back? Or Rafael Benítez at Liverpool? Or any manager worth his salt?

'Juande Ramos at Spurs would do it this way,' he said.

'Well, you need to find another Juande Ramos then,' I snapped.

It was a fiery meeting. Derek Llambias clearly thought I would drive home, have a think about it and be in the following day as if nothing had happened. Once he realised that might not be the case, he became very loud and confrontational, telling me I wasn't going to be allowed to walk out on the club. 'You don't know me,' I said, and then I left. He wasn't going to bully me.

As I drove away from St James' Park, I didn't see any possible way back, but then a message reached me that Mike Ashley wanted to meet, one on one, to see what could be done to put everything right. It would be a private meeting, I was assured. Nobody would know about it – just the two of us, at a secret address in London to thrash everything out.

At the back of my mind I was still thinking, *Well, maybe he's going to give me some control and the powers I need to do the job properly.* I was still clinging to the hope, more fool me, that he would tell me he understood all my frustrations and move out the people who were to blame. I went down to London and, as I turned the corner to where this supposedly confidential meeting was taking place, a Sky cameraman was waiting on the pavement. It had been leaked – and I had been stitched up. Newcastle, I assume, wanted pictures of me so they could tell the fans they had tried their best to talk me around.

Unfortunately for the cameraman, I learned that day I still had some of the old Kevin Keegan pace. I shot off straight away, ducked into the nearest restaurant, explained to the staff I needed an escape route and the chef let me go through the kitchens and out the back exit.

After that, I knew there was no way back for me at Newcastle. Maybe they thought I wouldn't dare walk away from a £3-million-a-year contract but they obviously didn't know me very well. They had made my job untenable and, when I officially announced my resignation, via the League Managers' Association, I wanted to make it clear to the supporters that I had been in office but not in power. 'I've been working desperately hard to find a way forward with the directors, but sadly that has not proved possible,' my statement read. 'It's my opinion that a manager must have the right to manage and that clubs should not impose upon any manager any player that he does not want. It remains my fervent wish to see Newcastle United do well in the future and I feel incredibly sorry for the players, staff, and most importantly the supporters. I have been left with no choice other than to leave.'

I knew my resignation was going to be big news, and straight away there was talk of fan protests. The Newcastle supporters knew that if I was going to leave the club after only eight months, there had to be a serious issue. I just wish the people running the club could have treated them better. The fans had not changed. But the club had.

Terry McDermott was distraught and told me he would resign as a matter of principle. I told him to sit tight because he hadn't done anything wrong. I had brought in Chris Hughton to be part of the backroom staff and it must have been tough for him, too. All I could do was explain and say sorry. Terry was called in the following week and they paid him off. They also got rid of Adam Sadler, the reserve team manager. I still don't know why.

After that, I started the long and difficult process of filing a claim for constructive dismissal and preparing to take Newcastle to an independent arbitration panel. Newcastle launched a counter-claim for £2 million, citing a breach of contract. Stories started being leaked. Newcastle had friends in the media. David Craig, Sky's north-east correspondent, was one of their go-to men. One story came out that if I won my case it threatened to bankrupt the club. Anybody with a modicum of common sense would have known where that leak originated. There were people trying to drive a wedge between myself and the supporters. It was so obvious what was happening, and why.

The case was certainly for a lot of money, but that was a problem Newcastle had made for themselves and, if I had lost, it would have bankrupted me. They could have settled without going to court, but when there was an attempt at arbitration, they insisted I would have to sign a confidentiality agreement. I turned it down. I wasn't willing to be gagged.

It took a year before the tribunal was heard and that long delay was difficult in so many ways. I always had it hanging over me. I had meetings with lawyers that would last a full day and leave me drained. I wanted to get on with my life but I was in a state of limbo. I couldn't understand, when the evidence was so overwhelming, why they hadn't settled out of court when they had the chance. Why couldn't they admit they had got it wrong when they obviously didn't have a leg to stand on? My lawyers kept looking at the evidence and shaking their heads in disbelief. 'They must have something up their sleeve,' they would say. But there was nothing up their sleeve. The club just didn't want to back down.

Every day for two weeks I would walk from my hotel in London to 70 Fleet Street, the offices of the International Dispute Resolution Centre, where the tribunal was heard. I used that walk to clear my head. It was a difficult, gruelling experience and I will never know how Dennis Wise, with absolutely zero shame, could possibly think on the day he was giving evidence that I would want to shake his hand.

Maybe I should have been the bigger man, but I was going into a tribunal against people who had betrayed me. The case had been festering for a year and there he was, hand stretched out, trying to greet me like an old friend. 'Dennis,' I said, looking him straight in the eye. 'I don't want to shake your hand.' Dennis had the nerve to say during the proceedings he was 'amazed' by my reaction. Well, it amazed me he could have so much front and so little self-awareness.

In the end, the three-man panel – Philip Havers QC, Lord Pannick QC and Ken Merrett, Manchester United's assistant club secretary – didn't need long to realise how lopsided all the evidence was. Their verdict was crushing for Newcastle because what it said, in short, was that the tribunal accepted my interpretation of events rather than the arguments made by the club. I felt vindicated. It was an enormous sense of relief; finally I could get on with my life and start putting it all behind me. But I was sad, too, that it had gone that far and appalled by some of the stuff that had come out.

It was certainly interesting to note the awkward body language as they gave evidence, under oath, and tried to explain the González loan at a time when Newcastle were supposedly trying to change the culture whereby agents had too much influence at St James' Park and were making extraordinary amounts of money out of the club.

Wise's argument was that it was not out of the ordinary for these kinds of deals to happen in football, referring to them as 'commercials', and telling a story about his time at Leeds to illustrate his point. According to Dennis, the Leeds chairman, Ken

Bates, approached him one day to suggest they offered a boy of seventeen a professional contract. The boy wasn't good enough to be a footballer but that, plainly, was not the most important detail as far as Leeds were concerned. The boy's father had a successful business and a lucrative deal had been arranged for that company to sponsor Leeds – on condition they signed the boss's son.

'It [the sponsorship] was a big amount of money to help out when the club were in financial trouble,' Wise explained. 'Ken came to see me. He said, "I need you to help me out here, I need you to take this boy." So I do understand these situations.'

The boy was never named. Yet Wise made it clear he was happy to go along with this sham. 'I said to Ken, "He won't play in the first team, he won't play in the reserves, is that OK?" And he said, "OK." It wasn't explained to the boy. His dad didn't tell him. And I didn't think it was my responsibility either.'

Can you believe it? We all do favours for friends sometimes, or even friends of friends, but there is a big difference between setting up someone with work experience and offering a professional contract when you know it is all a pretence. It was completely wrong. It might be the way Leeds worked back then. It wasn't the way I wanted Newcastle to be.

The case hinged on whether the club had gone back on their word that I should have the final say on transfers. Ashley's view was that it should have been 'blindingly obvious' from the start that I never had that privilege. Yet Mort had openly stated in an interview with *The Mag*, a Newcastle fanzine, that the final decision on signings would be mine and that Wise and Jimenez were there to recommend players before I had the ultimate say-so.

Ashley had also said it publicly, and Wise, I presume, must have found it awkward to explain another interview where he had declared exactly the same. 'I'm not here to be involved in the first team,' was the precise quote. 'I am not here to manage. I am here to help Kevin as much as possible in bringing young players through and also recommending certain players to him and he'll say yes and no. He has the final word and no one else. I'm not going to do things like bring players in behind his back – I'm not into that. Everything that happens will be run past him and he'll say yes or he'll say no.' And pigs might fly.

That interview took place during his first week at Newcastle. The headline was 'I'm here to help Kevin – he has the final word' and the interview appeared on the club website as well as being printed in the programme for the next game. 'I have never looked at the club website and I have to be exceptionally bored to read the programme,' Ashley told the panel. 'You will get more sense out of the *Beano*.'

Newcastle were taking their supporters for fools. One interview, ticked off by the club, had Ashley describing a 2–0 win against Sunderland as his favourite moment at Newcastle so far. 'It wasn't,' he told the panel. 'It was when we beat Spurs 4–1. If you want to refer to dealing with the media as lying, then I would say yes, but I don't think it's lying in the true sense of the word.'

If it wasn't such a tragedy that Newcastle were being run this way, it would have made a great sitcom. Dennis, it transpired, used to keep his notes in a diary with 'This Book Belongs to Mr Wise' written on the front cover. Even his own barrister seemed amused, describing it 'like a child's exercise book'.

When the relevant people were asked why they had gone on record saying I had the final approval for transfers, their stock reply was that they knew it was untrue even when they put it out. Yet they said it was worth telling a lie – and had decided as much in advance – because they thought it was what the fans wanted to hear. 'Was I conscious that I was involved in a PR exercise?' Ashley said. 'Yes.'

The panel described the club's explanation as 'profoundly unsatisfactory' and the verdict was damning. 'We do not understand why the club could not set out publicly and truthfully what they maintain was the true position,' it read. 'After all, Mr Ashley's vision for the club involved a change to a continental structure and it is clear from the evidence that there are managers of some continental clubs who do not have the final say. We do not understand why the club felt unable to make this clear publicly from the outset, regardless of what Mr Keegan himself may have said. For the club to have made these statements when they were, according to the club, untrue was in our view simply to store up trouble for the future.'

Newcastle were ordered to pay me £2 million, plus interest, as well as costs, with the panel condemning the club for 'repeatedly and intentionally misleading the press, public and the fans of Newcastle United', noting how the loan deal for González 'cost nearly £1 million in wages for a player who was not expected to play in the first team'.

They had dragged the club's reputation through the gutter and, when it came to González, I still find it difficult to understand how it didn't spark an investigation by the football authorities. Let me stress that no rules had been broken, as was made clear in the tribunal, but can you ever remember a deal that looked worse? We were talking about vast sums of money exchanging hands as a so-called favour. Not once did anyone from the FA seem to think, *Hang on, what the hell was all that about?*

I felt sorry for Chris Mort, and I know he had some sympathy for me. He was a decent guy who had been put in a difficult situation and he accepted I had legitimate reasons to be concerned. I also had a bit of sympathy for Dennis Wise, though I know that might surprise a lot of people. Maybe I should have nothing but contempt for the guy, but Dennis didn't really have any power. He was Jimenez's man. They had become friends and somehow Jimenez, who was the real problem, had got himself in a position that was way beyond his true capabilities.

What I could never understand was why Mike ever appointed me if that was the way Newcastle were going to operate. Why not name Wise as manager? They wanted a puppet, someone who would turn a blind eye and never complain. Despite his fiery reputation as a player, Wise was that person. He and Jimenez were best buddies, thick as thieves. It would have made a lot more sense to give Dennis the job and spare themselves all that trouble further down the line.

Sadly, I suspect Mike, being a newcomer to football, thought Jimenez seemed entirely plausible. Mike had so much happening elsewhere that he didn't seem to know half of what was going on at Newcastle. Maybe now he realises that appointing Jimenez was the worst thing he ever did. Perhaps he understands now why Jimenez, in my view, ruined Newcastle during my time at the club. He and his pals thought Newcastle was a toy they could play with. Nothing could have been further from the truth. Jimenez was against the club apologising to me for the Bafétimbi Gomis affair and was doubling up as a mole for the tabloid press, leaking what should have been confidential information about Michael Owen's contract negotiations. Impressive guy, Tony Jimenez.

What you need at a successful football club is harmony. All I had at Newcastle was the opposite, and a legal battle that scarred me so badly it changed my feelings towards the game I had always loved. That was the legacy of my second managerial spell at Newcastle – the lies, the broken promises, the scheming, the infighting, the back-stabbing and the gut-wrenching realisation that I was being taken for an idiot. Something like that leaves a scar and, even though I won my case, I knew after the tribunal that I didn't want to go back into management. It drained my enthusiasm and left me questioning my attachment to the sport. *If this is football now*, I thought, *I don't want any part of it.*

My eight months at Newcastle, and all the unpleasantness that followed, had left me with a cynical view, hardened by my experiences. I had to get out. I had won my case but, in another sense, I had lost so much. Football had given me everything except a happy ending.

21

GOOD TIMES

It wasn't pretty, was it? Yet if the story I have recounted over the previous two chapters has left anyone wondering whether it has soured me against Newcastle United, or changed the way I regard the beautiful game, then I must reiterate that the good memories will always far outweigh the bad ones. Yes, it was a fairly wretched period and, as the psychiatrist once said of Basil Fawlty, there was enough material for an entire conference. But I won't allow it to taint the happier times, and it doesn't change the fact I feel privileged to have made a life from the sport I would have played for nothing.

There have been too many exhilarating highs to dwell on one excruciating low, and now, when I look back on my life and remember all that I wanted from it as a young boy in South Yorkshire, I find myself reminiscing about some of the key moments and see more clearly than ever how lucky I have been that so much could come to one man.

I wonder which direction my life might have taken had it not been for the school report from Sister Mary Oliver, amid all the stern lectures from my other teachers, to recommend that 'Kevin's football must be encouraged.' I owe so much to my headmistress because, without that intervention, I wonder if my time chasing a football would have been rationed. My fondness for playing Jack the Lad had meant my school studies suffering – and so did my backside when my dad read the reports. Sister Mary's words at least persuaded him I shouldn't be prevented from play-ing the game that mattered so much to me.

As galling as it was at the time, what a stroke of fortune as well that my colleagues at Peglers Brass Works in Doncaster didn't think more highly of my football ability when I started my first job after leaving school. Imagine if they had seen my poten-tial and promoted me from the second team to the main works side. I would like to think I might have made the grade. Alterna-tively, it might have meant never playing in the game that led to Bob Nellis offering me the trial with Scunthorpe United that turned professional football from a dream into reality.

When I look at the faint scar beneath my right eye, I am reminded I wouldn't have even got that far if, on one of my many excursions to Doncaster's Hyde Park, when I tried to recreate my own King Harold moment with a bow and arrow, the impact had been a few millimetres higher.

Then consider how lucky I was that the Football Association's rules stopped Arsenal from taking me on trial from Scunthorpe to go on tour with their youth team. It didn't feel lucky at the time, and who knows where it might have led if I had been allowed to go? Maybe their manager, Bertie Mee, would have decided I was worth a punt and I would be reminiscing now about my years with Arsenal. With all due respect, however, that would have meant never meeting the great Bill Shankly.

Everybody needs a bit of luck, and my guardian angel was feeling particularly benign when Scunthorpe were drawn at Tranmere Rovers in the first round of the 1970–1 FA Cup. We drew 1–1 at Prenton Park, and when we came back to the Old Showground three days later it was 0–0. Those were the days when there were no penalty shootouts, so a coin was tossed to decide the venue for the second replay. Luckily, Scunthorpe couldn't win anything at the time – not even the flip of a coin – and Goodison Park, the home of Everton, was chosen as a neutral ground. That was a godsend for me because it gave Shanks the perfect opportunity to send Liverpool's scouts to have a look at

me. They liked what they saw and I am eternally grateful to whoever called heads or tails for Tranmere.

Above everything else, I will always consider how lucky I was
that when I went down to the Leger Fair with my friend Phil Niles
that same year, the two girls shouting and screaming as they
whirled around on the waltzers didn't mind too much when we
began to laugh at them. They even found some of our jokes relatively amusing when, boys being boys, we set about trying to
impress them with a non-stop barrage of humour. I was nineteen
at the time. Jean Woodhouse was sixteen, and when we started
courting it was nearly three months before I came clean and told
her I was a footballer. Until that point, I had said I worked at
the steelworks in Scunthorpe because I didn't want her to think
I was acting the big 'I am'. Once I had told that white lie, it was
hard to know how to correct it and I kept the pretence going
until one day she put me on the spot by asking to go ice skating
on a Saturday afternoon. Jean accepted my explanation, and, after
meeting on the waltzers, I am glad to say she has been going
round with me ever since.

I still remember Jean giving me a sad love record, Diana
Ross's 'Remember Me', when I signed for Liverpool. I told her I
had no intention of forgetting her. She wrote every day, posting
the letters on her way home from school, and we often met in
Manchester on Sundays. I would drive from Liverpool and Jean
would catch the train from Doncaster. I knew she was the one for
me and when her parents, Ernie and Molly, moved to Newquay
a couple of years later, Jean came to Liverpool to live in digs with
Mr and Mrs Roberts – or Gav and Lil, as we knew them. I went
down on one knee to pop the question on her eighteenth birthday, in the summer of 1972, but we never really talked about a
date until my eleven-game ban for the Charity Shield scrap with
Billy Bremner opened a window of opportunity.

Around that time, Dad was told he had a tumour and needed
an operation if he was to live for more than six months. Dad
made a deal with me. 'I'll go into hospital if you marry that lass

of yours', he said. 'You've kept her waiting long enough.' I still had to get Ernie's permission, and when I approached my prospective father-in-law, my nerves were not helped by the fact he had a huge knife in his hand. He and Molly ran a fish and chip shop in Owston and he was in the back room cutting up all the haddock.

We were married at Saint Peter-in-Chains Roman Catholic Church in Doncaster on 23 September 1974, and Jean looked beautiful in her long white dress. I scrubbed up quite well myself in a specially made white leather suit with huge lapels and even bigger bell-bottoms. I mean, could David Beckham pull off a white leather suit? What I didn't realise was that we would be sitting on leather stools, and every time I moved there was the most embarrassing sound to start Jean giggling and attract funny looks from the priest. I was terrified even to breathe. It was a special day but we had no time for a honeymoon. The next morning I was training at Melwood while Jean was back to work at the optician's where she was a receptionist.

Jean and I have always shared everything and she used to take the strain away from me when I was at the sharp end of football. My parents adored her and, years later, when Jean and I had moved into Wynyard with the girls, we bought Mum a bungalow on the same estate. Her mother, Molly, who had been widowed too, moved up as well. We would bring them over for tea and the two of them would end up in fits of giggles when they got together.

Mum lived for another twenty-four years after Dad passed away, and I am reminded of her sometimes when I look at the little finger on my left hand. It's Dupuytren's contracture, which is hereditary and means my finger is permanently bent in a flexed position. Mum had the same but a lot worse. She found it difficult to handle coins, so if she ever went into a shop she would always use a banknote and then hold out her purse for the change. When we cleared out her bungalow after her death we found piles of coins everywhere – every bag, every purse, every drawer.

It was a small fortune when we added it all up – around £1,000 – and we split it between our grandchildren.

Life shows no sign of slowing up, and nor would I want it to. Winston Churchill was seventy-six when he began his second term as prime minister. There is still plenty for me to do, plenty of places to see and plenty of work to be done. For a long time I guested as a football pundit in Qatar with Richard Keys and Andy Gray, who I still consider the best two in the business, whereas my diary now is filled mostly with company days and various other functions where I give motivational talks and presentations. I adapt my routine depending on the audience, but I always try to keep it light and humorous, and there will inevitably be a couple of gags about Alex Ferguson, the occasional photo of a referee wearing a Manchester United shirt and plenty of jokes at my own expense. I always send myself up. It's a lot easier to make people laugh when they can see you are willing to poke fun at yourself and there will always be someone – often myself – who slips in a 'love it' moment or mentions the famous performance on *Superstars* when I showed I was a far better footballer than a cyclist.

We haven't properly covered that crash yet, and the race against the Anderlecht captain, Gilbert van Binst, when I was going like the clappers to get to the first corner and ended up clipping his back wheel to send myself flying across the track. *Superstars* was great fun, taking on all these different sports personalities and, without any practice, having a go at kayaking, table tennis, weightlifting, shooting at the renowned Bisley range, cycling and running. That fall burned all the skin off my back and shoulder but I got up to take on Van Binst again. I beat him and then left everyone for dust in the final event, the steeplechase, from a group that included the downhill skier Franz Klammer, the Dutch footballer Rudi Krol, the Swedish world table-tennis champion Stellan Bengtsson and the Belgian heavyweight boxer Jean-Pierre Coopman. I collapsed over the finishing line as the winner, $2,000 richer, and toasted my success with a flute of champagne.

What the people tuning in didn't see was that when the gallant hero reached the M1 on the way home I had to pull in at Newport Pagnell services because I suddenly didn't feel well. Very soon I was out for the count. Jean called an ambulance and I was on a drip for three days in Northampton General Hospital, where the doctors told me it was a combination of delayed shock from my accident and a form of colic caused by pushing my body too hard on one of the hottest days of the year. That was the end of me and *Superstars*. I was invited to an international heat in Florida and fancied my chances but Jean, the sensible one, put her foot down.

As for Newcastle, that chapter of my life is closed now, but I can give you one last example of how petty the feud became. That year, the match-day programme had been producing a series of articles telling the history of Newcastle since the club's formation in 1892. I found out later the series was then withdrawn because they didn't want to tell the story of the Keegan years, even though they were the best times the vast majority of Newcastle fans will ever have experienced. Clearly it would have been far too galling to give me any form of public recognition, so the history of Newcastle mysteriously stopped pre-1992.

Xisco, the £5.7 million striker who was signed against my wishes on £60,000 a week, made nine appearances for Newcastle in four and a half years and scored once in all that time. He was loaned to Racing Santander and Deportivo de La Coruña once Newcastle had cottoned on that he wasn't good enough. His contract was terminated in January 2013 and the *Newcastle Evening Chronicle* named him as one of the worst centre-forwards in the club's history.

Ignacio González? He made two substitute appearances for Newcastle, totalling thirty-eight minutes, before getting injured and was never picked again. Newcastle decided not to take the £8 million option to turn his season-long loan into a permanent transfer and he went back to Valencia, who didn't want him either. The next stage of his career was on loan at Levadiakos of Greece, where he made fourteen appearances, and he eventually joined Standard Liège on a free transfer. Valencia didn't use him once and, unless I am missing something, how precisely did Newcastle benefit from that 'favour' with the two South American agents? Joe Kinnear took over from me as manager. Newcastle were relegated at the end of that season and more than a hundred honest, hard-working people lost their jobs. All those lives irrevocably changed for the sake of some South American backscratching.

I also note that some of the people who tried to gang up against me no longer appear to be such great friends. Indeed, Dennis Wise fell out so spectacularly with Tony Jimenez he ended up suing him at the High Court over a £500,000 investment in a French golf course. Jimenez had become the co-owner of Charlton Athletic by that stage, and was also the subject of litigation from Mike Ashley. Wise was paid off by Newcastle in the same season I left the club and Derek Llambias resigned in 2013, the day after Kinnear was appointed as the new director of football.

Unfortunately for Newcastle, it is still Mike Ashley's name above the door. He is the only one left from what the fans used to call the 'Cockney Mafia', and his popularity on Tyneside can probably be gauged by the various banners the supporters held up before a game against Burnley at St James' Park in January 2018.

Together, the banners read: 'Don't ever give up on your club. Keep supporting it, it's your club and, trust me, one day you will get your club back and it will be everything you wanted it to be. Newcastle United is bigger than anyone. It hurts, I know, but just keep going. He is only one man. We are a city, a whole population. Trust me.' That quote was one of mine, from an event in the north-east with the club's supporters.

Life will occasionally throw up these unexpected dramas.

Another one came when I took a call from the police to say they needed to talk to me about the phone-hacking scandal that had engulfed some of the biggest tabloid newspaper titles in the country. It turned out my details had appeared on the list of hacked numbers and various red-top journalists had been tapping into my answerphone messages to try to find something they could rev into a headline.

It was a terrible shock and it took a long time to get over the feelings of personal intrusion, especially because we believe Jean was also targeted. It was the same kind of feeling you would get if your house had been burgled, and what made it even worse was that it dated all the way back to when I was suing the *News of the World* because of their lies about me in Euro 2000. What if they had heard something I was telling my lawyers from that case? But then you realise these people had no scruples whatsoever when you see that journalists had also hacked the phones of the murdered schoolgirl Milly Dowler, as well as victims of the 7/7 London bombings and relatives of British soldiers who had been killed in combat. It was despicable. It had been going on for years, and who can even begin to calculate the true number of celebrities, sports personalities, MPs, members of the Royal Family and countless others who were targeted?

On the day when my case was heard in the High Court, there were forty-four separate claims from, among others, Lord Jeffrey Archer, the former home secretary Charles Clarke, the actress Patsy Kensit, the singer Sophie Ellis-Bextor and various television soap stars. Anyone who was anyone was being hacked. I received damages and an apology from Mirror Group Newspapers and came away with the firm impression, despite the many reputable journalists I have known, that it was a dirty industry.

Here's one last story, though, that never made it into the newspapers, thank goodness, and perhaps a chance for me to thank the kind person who noticed me on that crisp December morning in 2017, sitting on a wall just down the road from

Chelsea and Westminster Hospital, and didn't want to pass without having a word.

Jack, my fourth grandchild, was in the new-arrivals unit, and the previous night I had been out to wet the baby's head with his father, John. I was feeling a touch delicate that morning. I hadn't had a shave and there had been a few complications around the birth that meant Jean and I had stayed down longer than planned. I was tired. But life was good. The sun was shining, I had another beautiful grandson and, as I watched the world go by, I reflected how kind life had been to me.

I started looking at all the congratulatory text messages to 'Grandad'. Then I put my phone away and sat in peace, lost in my own thoughts, thinking again how great it was to be alive. I had a wonderful family, a lifetime of precious memories and another boy who might – who knows? – run out one day at some of the football grounds where I have played. I hadn't done too badly, had I?

I cannot remember precisely how long I was on that wall, but perhaps I wasn't looking at my absolute best. Jean told me afterwards she didn't like the big black coat I was wearing and my head was a little fuzzy from the red wine the previous night. I was starting to feel drowsy, wondering whether I could get away with closing my eyes for a few minutes, when I became aware that a man had stopped in front of me. I had my head down, hunched into my collar, so all I saw at first were his shoes. But then he leant over and pressed something cold and hard into my hand. 'Here you go, mate,' he said in a friendly voice. 'Go and get yourself a coffee.' It was a £1 coin, and when I did indeed buy myself a coffee later that morning, I was still chuckling.

INDEX

Picture Acknowledgements

1. © NMP 39
2. Author's own photograph
3. © Peter Robinson / EMPICS Sport
4. Author's own photograph
5. © *Daily Mirror*
6. © *Daily Express*
7. © PA / PA Archive / PA Images
8. © Keystone Pictures USA / Alamy Stock Photo
9. © PA Photos / PA Archive / PA Images
10. © S&G / S&G and Barratts / EMPICS Sport
11. © *Sun* / News Licensing
12. © Associated Newspapers / REX / Shutterstock
13. © Peter Robinson / EMPICS Sport
14. © S&G / S&G and Barratts / EMPICS Sport
15. © Colorsport / REX / Shutterstock
16. © akg-images / picture-alliance / dpa
17. © Mike Hollist / Associated Newspapers / REX / Shutterstock
18. © Michael Hollist / *Daily Mail* / REX / Shutterstock
19. © Trinity Mirror / Mirrorpix / Alamy Stock Photo
20. © Trinity Mirror / Mirrorpix / Alamy Stock Photo
21. Author's own photograph
22. © Ted Blackbrow / *Daily Mail* / REX / Shutterstock
23. © Agent / *Daily Mail* / REX / Shutterstock
24. © Mirrorpix
25. © Jeremy Selwyn / *Evening Standard* / REX / Shutterstock
26. © Ted Blackbrow / *Daily Mail* / REX / Shutterstock
27. © Andy Hooper / *Daily Mail* / REX / Shutterstock
28. © MICHAEL PROBST / AP / REX / Shutterstock
29. © Jack Dawes / *Daily Mail* / REX / Shutterstock
30. © Owen Humphreys / PA Wire / PA Images